Critical Terrorism Studies

This book is an introduction to critical approaches to terrorism studies. While there is a growing body of critical terrorism studies literature devoted to empirical examples and conceptual development, very little has been written about how to systematically carry out this kind of research. *Critical Terrorism Studies* fills this gap by addressing three key themes:

1. the position of terrorism studies and critical terrorism studies in the discipline of international relations;
2. theoretical and methodological elaborations of critical approaches to the study of terrorism;
3. empirical illustrations of those approaches.

Drawing upon a range of engaging material, the volume reviews a series of non-variable-based methodological approaches. It then goes on to provide empirical examples that illustrate how these approaches have been and can be utilized by students, teachers, and researchers alike to critically and rigorously study terrorism.

This textbook will be of much interest to students of terrorism studies, sociology, critical security studies, and international relations in general.

Jacob L. Stump is Assistant Professor of Political Science, Shepherd University, USA.

Priya Dixit is Assistant Professor of Political Science, Virginia Tech, USA.

Critical Terrorism Studies

An introduction to research methods

Jacob L. Stump and Priya Dixit

Routledge
Taylor & Francis Group

LONDON AND NEW YORK

First published 2013
by Routledge
2 Park Square, Milton Park, Abingdon OX14 4RN

Simultaneously published in the USA and Canada
by Routledge
711 Third Avenue, New York, NY 10017

Routledge is an imprint of the Taylor & Francis Group, an informa business

British Library Cataloguing in Publication Data
A catalogue record for this book is available from the British Library

Library of Congress Cataloging in Publication Data
Stump, Jacob L.
Critical terrorism studies : an introduction to research methods / Jacob L. Stump and Priya Dixit.
p. cm.
Includes bibliographical references and index.
1. Terrorism--Research--Methodology. 2. Terrorism--Study and teaching. I. Dixit, Priya. II. Title.
HV6431.S785 2013
363.325072--dc23
2012026888

ISBN13: 978-0-415-62046-8 (hbk)
ISBN13: 978-0-415-62047-5 (pbk)
ISBN13: 978-0-203-07357-5 (ebk)

Typeset in Times
by Taylor & Francis Books

MIX
Paper from
responsible sources
FSC
www.fsc.org FSC® C004839

Printed and bound in Great Britain by
TJ International Ltd, Padstow, Cornwall

Contents

List of Illustrations

Tables

Acknowledgments

Writing a book can be a daunting task. This project could not have been imagined, written, or completed without a great deal of help. We have been fortunate over the years to have the incredibly supportive sets of friends and family, colleagues, and professional and social networks.

In particular, Patrick Thaddeus Jackson at American University's School of International Service has been a constant point of support for the book. From the start he has instructed, supervised, mentored, and opened doors. Jackson has made good things possible for us.

Our time spent dissertating at the School of International Service has also been important for us. It was in that environment that Priya and I first talked about and conceptualized this book project and put together a book proposal.

The Department of Political Science at Shepherd University, especially the Chair, Dr. Stephanie Slocum-Shaffer, has helped Jacob by making an office environment that is collegial and conducive to getting things done. Theresa Smith and Joshua DiSalvo at Shepherd University's Scarborough Library were exceptionally helpful in locating and providing Jacob with a variety of books and journal articles. Similarly, Priya would like to thank the people at the Department of Political Science, Virginia Tech, for assisting in the transition to a new job, new classes and providing encouragement for writing.

Also, Jacob would like to give a very special thanks to his wonderfully supportive wife, Rebecca Stump.

Abbreviations

CDA	Critical Discourse Analysis
CIA	Central Intelligence Agency
CSS	Critical Security Studies
CT	Critical Theory
CTS	Critical Terrorism Studies
FSS	Feminist Security Studies
IR	International Relations
IRA	Irish Republican Army
MILF	Moro Islamic Liberation Front
NGO	nongovernmental organization
PFIR	Postcolonial Feminism in International Relations
SNA	Social Network Analysis
TS	Terrorism Studies

1   The Critical Terrorism Studies Project

Introduction

Since the 1970s and especially in the 2000s, the topics of terrorism and counterterrorism have become the focus of a considerable amount of research. Terrorism Studies (TS) has been described, debated, criticized, and defended by a number of different authors (Jackson et al. 2009a; Gunning 2007a; Ranstorp 2009; Reid and Chen 2007; Weinberg and Eubank 2008; Horgan and Boyle 2008). Not all research on terrorism and counterterrorism, however, operates from this orthodox or traditional TS perspective.

More recently, a Critical Terrorism Studies (CTS) research agenda has been introduced (Jackson et al. 2009a, 2012) and subjected to various criticisms (Weinberg and Eubank 2008; Horgan and Boyle 2008; Gunning 2007b; Michel and Richards 2009). While there is a growing body of CTS literature devoted to empirical examples and conceptual development, very little has been written about *how* to systematically do this kind of research. This book directly addresses that gap. In particular, our focus is on:

1. sketching out a consistent methodological framework;
2. describing in detail particular methods of data analysis and data gathering;
3. showing illustrative examples and suggesting future avenues of research;
4. providing basic research strategies for different methods.

The remainder of this chapter is divided into three parts. Because CTS has engendered a great deal of debate and to help the reader see more clearly what is at stake in these debates, the next section is concerned with outlining some of the key arguments that have been advanced *for* and *against* the CTS project. After that, our focus shifts to clarifying some important issues that CTS approaches grapple with, such as emancipation, identity, and defining terrorism. Finally, the last section briefly sketches out the remaining chapters of the book.

CTS: Arguments For and Against

Over the past few years, a number of authors have debated whether or not CTS is warranted. Some argued in the affirmative and suggest that any problems with the CTS project are risks to avoid or overcome in the future (Jackson 2007b; Jackson et al. 2009b; Gunning 2007a; Smyth 2007). Others argued in the negative and suggest that some problems facing the development of CTS undermine the very basis of the project or, at least, certain points should be corrected (Horgan and Boyle 2008; Weinberg and

Eubank 2008; Gunning 2007b). In this section, we briefly sketch out both perspectives so that readers have a clearer picture of the debates surrounding CTS.

Arguments Against CTS

We briefly describe four arguments made against CTS or problems identified with the development of the project. These problems are not exhaustive, but offer a solid starting point for discussion.

1. The novelty of CTS criticisms of TS, such as limited primary data, theoretical naivety and state centricity, are overstated. Scholars studying terrorism have been well aware of these concerns and, over the past couple of decades, have provided their own criticisms of the field that encompass CTS concerns (Horgan and Boyle 2008).
2. Defining the boundaries of CTS in relation to TS is risky because CTS could ghettoize itself and completely break away from more conventional ways of studying terrorism (Gunning 2007b: 237–238). John Horgan and Michael J. Boyle make this point further. They argue that CTS has, in fact, made this very ghetto. In their words, CTS has "created a false dualism" between a critical approach to the study of terrorism and a conventional (or orthodox) way to study terrorism (Horgan and Boyle 2008: 61). The false dualism created by CTS, in other words, blinds CTS to the criticisms already raised by authors writing from within TS, which basically undermines "the claim that CTS is fundamentally 'different'" (Horgan and Boyle 2008: 61).
3. The notion that there is an orthodox TS is a "recent intellectual" fabrication built on a selective reading of the extant literature on terrorism (Horgan and Boyle 2008: 57). For instance, CTS is often critical of the way TS researchers handle the concept of causation, while CTS fail to closely address "previous work on the subject" (Horgan and Boyle 2008: 58). Similarly, the CTS claim that TS research is often ahistorical fails to seriously engage the work of historians of terrorism, such as Walter Laqueur and David Rappaport, who have traced terrorism to ancient times and strongly made the case that it is "hardly new" (Weinberg and Eubank 2008: 189). The CTS claim that TS has too often avoided state terrorism and overly emphasized group terrorism is also a result of a selective engagement with the literature on terrorism. Weinberg and Eubank argue that TS has, to the contrary, "extensively" studied state terror in the context of Latin America, apartheid South Africa, and the abuses of power by American and British governments (2008: 191). CTS scholars, in other words, "have a responsibility to offer a more textured and careful review of the literature than they have offered so far" (Horgan and Boyle 2008: 58).
4. CTS shows a suspicion of policy relevant research (Horgan and Boyle 2008: 59). In particular, as Gunning notes, the concern is that CTS scholars working too closely with policy-makers will become coopted into generating rational choice, problem solving work that loses its critical edge. But, especially for those advancing an emancipatory agenda, policy relevance is necessary (Gunning 2007b: 239–240). In response to this concern and discussed in Chapter 4 of this book, some CTS advocates have identified ways to work with policy-makers and advance an emancipatory agenda (Toros and Gunning 2009). Similarly, policy relevance does not necessarily mean working with policy-makers. It could also mean working with non-governmental organizations and other civil society organizations (Horgan and Boyle 2008: 59).

Reasons for CTS

Why develop a CTS? Supporters of CTS offer a number of reasons in support of their position. While not exhaustive, we sketch out four closely related reasons that should encourage further discussion.

1. Much of the TS literature operates from a problem-solving perspective (Gunning 2007b), but clearly not all TS writing works in this vein (Horgan and Boyle 2008: 53–55). Drawing from Robert Cox, a problem-solving perspective takes existing actors and relations, such as the state (its interests and identity) and their relations of insecurity with terrorist groups, as given, objective features of world politics. It does not attempt to account for the historical emergence of the state, its interests, identity, or its relations of insecurity with terrorist groups. Rather, a problem-solving approach works to explain why present problems exist and how those problems can be overcome with specific policies the state can implement (Cox 1981; Gunning 2007a). CTS-inspired work, in contrast, might investigate the subjectivity of the militant (Zulaika and Douglass 2008; see also Chapter 6), explore the various ways that people make sense of terrorism and counterterrorism (Chapter 7), or map networks of policy-makers and institutions and explore how these actors garner sociopolitical benefit from issuing terrorist warnings (Chapter 10).
2. Much of the TS literature is state-centric (Smyth 2007: 261), which is closely related to the criticism of problem-solving that we noted above (Gunning 2007a: 371). State-centric work presumes the state is the basic unit to be secured against the threat of terrorism. The means to secure the state center on military and police agencies. CTS approaches, in contrast, might focus on non-state actors. For instance, as we discuss in Chapter 4, critical-theory-inspired CTS might focus on marginal voices within civil society, terrorist groups, or attentive citizens in the USA. Or, even more broadly, human security as opposed to state security might be a concern of approaches that avoid state centrism.
3. Much of the TS literature is ahistorical (Smyth 2007: 260), which has two meanings in the context of CTS critique. First, while the general history of terrorist violence has been investigated (Weinberg and Eubank 2008: 189; Laqueur 1977; Rapoport 1984), there is the presumption that the events on September 11, 2001, were exceptional (Smyth 2007: 260). Second, the TS literature is ahistorical insofar as it ignores the historical trajectory of the state (Gunning 2007a: 371), the genealogy of terrorism (Blain 2007; Jackson 2006), and the historical development of terrorism and the state (Jackson 2006; Oliverio 1998; Dixit 2010; Stump 2010). CTS approaches drawing from ethnography and discourse analysis might, for instance, show how the counterterrorist state is composed in the present or how the state historically developed in relation to terrorism. We discuss these research possibilities in Chapters 7 and 9.
4. Since the development of TS in the 1960s and 1970s, writing on the topic has grown dramatically. Starting in the 1980s and especially after September 11, 2001, explicitly "critical" approaches to the study of terrorism have emerged. Classes focused on the critical study of terrorism have been developed, papers presented at conferences, conferences devoted to CTS have been organized, global networks of scholars have taken shape, research institutions are actively studying terrorism from an explicitly critical angle, a CTS-dedicated journal is in place, and articles, books, and chapters have been published.

Clarifying Some Key Issues

"Critical": What Does That Mean in CTS?

A continuing challenge for CTS centers on how most usefully to conceptualize the meaning of "critical." Critics have noted the ambiguity and vagueness of the meaning of "critical" for CTS-related publications (Jones and Smith 2009: 93–95; see also Chapter 4 of this book). The most vocal supporters of CTS have been explicit about their "relatively heavy reliance on Frankfurt School Critical Theory" as it has been filtered through the Critical Security Studies (CSS) of the Welsh School, especially the work of Ken Booth (Jackson et al. 2009a: 234). At the same time, these supporters have voiced apparent surprise that "there appears to be a perception among many US scholars that it relates specifically to Frankfurt School Critical Theory or some variant of either Marxism or post-structuralism" (Jackson et al. 2009a: 235).

In an effort to answer Jones and Smith's relevant critique and to push against the over-emphasis on Frankfurt School-informed conceptualizations of "critical," Priya Dixit and Jacob L. Stump have argued that there are other ways of understanding the meaning of "critical" work on terrorism (2011: 505). For example, well before the post-September-11 instantiations of CTS were taking shape, Karin Fierke defined "critical" in these terms:

> the analysis is not primarily critical because it includes a range of practices that in the past have been ignored. There is not necessarily anything critical about the mere descriptions of a change, even it if includes dissident voices. This volume is first and foremost critical because it makes us *look again, in a fresh way, at that which we assume about the world because it has become overly familiar.* In this way, new spaces are opened for thinking about the meaning of the past and the present and, therefore, how we construct the future.
>
> (Fierke 1998: 13; emphasis added)

Here, in Fierke's definition of "critical," it means using different methods to study how meanings are formulated, identities produced and actions legitimated. Specifically in relation to the problem of a "critical" study of terrorism, Fierke wrote:

> While the term "Critical Security Studies" sometimes refers to a school of thought that draws on post-Marxist traditions, and to the Frankfurt School in particular, I use the term in the broader sense to include a range of approaches whose point of departure is a critique of traditional security studies.
>
> (Fierke 2005: 51, note 1)

Thus, as Dixit and Stump claimed, "this re-understanding of "critical" does not automatically equate with a discussion of the ideological foundations of orthodox terrorism scholarship or the goal of emancipation" (2011: 505) – though, as we argue in later chapters of this book, the meaning of "critical" can certainly connect closely with the concept of emancipation and the Frankfurt School.

In other words, then, we argue that it is analytically useful to conceptualize "critical" for CTS as operating along a spectrum. At one end of the spectrum, "critical" is closely associated with the Frankfurt School. We go over this understanding of "critical" in much more detailed terms in Chapter 4. But basically, we argue that from the perspective of the Frankfurt School, "critical" means that the researcher should align their selves with some unfree group, elaborate on the everyday critiques made by those suffering under the unfree conditions, help them reflect on their understandings and conditions and try to provoke them to change their situation and effectively emancipate their selves. At the other end of the "critical" spectrum and more in line with Fierke's suggestions, "critical" can avoid the association with the Frankfurt School and have a wider meaning that has nothing to do with emancipation. "Critical" in this broader sense of the term means to interrogate the commonsense assumptions that inform our analyses of security issues more broadly and terrorism in particular. We illustrate this broader meaning of "critical" in various chapters throughout this book and illustrate different methods for doing CTS.

Causation and Constitution

While there is no unified set of methods for making causal and constitutive explanations, Richard Jackson has argued that CTS is able to deal with both causation and constitution (Jackson et al. 2012: 202). In the social sciences (including political science and International Relations [IR] more specifically) "understanding" is often contrasted with "explanation" (Hollis and Smith 1990). Following Alexander Wendt (1998), however, we argue that both explanation and understanding are different *types* of explanations. Thus, using different methods discussed within this book, CTS should be able to explain these kinds of questions and more:

1. How do some actor(s) come to be (or not be) a terrorist and/or counterterrorist?
2. How does becoming a terrorist and/or counterterrorist change the kinds of actions one performs?
3. How does some specified community make sense of events deemed terrorism and/ or counterterrorism?
4. How do some actions come to be called terrorism and some do not?
5. How do violent actions mean to the actors who carried them out and/or to the community on which the violent actions were perpetrated?
6. How does the rhetoric of terrorism and/or counterterrorism legitimate certain actions and constitute particular actors and identities?
7. How has the meaning of terrorism and/or counterterrorism changed over time and in different places?

Note that the above questions are all *how* questions as opposed to *why* questions. Why questions, as critically oriented scholars have noted, take as unproblematic the possibility that certain actions and policy courses could happen. They presume the actors' identities and the meaningful social contexts in which the actors conduct their selves (Doty 1996: 4). In contrast, how questions help us explain an important aspect of power that why questions too often miss. That is to say, how questions enable us to explain the way that "power works to constitute" particular actors, identities, meaningful orientations, relationships, and modes of conduct (Doty 1996: 4).

How questions, furthermore, help us explain causation. To be clear, though, because we reject the possibility of ahistorical, acultural laws, we are not talking about the cross-case, covariational causation advocated by neopositivists. As Wendt has argued, "the 'independent variable/dependent variable' language that characterizes [neopositivist] causal inquires makes no sense, or at least must be interpreted very differently" (1998: 106). Rather, to the extent that CTS researchers are interested in explaining causation, at least two related possible routes are open to them:

1. "Sherlock Holmes causality," which is the "mapping of clues in context" and "tracing of connections among events" as a means of recounting a specific causal story about how a policy was implemented (Schwartz-Shea 2006: 108);
2. human meaning-making causality, which focuses on explaining individual actions (Jackson 2006c) and/or the "broad patterns" of action connected with "social movements" and organizations (Bevir 2006: 285).

In short, as Charles Tilly put it, "how things happen is *why* they happen" (2006: 410). How questions informed by an appropriate methodology and answered with appropriate methods of data gathering and analysis, in other words, can help CTS scholars explain causation and constitution.

Emancipation

Jackson and a number of other voices in the CTS debate have argued that emancipation is one of the core commitments of the project (Jackson 2007c; Jackson et al. 2009a; Smyth 2007; McDonald 2007). Drawing from the Frankfurt School as heavily as these researchers do, this commitment to emancipation should not be a surprise.

From the beginning of the debate, emancipation has been recognized as a posing a potential problem. Gunning, for instance, noted that a tension existed between the ethical commitment to emancipation and cultural sensitivity to particular locales. If not careful, CTS could "end up imposing its particular normative agenda and so become just another (neo)-colonial project" (Gunning 2007b: 241). Jones and Smith have taken this argument a step further and said that, in effect, the commitment to emancipation that Jackson and company have advanced lacks rigor, weakens the dispassionate study of terrorism, and "undermines any ostensible claim to pluralism and diversity" (2009: 299).

Clearly, emancipation plays an important part of the Frankfurt School perspective and for those who explicitly draw from that perspective in their formulations of CTS. However, as we noted in regards to the meaning of "critical" for CTS, not everybody critically studying terrorism operates in that mode. Therefore, in contrast to Jackson's claims of a core commitment to emancipation, we argue that not all CTS must be committed to emancipation. In line with Buzan, Waever, and de Wilde's discussion of securitization theory and its relationship to emancipation,

> [we] abstain from attempts to talk about what "real security" would be for people, what are "actual" security problems larger than those propagated by elites, and the like. To be able to talk about these issues, one has to make basically different ontological choices than ours and must define some emancipatory ideal. Such an approach is therefore complementary to ours; it can do what we voluntarily abstain from, and we can do what it is unable to: understand the mechanisms of securitization while keeping a distance from security – that is, not assuming that security is a good to be spread to ever more sectors.
>
> (Buzan et al. 1998: 35)

A CTS closely wedded to the Frankfurt School might well, for instance, talk about what counts as "real" terrorism and "real" interests and they may have emancipatory goals. Strictly speaking, however, all voices in CTS should not debate over what counts as "real" terror, terrorists, and terrorism and the goal should not be focused on emancipatory politics. As we demonstrate throughout this book, ethnography, Social Network Analysis (SNA), and discourse analytic approaches critically study terrorism, but are not necessarily committed to emancipation. A stance regarding emancipation such as this does not pin the core of CTS to the Frankfurt School and, simultaneously, makes space for a wider set of methodologically legitimate ways to approach the topic of terrorism.

Identity

One of the important points that CTS brings to the table is the study of identity. Interpersonal, group, national, state, and civilizational identities are all relevant for CTS. In this book, especially in Chapters 8, 9, and 10, we highlight the significance of studying identity in relation to terrorism and counterterrorism.

Similar to traditional security studies, writing in TS has often posited the existence of certain entities (often but not always individuals and states) in an environment in which they experience the threat of terrorism. Those posited as threatening are assumed or asserted to have a stable terrorist identity – "they are terrorists," the claim goes. Similarly, the actors experiencing the threat of terrorism are claimed or assumed to have some sort of stable identity – "America is freedom loving," the claim goes. Much like traditional security studies, in other words, TS naturalizes actors and their insecurities in the sense that they are treated as obvious facts "given by the nature of the interstate system" (Weldes et al. 1999: 9).

Moving beyond this naturalized conception of identity was an important component of the development of CSS (see Weldes et al. 1999; Krause and Williams 1997; Campbell 1998a). We argue that the development of the study of identity is an important component for the development of CTS as well. To make this move, identity must be re-conceptualized and made available to empirical analysis rather than assumed or asserted as an essential component of the actor(s) in question. Identity, in other words, should be seen as an ongoing, contextually dependent process that is established and reestablished in relation to difference. Difference, in this sense, is whatever identity is not – it can be mundane or extraordinary. "Thus, there is always a politics of identity and difference through which difference can, but need not, be transformed into otherness (Weldes et al. 1999: 11).

Identity has played an important role in some of the foundational CTS studies. Richard Jackson's seminal book, *Writing the War on Terrorism,* for instance, devotes a considerable amount of space to identity construction. Jackson closely examines how the language of counterterrorism regularly appeals to identity: "terrorists are endlessly demonized and vilified as being evil, barbaric and inhuman, while America and its coalition partners are described as heroic, decent and peaceful – the defenders of freedom" (2005: 59). Since then, while still being mentioned in some writings (e.g., Jackson 2006, 2007b, 2007d), identity has played a less significant role in the development of CTS. Identity was not, for instance, noted as a core commitment of CTS (Jackson 2007c). While clearly not equally significant for all writers critically studying terrorism, just as emancipation is not equally significant for CTS, identity should continue to play an important role in the project.

Defining Terrorism

It has become a cliché to note that terrorism is an essentially contestable concept with no universally accepted definition. In 1988, Schmid and Jongman asked 100 researchers working on the topic of terrorism to define terrorism. They received back 109 different definitions (2006: 1–38). That terrorism is essentially contested has led some to advocate the abandonment of the term altogether because it lacks analytical value or because research can be conducted without employing the term (Jackson 2011). Against the abandonment of the term and in an effort to offer a more nuanced understanding, Richard Jackson (2011) has offered a "minimal foundationalist" redefinition of terrorism. In his words, "Terrorism is violence or its threat intended as a symbolically communicative act in which direct victims of the action are instrumentalized as a means to creating a psychological effect of intimidation and fear in a target audience for a political objective" (Jackson 2011: 8).

However, such a definition fundamentally differs little from those offered by TS scholars such as Walter Laqueur and Bruce Hoffman. Indeed, most all definitions of terrorism, including Jackson's suggested CTS redefinition, "reify terrorism as a particular type of violence" (Stump 2013 forthcoming).

Researchers, we argue, should avoid the intentional or unintentional reification of terror, terrorists, and terrorism (Dixit and Stump 2011; Stump and Dixit 2012; Stump 2011) for at least two reasons. One reason is that reifying terrorism closes down the possibility of certain research questions, such as: how do certain acts of violence become constituted as terrorism and other acts of violence do not? Under what social conditions can the label terrorism be successfully applied to particular acts – violent or otherwise? What (violent) policies are legitimated and foreclosed by the construction of terrorism? What identity boundaries are produced and reproduced with the invocation of terrorism? And so on (Stump 2013 forthcoming). The second reason is that reifying terrorism blinds researchers to the possibility of examining nonviolent, mundane examples of terrorism, such as the "banal terrorism" explored by Katz (2007), the "terrorist warnings" spoken by policy-makers and intended to instill fear for political gain (Goodin 2006), or the teaching-learning processes in classrooms that give shape to a culture of fear in places like Guatemala (Salazar 2008).

Our argument is that to keep open the possibility of systematically studying violent and nonviolent, extraordinary and mundane phenomena, it is most useful to treat terrorism as an analytical practice. More specifically, making an important distinction between an *analytical practice* and a *political practice* helps avoid the problem of reification. As an analytical practice, in other words, terrorism should be understood as a more or less useful, ideal typical tool employed by researchers to study some empirical events. Conversely, a political practice is what the subjects of our research do or say. In short, it is important to keep separate the analytical tools we use from the phenomena we study. Our suggestion for CTS falls in line with the Copenhagen School's securitization theory that systematically treats security as a practice (Hansen, 2006; Buzan et al., 1998). In this way, a single, unified definition that claims to capture the total substance of terrorism or even the minimum foundation of terrorism is not required to study the practice of terrorism from a critical perspective. To be clear, this is not to say that a definition of terrorism as an analytical tool cannot be used but, rather, a definition that attempts to define the substance of terrorism (no matter how minimal) is not required.

Organization of the Book

This book is organized into two parts. Part I, including Chapters 2 and 3, sketches out the history of TS in the context of IR, with an emphasis on when TS formed (1970s and 1980s), how it has developed since September 11, 2011, and its primary focus on countering the objectified danger of terrorism via policy guidance to government agencies. We discuss the drawbacks of such an approach to the study of terrorism and how those limitations parallel the problems of mainstream IR. Conversely, we argue that the diversity of non-mainstream IR, particularly the development of CSS in IR, can benefit the critical study of terrorism. To help the reader get a firmer grasp on the wide breadth of critically oriented TS, we also describe current CTS research using prominent scholars' own words and how they see their work. Then, we describe the study of terrorism and terrorists in non-IR disciplines, including anthropology, history, literature, philosophy, geography, and rhetoric and cultural studies, while indicating possible research avenues and ways that CTS might benefit from geographic and methodological plurality.

Part II of the book closely explores some of the key methods of data gathering and analysis used to study terrorism from a critical perspective. Chapter 4 looks at the contributions of the Frankfurt School's CT to CTS. In particular, we emphasize the meaning of "critical" from the Frankfurt School's perspective; that is, the researcher becomes an agent of revolutionary practice that makes an ethical commitment to aid some group of people to overcome their unfree conditions. This emancipatory aim is less utopian and more a practical matter of helping the people suffering from certain conditions to transition into another situation. We outline two critical methods for accomplishing these emancipatory goals: first, immanent critique, which helps identify and clarify lived contradictions and, second, functional critique, which helps explain how certain words, practices, and ideologies function to stabilize the status quo.

Chapter 5 explores postcolonial and feminist influences on CTS and areas where CTS would benefit from their insights. Drawing our attention to the less visible sites and peoples involved in the study and experience of terrorism and violence, this chapter shifts our attention to everyday life. In particular, concern is placed on the ways that race, gender, and class inform the experience of terrorism and violence in different locations around the world. We also examine the role of standpoint epistemology in shaping knowledge of terrorism and, similarly, how power relations impact whose view of terrorism counts as relevant and whose view of terrorism does not. This chapter also considers the role of the "other" and, in particular, the way the "other" is constituted by dominant racial, gendered, and classed perspectives, including the imperial gaze of the colonial "other." In addition to providing an overview of the existing research on terrorism, we locate postcolonial and feminist concepts and issues in their historical development in IR and, especially, security studies.

Chapter 6 looks more closely at ethnography. In particular, the chapter defines ethnography as a methodology, method, and finished product, with an emphasis on the first and second elements of this definition. We discuss the process of identifying a terrorist group to study, indicate some strategies for gaining access to those communities and the risks associated with such an activity, and how one might develop and maintain a rapport with their subjects. We also focus on the methods and sources of data appropriate to this approach, including participant observation, semi- and unstructured interviewing, and the gathering of archived documents. The chapter ends with a discussion of three ethical relationships that a researcher using ethnography should consider, including the researchers' relation to their self, their subjects and bystanders, and their colleagues.

Chapter 7 continues with the exploration of ethnography, but the focus of this chapter is on the study of counterterrorist policy-makers, policy implementers, and those people affected by events deemed terrorism and counterterrorist policies. The problems of identifying a community to study, gaining entrance into a particular community, and developing and maintaining a rapport are discussed within the context of this new focus on policy-makers, policy implementers, and affected subjects.

Chapter 8 introduces the reader to the study of discourse, especially as it relates to IR, security studies, and CTS. In particular, the chapter outlines Critical Discourse Analysis (CDA) and poststructural, or Foucauldian, discourse analysis, with an emphasis on their differences and similarities. In greater detail, the poststructural approach to the study of discourse is outlined and suggestions are made as to how this approach can be used to critically study terrorism. We argue that discourse analysis is useful at explaining how particular identities are produced and policies deemed normal or commonsensical, while other identities and policies are excluded and deemed impossible.

Chapter 9 continues with a discussion of discourse analysis, but focuses specifically on state and terrorist identity-formations and the analysis of counterterrorism. The chapter begins by locating the role of the state in the study of terrorism. Then, our discussion turns to particular ways that state and terrorist identities can be studied using discourse analysis. We look more closely at the method of genealogy and provide examples of the genealogy of state counterterrorist identity and policy. The chapter ends by discussing some other relevant issues that the discourse analysis of terrorism entails.

Chapter 10 outlines the study of terrorism using SNA. In particular, the chapter discusses in detail some of the relevant concepts, such as ties, sites, and networks that are appropriate to this approach. We also indicate techniques and formulas for making structural and interactional measures common to SNA, such as size, density, degree, centrality, strength, duration, content, and so on. Furthermore, we discuss the differences between structural and interactional approaches to the study of networks, with an emphasis on the role of sense-making and identity in interactional approaches. The chapter also talks in depth about the methods and sources of data, including participant observation, different types of interviewing, and gathering documents from archives, which are regularly used in SNA. All of this information is related to CTS.

Questions to consider

- What are some of the arguments for and against CTS?
- What does "critical" mean for CTS?
- What are the types of research questions that drive CTS? And why those types of questions?
- Why is identity an important component of CTS?
- What CTS approaches adopt a political emphasis on emancipation?
- Why not reify terrorism? How can we avoid reifying terrorism?

Weblinks

Richard Jackson is one of the leading thinkers working on CTS. He blogs at http://richard jacksonterrorismblog.wordpress.com.

Anthony Burke writes about critical security and CTS at http://worldthoughtworldpolitics. wordpress.com.

The journal *Critical Studies on Terrorism* can be found at http://www.tandf.co.uk/journals/titles/ 17539153.asp.

Part I

The History and Transdisciplinarity of (Critical) Terrorism Studies

2 Terrorism Studies in International Relations

Introduction

In this chapter, we outline the history of terrorism scholarship in IR. It developed in the 1970s as a separate subfield and became more popular throughout the 1980s. However, it was the events of September 11, 2001 in New York that led to a growth of scholarship on terrorism. Despite this growth, much of TS remains focused in countering so-called terrorism, providing policy advice to governments and is definitionally limited in that it considers terrorism an act performed by non-state actors. These drawbacks of mainstream TS parallel the limitations of security studies during that subfield's development. In the second section of this chapter, we draw upon critical approaches to security to outline some ways in which CTS could proceed. In doing this, we argue that the diversity of CSS is not a drawback but indicates a thriving subfield, something that CTS could emulate.

A Brief History of Terrorism Studies in IR

While the study of violence and violent actors labeled as terrorism and terrorist is not new, the growth of "Terrorism Studies" as a subfield is relatively recent in IR. Scholars have associated the 1970s, with the rise in terrorism in Western Europe, as the time when scholarship on terrorism increased. There were also studies on how anti-colonial groups were labeled terrorist and some attention paid to terrorism by the state, with the state in discussion usually Nazi Germany or the Soviet Union. Even after the growth of scholarship on terrorism, its study tended to be seen as "problem-solving" and outside the realm of the more theoretically inclined subfield in IR such as security studies.

Indeed, as Richard Jackson points out, the study of terrorism was part of strategic studies and based on formulating policies to deal with terrorists, not understanding them or understanding how different social actors make sense of them. R. Jackson draws attention to the origins of TS in (orthodox) security studies and strategic studies, including counterinsurgency studies (2007c). He refers to Schmid and Jongman who wrote that much of early TS was "counterinsurgency masquerading as political science" (quoted in Jackson 2007c: 245) Jackson himself adds, "as a consequence, much terrorism research adopts state-centric priorities and perspectives and tends to reproduce a limited set of assumptions and narratives about the nature, causes and responses to terrorism" (2007c: 245). Additionally, Jackson points out that the embedded nature of terrorism "experts" is another drawback in traditional TS since these scholars are allied to institutions which are part of or funded by governments or have close links to government funding. In other words, "problem-solving" theory – where the problem is terrorism and the problem solver is (usually) the state – dominates traditional research on terrorism (Jackson 2007c).

There was a small group of scholars – mostly in Western Europe and linked with various government or strategic think tanks in the USA – who formed an "invisible college" of terrorism "experts", circulated information about terrorism, provided advice to government organizations and often served as "experts" on terrorism for media-related purposes. This prevented critical research. Ranstorp clarifies this further:

> The field of terrorism studies has been largely the confines of a rather varied collegiate of scholars hailing from diverse disciplinary backgrounds since its emergence as a specialization in the mid-to-late 1970s. Largely atomized and peripheral to the major disciplinary debates within the social and behavioral sciences, and confined to a few dozen core scholars worldwide, it is not surprising that there has been a relative absence of core debate and critical challenges of assumptions necessary to intellectually push the field forward with new waves of innovative research.
>
> (2009: 19)

Box 2.1 Mapping terrorism studies

Various scholars have recently "mapped" the development of terrorism studies as a growing subfield. Along with Ranstorp, Schmid and Jongman (2006), and Reid and Chen (2007) have outlined a history of terrorism studies. Ranstorp refers to Reid and Chen's work (based on the ISI citation database) and their claim that "there were forty-two core researchers in all between 1965 and 2003," a group he calls an "invisible college" (Ranstorp 2009: 20). The subfield of terrorism scholarship was dominated by this "invisible college" for much of the 1980s and 1990s: "Many of the same core terrorism researchers continually met and presented their findings at the same conferences for over two decades" (Ranstorp 2009: 20). Lisa Stampnitzky's work supports this claim and the interrelationship between knowledge about terrorism, this small "invisible college" (made up mostly of scholars from the Global North) and subsequent production of terrorism databases. In a sociological analysis which includes interviews with terrorism scholars, Stampnitzky claims that "Terrorism studies fails to conform to the most common sociological notions of what a field of intellectual production ought to look like, and has been described by participants and observers alike as a failure" (2011: 1).

However, Stampnitzky's work leaves out critically-oriented terrorism researchers. For this, Lee Jarvis in "The Spaces and Faces of Critical Terrorism Studies," (2009) outlines some of the main proponents and claims of critical terrorism studies. A similar but updated survey of terrorism scholarship is "The Orthodox Study of Terrorism," in Jackson et al.'s *Terrorism: A Critical Introduction* (2012). In it, Jackson et al. describe the development of terrorism studies and point out how the study of terrorism is now an "industry," where a small group of researchers circulate between think tanks, academia and the government and provide expert advice. Relatedly, they indicate how terrorism studies remains dominated by "problem-solving theory" to the detriment of critical scholarship. However, as Jackson et al. also point out, there is critical scholarship on terrorism, both from "within" IR but especially from outside of IR, in disciplines such as sociology, cultural studies and anthropology. We refer to some of these scholars in subsequent chapters. While a comprehensive list of these scholars would be beyond the scope of this short outline, scholars such as Adam Hodges, Alex Tickell, Cynthia Mahmood, Neluka Silva, and others have been and are studying terrorism. Postcolonial scholar Ashish Nandy's short essay "Narcissism and despair", also questions some of the orthodox understandings of terrorism.

Despite this ongoing development as a subfield, the relationship between IR theorists and TS remains somewhat distant. It can be noted that the two core journals in TS do not "contain articles that are directly concerned about applying IR theory to terrorism and a brief look at six leading IR theory journals seems to confirm this trend" (Spencer, quoted in Ranstorp 2009: 24). A review of articles in the issues from summer 2010 to winter 2011/12 of the journal *International Security* indicates only one article specifically with terrorism in its title. This article, entitled, "Muslim 'Homegrown' Terrorism in the United States: How Serious Is the Threat?" examines terrorism from the perspective of the state (how threatening "Muslim 'homegrown' terrorism" is to the US state). A critical approach might question the phrase "Muslim 'homegrown' terrorism" and ask questions such as: a threat to whom? As disclosures of communities of US citizens being put under surveillance and being treated as dangerous have indicated, "homegrown terrorism" is not just a threat *to* the state but a source of insecurity to various communities who are then linked with "homegrown terrorism" and face danger *from* state practices such as surveillance and worse.

The issues from winter 2000/1 to summer 2001 of the same journal (*International Security*) indicate a focus on democracy-promotion and international institutions apart from an article in the spring 2001 issue asking how prepared the USA is for a "domestic terrorist attack" (Falkenrath 2001: 147–186). The winter 2001/2 issue, however, is all about terrorism but overwhelmingly from a US–Western-centric standpoint. A subsection is entitled "The Threat of Terrorism: US Policy After September 11," thus erasing that "September 11" was of concern to peoples and actors outside of the USA and that there were other "September 11's" elsewhere. Of more concern is another subsection entitled, "The New War on Terrorism: South Asian Perspectives." This includes five articles, three of which are about the USA in Southwest Asia and Japan. Another is about the rise of the private military industry. The final article entitled, "Fighting Terrorism in Southern Asia: The Lessons of History," again focuses on how terrorism has been fought in the region, emphasizing the role of the states in doing the fighting. A critical approach to a similar topic could ask for different meanings of violence and terrorism as in Sluka (1989) and Warren (1993). It is of concern that one of the top security journals in the field has either ignored terrorism altogether or provided an overwhelmingly US- and state-centric standpoint from which to study terrorism. A quick glance through one year of issues of *Security Studies* (mid-2010 to mid-2011) reveal a similar lack of interest in terrorism as a topic of research. Among the few articles on terrorism is one in vol. 19, no. 1 about terrorism in different states of India. But this is a straightforward article, in which a simple hypothesis-testing is performed.

There is also a stigma attached to being a terrorism researcher as "many who publish elsewhere do not wish to be identified with 'terrorism studies'" (Gunning, quoted in Ranstorp 2009: 24). This lack of interest in being associated with terrorism scholarship is seen as due to TS's characterization as biased and uninterested in theoretical development or empirical research. Ranstorp reasons:

> it [the lack of IR theorists writing about terrorism] can probably be attributed to the fact that many non-specialists are turned off by the political bias and analytical shallowness on offer, as they often complain that similar empirical tapestries are woven together *without* much reference to other literature, critical debates, or interviews in the field with actual terrorists.
>
> (Ranstorp 2009: 24)[1]

A similar point was made in their book by Keith Krause and Michael Williams regarding security, as they wrote, "Yet lurking in the interstices of the discipline, one can without much effort find a wide range of scholarship that is 'about' security (and its core subject matter), but that its authors, or the discipline, refuse to label as such" (1997: vii). We claim that TS is even more in the interstices of IR and that critical research on terrorism is more commonly found in non-IR disciplines.

Critical Security Studies and Critical Terrorism Studies

Since the 1990s, while there has been a rise in researchers studying security from various critical perspectives, there was no concurrent rise in critical scholarship on terrorism in IR. Debates emerged in CSS about meanings of the term "critical," new referent objects, studying the state as a social construction, and expanding the meaning of security to include human, societal and global security. These dialogues offer potential avenues for CTS to explore.

Some CTS scholars are, however, critical of CTS's potential links with CSS. For example, Jonathan Joseph claims "CTS makes a clean break with prevailing views within IR theory to be truer to CT [Critical Theory]" (2011: 24). He critiques how the term "CT" has been used as an "umbrella term" for a diverse range of approaches which include historical sociology, feminism, poststructuralism, etc. and this leads to "the lack of any clear focus or direction" for CSS or CTS (2011: 28). He then calls for the "critical" in CTS to be linked with a Frankfurt School-oriented CT approach.

In Chapter 4, we address how a research project based on a Frankfurt School-oriented CT approach to terrorism could proceed. While Joseph's points about the lack of clarification of many critical terrorism scholars about what they mean by "critical" and their own methodological standpoints are worth following up, it is also important to keep in mind that ignoring the history of the development of other subfields in IR might be detrimental to the development of CTS. For now, we point out that ignoring the debates that have occurred and are occurring in CSS in order to claim that the "critical" in CTS should be defined in one particular way (as Joseph seems to do) is to attempt to establish an orthodoxy, one that CTS should be wary of. At the same time, narrowly linking "critical" TS with the Frankfurt School of CT may serve to silence non-Western (the Frankfurt School emerged from a specific historical and political background) standpoints on knowledge, thus illustrating the (hegemonic) workings of power; this is a practice that Frankfurt School-oriented researchers would themselves critique.

There is no reason why a Frankfurt School-oriented CT approach should be the *only* way to do critically oriented research on terrorism and that is something to which CSS scholarship, with its diverse approaches and geographical "schools," draws our attention. In that spirit, we provide here *six* ways in which the debates and dialogues in CSS might be helpful for the growth and development of CTS. Various aspects of these will be detailed further in the subsequent chapters of this volume and these are, of course, not exhaustive but they serve as a starting point for a dialogue on contributions (and warnings) of CSS for CTS. For future CTS researchers, the development of CSS can be useful in terms of learning from some of the debates in CSS and reminding them that clarifying one's methodological standpoint is important prior to conducting and communicating research. Then different "critical" scholars can dialogue and debate amongst themselves and also indicate how their work differs from those of orthodox scholars.

1. Methodological clarification.
2. Who or what is to be secured from terrorism?
3. How to study terrorism?
4. A "terroristization" approach.
5. Reflexivity.
6. Non-mainstream/non-Western ways of knowing.

Methodological Clarification

Some CTS scholars have called for the formation of a "broad church" (Jackson 2007a: 226; Jackson et al. 2009a) while others (Joseph 2011) have been critical of this call. Indeed, Joseph points out, "This desire for everything to be post-positivist and critical simply leads to ontological, epistemological and methodological confusion" (2011: 28). Undeniably, labeling one's work as "post-positivist" is insufficient to provide information on the researcher's methodological standpoint. But, instead of calling for a narrow definition of "critical" as Joseph ends up doing, a quick glance at CSS helps the researcher to indicate her own methodological standpoint prior to analysis. The answer (contra Joseph) is not linking "critical" in CTS with Frankfurt School CT. The answer is making it clear what the researcher's ontological (e.g., social interactions as foundational to analysis?) and epistemological (e.g., Foucauldian discourse analysis? Ethnography?) standpoints are. Making clear what *type* of post-positivist analysis is being done is key to clarification.

This is where CSS is helpful; a review of CSS's development since the late 1980s allows CTS researchers to acquire and hone a language in which their particular research standpoint can be presented and justified. At the same time, CSS's division into different branches (see Table 2.1) provides a template for how CTS might develop and pitfalls to be avoided. In this sense, the diverse ways in which CTS scholars conduct research is not a drawback or a weakness but a sign of the robustness of the emerging subfield. The goal for CTS scholars should be to clarify one's ontological and epistemological position so similarities and differences with others in this "broad church" and beyond it can be noted (Stump and Dixit 2012).

The debates that have occurred as CSS subdivided into various regional branches and standpoints are also useful for CTS in order to note how a thriving subfield can and does include different ways in which "critical" or interpretive methodologies can be used to study terrorism. Concepts have been expanded, critiqued and adapted for use in different situations. For example, the Copenhagen School's securitization approach has

Table 2.1 Some "sub"-schools of critical security studies

Subdivisions	Major influence(s)	Concepts	Theorists
Welsh	Jürgen Habermas, Frankfurt School	Emancipation	Ken Booth, Richard Wyn Jones
Paris School	Pierre Bourdieu	Habitus-field	Didier Bigo
Copenhagen School	Michel Foucault J. L. Austin	Foucauldian discourse, Securitization	Ole Waever, Lene Hansen
Feminist security	Judith Butler, the Frankfurt School, Michel Foucault	Emancipation (See Chapter 4 and Chapter 5)	Ann Tickner, Cynthia Weber, Christine Sylvester
Postcolonial security	Karl Marx, Gayatri Spivak, Franz Fanon	Subaltern, Hybridity (See Chapter 5)	Mohammad Ayoob, Ashish Nandy

been expanded, critiqued, adapted beyond Europe (e.g., Bilgin 2011; Pram Gad and Petersen 2011a and 2011b; Hansen 2011; Guzzinni 2011; Knudsen 2001; Wilkinson 2007; Vuori 2008). Similarly, discussions among and by critical security scholars can provide examples for CTS scholars in doing different types of "critical" analysis.

Who or What Is to Be Secured from Terrorism?

CSS had its beginnings when scholars realized the referent object (almost always the state) could be opened up for questioning. Research then focused on social construction of states, societies, groups, gender, races, and on the interconnections among these. A related focus was on the definitional process of security itself. This was unlike traditional security studies which maintained the state had a pre-given identity and security was almost exclusively defined as keeping the state secure from external, often military, threats.

Krause and Williams point out the implications of taking security for granted:

> To be a member of the security studies community has traditionally meant that one already knows what is to be studied. Both the object of security (what is to be secured) and the means for studying it are treated as largely given and self-evident. ... The security of the discipline ... is made into an element – perhaps even a prerequisite – of security itself!

(1997: ix)

As it was with security, so it is with terrorism where orthodox terrorism scholars often deem questions about social meanings of terrorism and terrorists as illustrating moral relativity and even sympathetic to so-called terrorists (Jones and Smith 2006). Reading texts like Krause and Williams allows CTS scholars to expand their vocabulary for positioning their own work in the field especially regarding how their research questions are fundamentally different to many of the "mainstream" questions asked in terrorism scholarship. This opens up the possibility for dialogue with the TS in general (if CTS researchers are so inclined). Discussing research questions in CSS, Weldes et al. write in *Cultures of Insecurity,*

> If conventional analyses in security studies begin with a set of pre-given entities and ask "how can they be secured?" the papers in this volume flip this strategy on its head. We take discourses of insecurity, or what David Campbell (1992) has called "representations of danger," as our objects of analysis and examine how they work. Analysis begins with a set of discourses and asks "what do they do?"
>
> (1999: 10)

By asking such questions, critical scholars interrogated the commonsensical understanding that threats emanated from outside the state as well as the inside/outside distinction that separated the state from the international system in much of security studies. One result of doing a critical analysis was then to open up discussions of what security means and ask questions such as: who is secure? Who is doing the securing? What is being secured? This destabilizes security and focuses attention on the meaning-making practices that produce something (and someone) as a security issue. For CSS, as quoted above, security does not have a pre-given meaning and is not a set of preferences such as rational choice theorists might claim; instead, security is practice – the practice of speaking, doing, acting in relation to what is considered security. The focus of research then shifts from linking security with a series of things (jobs, a strong army, financial well-being, etc.) to seeing it as a process or, as Waever called it, a "field" (Waever 1995). This allows security to be examined (or, in our case, terrorism) in relation to other actions and identities and as a field where various seemingly unconnected practices may emerge and coalesce during social interactions relating to terrorism.

Terrorism scholars can refer to these CSS debates of what security "is" and the related shift from understanding security as an external threat to a pre-existing bounded entity of the state, to security as how social actors define and act in relation to it. By shifting the focus from *what* terrorism "is," whether a material reality or resistance or radicalized violence, to *how* terrorism is conceptualized in practice by various social actors – states, different ethnic groups, regional and global organizations, etc. – the researcher can examine the spaces and politics of naming and reacting to terrorism. Here, the goal may be to illustrate the ideological underpinnings of the counterterrorism industry or calling for emancipation (if one is adopting a CT approach). But, it may also be outlining the mechanisms of governmentality and illustrating how terrorism is used as a technique of ordering and organizing (if one is following a more Foucauldian approach). The point being there are diverse ways in which terrorism can be studied and understood even within a "critical" orientation.

How to Study Terrorism?

Once the researcher has decided upon her ontology of terrorism, whether "rump materialism" (or "more ontological") as some CTS scholars have called for (R. Jackson and more explicitly J. Joseph) or an anti-foundationalist reflexivist approach, then the question of how to study terrorism arises. CSS can provide valuable pointers here in the types of discussions that may emerge as researchers with similar and yet different ontological commitments use the same concepts (e.g., discourse, social actions) differently. By making emerging CTS scholars more conscious that their use of a specific concept may not be shared by all critically oriented terrorism scholars, CSS helps remind CTS scholars to clarify their ontological and epistemological standpoints prior to analysis.

Karen Fierke writes that one of the goals of a CSS approach that outlines a series of different ways to study security "critically" is "to construct and facilitate a dialogue between different approaches regarding the various concepts" (2007: 3). It is a similar task that CTS scholars can pursue as well. There can be a dialogue about concepts such as "state terrorism," "insurgency," "reconciliation" and especially "emancipation" (Box 2.2).

Box 2.2 Being critical: deconstruction

As we have indicated elsewhere, it is important for researchers interested in doing critical work on terrorism to realize that the Frankfurt School's Critical Theory approach is not the only way of doing critical scholarship. Others include Foucault-influenced research (described more in Chapters 8 and 9) as well as other approaches drawing from anthropology and sociology (Chapters 6 and 7) and Derrida-inspired deconstruction. Since most of these other ways of doing research will be detailed further in chapters to follow, we will now briefly outline how a deconstructionist research program could proceed.

Deconstruction is one of Derrida's best-known concepts. Simply put (if one may be permitted to simplify what is a complex concept), if language is a series of signs which refer to each other, then meanings (and categories) are made up of binary dichotomies. For example, developed/underdeveloped, secure/insecure, The West/Muslim World. As can be noted here, these binaries are not neutral. Instead, one side is privileged over the other and there is a hierarchical relationship between one side of the binary and the other. Deconstruction then refers to an ethos which brings to our attention this non-neutrality of how "we" categorize the world around us. It decenters the binary formulation of meanings. At the same time, deconstruction also "centers" the previously-marginalized side of the dichotomy. However, this does not mean a new center is created. Instead, deconstruction points towards the unstable nature of these categorizations and, as such, questions the new center as well.

For IR, drawing on deconstruction David Campbell writes,

> deconstruction signifies, on the one hand, the determinate strategies that can be variously deployed to disturb and unsettle, while, on the other hand, it marks the undecidable nature of the context in which those strategies are required to operate – as well as the process and provocation that take place in between.
>
> (1998b: 21)

A researcher who uses deconstruction thus needs to be continually aware that any fixity of meaning and the subsequent categorization of identities and issues are themselves unstable in the long term. Deconstruction is therefore anti-foundational while allowing for the possibility of studying temporarily "fixed" identities, whether of "terrorists" or "counterterrorism." CSS scholar David Campbell's *National Deconstruction: Violence, Identity and Justice in Bosnia* (1998b) uses Derrida's work to analyze events in the former Yugoslavia and, as such, is exemplary of how deconstruction can be useful for analysis. A similar study on terrorism could be conducted in which the "unsettling" of issues related to terrorism and counterterrorism and how we come to know these can be scrutinized. Another possible research concern is a deconstructive analysis of the West/Muslim World (or West/Non West) dichotomy.

As Campbell points out, deconstruction is not a method or a philosophy, discourse, act or practice. "It is what happens, what is happening today in what they call society, politics, diplomacy, economics, historical reality and so on and so forth" (Derrida, quoted in Campbell 1998b: 24). This thus draws attention to the ethos of critique as well as to the critique of the current sociopolitical condition itself.

For examples of scholars outside of IR who have used deconstruction in their own work, Barbara Johnson in feminism, Homi Bhabha in cultural theory/postcolonial studies and Judith Butler in feminist/cultural studies are exemplary for researchers interested in pursuing a deconstructionist analysis. Deconstruction is not limited to sociology, anthropology, feminism and IR, however; in architecture, a deconstruction-inspired movement exists with proponents calling for designing structures which reflect the unstable nature of social world as deconstructionists see it, while also ensuring the building remains useful for various purposes. Thus deconstruction is useful not just for texts and discourses but also for spatial reimagining.

A "Terroristization" Approach

In CSS, securitization has been discussed, debated and attempts have been made to debunk it. However, it remains a well-known and well-traveled concept since its early usage in the 1990s. Drawing from those discussions, a similar approach to the processes which socially construct an issue, individual, states, regions, races and ethnicities, religion, etc., as terrorist can be adopted. Perhaps this approach may even be called "terroristization." Securitization began by focusing on the state as the main actor doing the securitizing but has since expanded to include other levels of analysis as well as other social actors who may do the securitizing. It assumes security is a "speech act" and thus emphasizes the role of language and social practices in relating to security. In *On Security,* Ole Waever writes, "In naming a certain development a security problem, the 'state' can claim a special right, one that will, in the final instance, always be defined by the state and its elites" (1995: 54). He goes on to ask:

> What then *is* security? With the help of language theory, we can regard security as a *speech act.* In this usage, security is not of interest as a sign that refers to something more real; the utterance *itself* is the act. By saying it, something is done (as in betting, giving a promise, naming a ship). By uttering "security," a state-representative moves a particular development into a specific area, and thereby claims a special right to use whatever means are necessary to block it.
>
> (1995: 55)

Similarly, CTS scholars might want to study practices of terroristization. Drawing on and adapting the securitization approach, terroristization would emphasize the process by which terrorism is defined and communicated and how terrorist threats are made sense of by different social actors. Relatedly, the focus is on who (states, ethnic groups, individuals) becomes categorized as "terrorist" and the implications of such labeling practices on societies as well as the "special rights" then conferred – often to states but also to certain ethnic groups, regional and international organizations, etc. – to counter such terrorists. Adopting a terroristization approach, the state would still be important to analysis since the state does represent and communicate information about terrorist threats.

But other levels of analysis, such as popular culture and its representations of danger, populations and their understandings of terrorism as well as regional and global actors could also be studied for terroristization. For example, while recent big budget Hollywood films have included a multicultural set of villains, the role played by Arabs remains linked with villainy and danger (Earp and Jhally 2006). Similarly, Muslims in the USA have become "terroristized" in the aftermath of an event (September 11, 2001) after which their "Muslimness" has been seen as a sign of danger. Terroristization is not just limited to peoples, but spaces can become terroristized as well. The debates over the future of the Maze prison in Northern Ireland indicate the emotional and often controversial question of how a formerly terroristized place, in this case, a well-known prison, could (or should not) be "de-terroristized" during peace-building.

The terroristization of various spaces within the USA can also be noted in different texts. A January 2012 report by the National Consortium for the Study of Terrorism and Responses to Terrorism (START), an institution which is linked with the US Department of Homeland Security, listed all events considered terrorism in the United States from 1970 to 2008. They then listed "hot spots" of terrorism, with a "hot spot" being areas where more than the US average (of six incidents) of terrorism had occurred. The conclusion included information that all states in the USA had suffered from at least one act of terrorism in this period, with Denver and Boulder (for example) being "hot spots" of "left-wing terrorism." A deeper look at the report indicates the definition of terrorists in this report is quite broad and is limited to "non-state actors" (START 2012). The report bases its definition of terrorism on that of the global terrorism database (which forms a large part of the data for the START report). The definition of terrorism used by the global terrorism database is as follows: "the threatened or actual use of illegal force by non-state actors, in order to attain a political, economic, religious or social goal, through fear, coercion or intimidation." Page 9, Footnote 3 of the report indicates how START expanded this definition. But the main focus remains on non-state actors and on "threats" and "coercion" as part of the definition. A related outcome here is, of course, the "de-terroristization" of the state as its actions are erased from the report's definition of what counts as terrorist.

Reflexivity

Critical approaches to studying political violence, especially in non-IR disciplines, provide guidelines on how to incorporate reflexivity into choosing texts (and research participants), doing fieldwork and communicating knowledge. Ethnographers such as Michael Burawoy, James Clifford, George Marcus and Charlotte Aull Davies have written extensively about the practice and challenges of reflexivity in the process of doing fieldwork. Scholars concerned with reflexivity also draw attention to broader processes and networks within which the individual researcher is situated and which shape the agency of the researcher in the process of choosing research topics and doing research (Eagleton-Pierce 2011). (Chapter 4 has more on reflexive analysis.) Mark

Neufeld's "Reflexivity and International Relations Theory" (1995) claimed "reflexivity" was "reflection on the process of theorizing" (1995: 40). Feminist IR scholars including Ackerly and True (2008) and Hesse-Biber and Piatelli (2007) developed the concept of reflexivity further and encouraged its usage to produce ethical, self-reflective research. CTS scholars, too, could build upon Neufeld and feminist scholars' work in this regard.

An example of critically oriented research that emphasizes reflexivity could be a research project that uses autoethnography to study terrorism. In security studies, feminist security scholars often centralize the researcher's own experiences in the world as a way of accessing and gaining data. In terrorism research, Richard Jackson has used it in his own research as has Marie Breen Smyth to study the concept and practices related to "suspect communities" in the UK (Smyth 2009).

Non-mainstream and Non-Western Ways of Knowing

Political violence, even if not explicitly labeled terrorism, has been studied extensively from beyond IR's mainstream. Much of this research has emerged from other disciplines such as sociology, anthropology, cultural studies, literature, history and geography (see Box 2.2). There is geographical diversity as well, not in terms of studying "other" peoples and places from Western standpoints but being aware of how different social actors may and do make sense of security (or, in our case, terrorism) differently in different places and times.

An example of interest here would be studies of indigenous meanings of nation and violence that have emerged. In Australian Aboriginal communities, the concept of "lateral violence" has been used to refer to: "behaviors that might include bullying, gossiping, jealousy, shaming, social exclusion, family feuding and organizational conflict, which often escalate into physical violence" (Gooda 2011). This is one of many illustrations of how violence is made sense of locally. Examples of lateral violence relating to the state include having to repeatedly prove one's identity when claiming native title rights. Furthermore, "In some states Aboriginal groups have a say in who belongs to a particular land and who doesn't, a right which can stir lateral violence when native title claimants are not sure of their Aboriginal identity. The native title process can also lead to feelings of dispossession" ("Bullying and lateral violence"). Here, colonial practices (erasure of Aboriginal identities) allied with modern state apparatus (needing to "prove" Aboriginal identity and the increased monetary value of settled land in a global capitalist system) can create mistrust – lateral violence – within and among communities. Insecurity is not produced directly from military or economic sources but from having to prove an identity that may have been silenced or obscured by the colonial state. The experiences of violence (and terror) are thus locally produced and made sense of.

Conclusion

On the whole, a clear specification of what the researcher means by "critical" – whether Frankfurt School-influenced (See Chapter 4) or other understandings of critical (e.g., poststructural) – is necessary for a robust and growing CTS subfield. If researchers state their ontological and epistemological standpoints prior to analysis, dialogue and dissent can be better articulated. Looking at the development of CSS, critical terrorism scholars can work towards redefining and reworking theories on terrorism. Different ways of understanding terrorism, drawn from CSS, can be pursued. CTS scholars can also expand topics and sites for empirical research, following on from research in other disciplines (see Table 3.1). These potential research avenues could address the current gap in security studies (and IR) regarding theoretically and empirically rich research on terrorism.

Questions to consider

- What are some lessons that researchers can learn and some pitfalls to avoid from the development of CSS for CTS?
- Why has TS occupied a marginal position in IR? What are some implications of this for the development of a robust subfield?
- Write some features of a "problem-solving" approach to terrorism; compare this with a critical approach to terrorism.
- Can you think of some examples of "terroristization" in the world today? What are some ethical, sociopolitical and normative implications of such practices for research on terrorism?
- Search for some non-Western sources on political violence and terrorism. How do they understand terrorism?

Note

1 Ranstorp also refers to Vallis, Yang and Abbas (2007) and their survey of the field.

Further Reading

Bleiker, R. and Brigg, M. (2010), "Autoethnographic International Relations: Exploring the Self as a Source of Knowledge," *Review of International Studies*, 36 (3): 779–798.

Buzan, B., Waever, O., and de Wilde, J. (1998), *Security: A New Framework for Analysis*, Boulder, CO: Lynne Rienner.

Campbell, D. (1998), *National Deconstruction: Violence, Identity and Justice in Bosnia*, Minneapolis, MN: University of Minnesota Press.

Krause, K. and Williams, M. (Eds.) (1997), *Critical Security Studies: Concepts and Cases*, Minneapolis, MN: University of Minnesota Press.

Kurki, M., Stavrianakis, A., Klabbers, J., Eschle, C., Maiguashca, B., and Grovogui, S. N. (2009), "Roundtable: The Limits to Bridge-Building," *International Relations*, 23 (1): 115–140.

Onuf, N., Burke, A., Sjoberg, L., Finney, P., Stokes, D., Joseph, J., Wight, C., and Dunne, T. (2009), "Forum: Bridge-Building and Terrorism," *International Relations*, 23 (1): 51–114.

Weldes, J., Laffey, M., Duvall, R., and Gusterson, H. (1999), *Cultures of Insecurity: States, Communities and the Production of Danger*, Minneapolis, MN: University of Minnesota Press.

Weblinks

A longer bibliography on autoethnography can be found at http://h2obeta.law.harvard.edu/65082 (accessed January 22, 2012).

For a view of security from non-Western perspectives, see http://www.littlemag.com/security/index.html.

D. Campbell blogs at http://www.david-campbell.org.

"Collaboratory in Critical Security Methods," http://www8.open.ac.uk/researchprojects/iccm.

The journal *Security Dialogue* can be found at http://sdi.sagepub.com.

3   Introducing Critical Terrorism Studies

Introduction

CTS has generally been linked with Richard Jackson and his colleagues (see Chapter 1) who have argued for a study of terrorism that does not privilege the state and includes methodological plurality (Jackson et al. 2009a, 2012). In the first part of this chapter, we refer to current CTS scholars' own words in describing what they do and how they see their work as different in relation to "orthodox" TS. In the second part, we draw from the study of terrorism and terrorists in non-IR disciplines, such as anthropology, history, literature, and philosophy to indicate possible research avenues for critical research on terrorism. In the final part of the chapter, we discuss geographical and methodological plurality and end by briefly indicating how a methodologically plural CTS could take shape.

The Current State of Critical Terrorism Scholarship

Since the publication of *Writing the War on Terrorism* (2005), there has been a wide move by Richard Jackson and his colleagues in promoting critical terrorism scholarship. Two recent books, *Critical Terrorism Studies: A New Research Agenda* (2009b) and *Terrorism: A Critical Introduction* (2012) provide overviews of the current state of CTS. This current CTS is characterized by:

1. Being critical of "orthodox" or traditional terrorism scholarship: In *Terrorism: A Critical Introduction* (2012), Jackson et al. claim their use of "critical" refers to "trying to stand apart from the existing order, questioning what passes for commonsense or accepted knowledge and how it is sustained" (2012: 31). They go on to say, "'critical' refers to approaches which draw upon the tools and insights of Critical Theory" (Jackson et al. 2012: 31).
2. Ontologically, current CTS considers terrorism a "social fact" (Jackson et al. 2012: 35) but also a means to some sort of political end as well as a strategy that different social actors can employ (2012: 35). Thus, for current CTS, terrorism is both a social fact and something that is out there (see Dixit and Stump 2011, as well as Chapter 1 for our thoughts on this issue). For researchers, the important point is that assuming terrorism as a strategy or a tactic assumes its "realness," which may contradict the notion of it as a "social fact." On a related note, current CTS has called for a maintaining of terrorism as "rump materialism," which falls under a critical realist ontology.

3. Epistemologically, current CTS argues the knowledge about terrorism is social and is linked with power (Jackson et al. 2012: 36). It also emphasizes a specific notion of reflexivity and personal subjectivity in making claims about terrorism (Jackson et al. 2012: 37). The key point is that current CTS acknowledges the interconnections between knowledge and power in designing research questions and that is something that CTS overall focuses on. As Jackson et al. write, "CTS scholars are concerned with questions like: Who is terrorism research for? How does terrorism research support particular interests? What are the effects of terrorism research on society?" (2012: 37). Questions that current CTS alludes to and that future research could expand upon include: how does terrorism research *construct* (and not just reflect) particular interests and identities? How are these (new) interests *legitimated* and *maintained?* What are the discursive mechanisms that allow for the legitimation of particular interests and identities during the research on terrorism and terrorists? These are the types of research questions that our notion of CTS point towards.
4. Emancipation: current CTS scholars have called for a "continuous immanent critique and the broader project of emancipation" (Jackson et al. 2012: 42). They describe emancipation as, "a continuous *process* of struggle and critique, rather than any particular endpoint or universal grand narrative. Emancipation, then, can never be fully and finally achieved; it is something for us as scholars, students and practitioners of global politics to continuously aim *towards*" (Jackson et al. 2012: 41–42).
5. Implications of current CTS research on the broader TS agenda: current CTS has focused on broadening the study of terrorism to include topics that are usually out of the mainstream, which includes deepening TS by "uncovering the field's underlying ideological, institutional and material interests" (Jackson et al. 2012: 43). It also includes a commitment to "*emancipatory praxis* central to the terrorism research enterprise" (Jackson et al. 2012: 43). Indeed, current CTS's summing up of "a future research agenda" is worth quoting in full here:

> A future critical research agenda calls for more systematic research on the underlying conditions and material interests of the TS field, state terrorism, the social and historical context of terrorism, gender and terrorism, the experience and perspectives of the developing world, and the impacts and ethics of counterterrorism, particularly the war on terrorism.
>
> (Jackson et al. 2012: 45)

In the next section, we outline some of the ways in which terrorism has been studied in fields outside of IR, providing examples from anthropology and sociology, geography, history, rhetoric and cultural studies, philosophy, and literature.

(Inter)Disciplining Critical Terrorism Studies

Anthropology and Sociology

There has been extensive research on terrorism in anthropological and sociological fields. Indeed, these were two of the fields where research on terrorism and terrorists was common even before the expansion of terrorism-related research since September 11, 2001. Some examples include Joseba Zulaika and William Douglass's *Terror and Taboo: The Follies, Fables and Faces of Terrorism* (1996), Jack Santino's research on Northern Ireland in *Signs of War and Peace: Social Conflict and the Uses of Symbols in*

Table 3.1 Examples of research on terrorism from non-IR disciplines

Academic discipline	Selected scholars	Research method(s)
Anthropology	Feldman, Santino, Zulaika and Douglass, McEvoy, Aretxaga	Participant-observation; interviews
Cultural Studies	Kumar, Temple-Raston	Drawing on fiction; personal narratives; visual analysis
Literature	Tickell, Kumar, Rockwell, Clymer	Poems and novels; writing; discourse analysis
Philosophy	Butler, Žižek, Nandy, Derrida and Habermas	Engagement with texts
History	Jackson, Lincoln	Textual analysis, genealogy
Geography	Elden, de Goede,	Studying flows and networks; spatiality as a mode of analysis
Media studies/rhetoric	Altheide, Oliverio, Hodges	Interrogation of texts and concepts; visual analysis
Sociology	Zulaika and Douglass, Altheide, Oliverio, Wagner-Pacifici	Symbolic interactionism; ethnography content analysis; discourse analysis

Public in Northern Ireland (2004), and Begonia Aretxaga's *Shattering Silence: Women, Nationalism and Political Subjectivity in Northern Ireland* (1997). Allen Feldman's *Formations of Violence: The Narrative of the Body and Political Terror in Northern Ireland* (1991) was one of the earliest terrorism-related ethnographies.

Anthropologists have also studied the effects of violence by the state. As such, anthropologists have been one of the few terrorism scholars who have focused on the state and its actions in creating fear and terror for (some) people, including often its own citizens instead of taking for granted orthodox terrorism scholars' view of the state as a safeguard against terrorism. Jeffrey Sluka's edited collection *Death Squad* (2000) includes essays on India, Argentina, Guatemala, and Spain, among others. In it, various meanings of terror and terrorism from the perspective of communities and individuals are outlined and there is an interrogation of the role of the state and its relationship to violence.

Anthropologists and sociologists detail their own feelings and reflections during the process of researching terrorism. Ethnography is a common methodological approach. Critical terrorism research drawn from anthropology and sociology may include:

• Outlining different meanings of "emancipation," "freedom," "terrorism," and "democracy" in different sociocultural contexts. For example, Stump (2010) examines everyday orientations towards terrorism in the USA. Dixit has studied meanings of "terrorism" in a context (Nepal) where such a word was not commonly used, and where the local word (*atankakari* in Nepali) has the same meaning for terrorist and "revolutionary."

• Accessing and describing cultural meanings of "terrorism," at the levels of the state or at everyday levels. For example, Alex Argenti-Pillen's *Masking Terror* (2003) examines the effects on people of a rural community when most of its young men become soldiers of the Sri Lankan state. Here, the impact of (fighting) terrorism upon those who do the fighting itself is laid out. Argenti-Pillen also looks at the related impact on women of the community and how they respond to violence.

- Detailing the effects of violence – both by terrorists and the state – amongst different ethnic groups, communities, genders: In addition to Feldman (1991) and Aretxaga (1997) indicated above, other examples include *Karaoke Fascism* (2004) where Monique Skidmore conducts "an ethnography of fear" in Burma. The strategies and policies by which the state operates to create fear amongst the citizens and also among tourists and visitors are outlined, along with examples of resistance. Here, too, anthropologists direct our attention to how terrorism and terror do not just emanate from non-state groups but are key to how a state operates and maintains its identity. Skidmore's research participants include those who are often "invisible" in studies of terrorism: addicts, prostitutes, children, and women.
- Looking at how the state makes sense of its actions and also at the meaning of post-conflict reconciliation in different societies. For example, the Israeli state's actions in creating a surveillance state and thus increasing the insecurity of its citizens is one of the themes of Juliana Ochs' *Security and Suspicion: An Ethnography of Everyday Life in Israel* (2011).
- Examining the challenges of being a researcher and doing research in situations of conflict and terrorism, including debates about the involvement of anthropologists in the US Human Terrain System. An example is Ivana Macek's *Sarajevo Under Siege: Anthropology in Wartime* (2011). Macek's book describes the lives of "ordinary people" in Sarajevo. Her focus is on how people continued with their lives in the midst of conflict and chaos. On a similar note, Carolyn Nordstrom's *A Different Kind of War Story* (1997) looks at Mozambican civil war, and the Iraq War is the central theme for *Iraq at a Distance: What Anthropologists Can Teach Us About the War* (Robben, 2010). This last example does not include fieldwork in Iraq but compares the situation there with other "cases," including Northern Ireland, Palestine and Israel. The editors call their approach "ethnographic imagination," indicating an innovative research approach to the issue of studying areas which may be deemed "off limits" by Institutional Review Boards of US academic institutions (such as Iraq during wartime).

Geography

Similar to anthropology and sociology, geographers have taken up the challenge of studying terrorism from a critical perspective. Geographers draw attention to spaces and places where reactions to and practices of terrorism and counterterrorism operate. They often focus on "making visible" sites which often remain out of sight in TS and examine flows and movements of people, money, ideas, etc. We will briefly outline each of these in turn:

- **Space and place**: questions of space and place take priority in geography and this is reflected in geographical research of terrorism. Stuart Elden's *Terror and Territory: The Spatial Extent of Sovereignty* (2009) studies how the "war on terror" relates to and challenges mainstream understandings of sovereignty and territory. Derek Gregory, in his own words, says he is interested in studying "the spatial modalities of late modern war" and "cultural and political geographies of bombing".[1] His book *The Colonial Present: Afghanistan, Palestine, Iraq* (2004) connects different spaces together in terms of their commonalities (experiences of colonialism and violence). Lunstrum studies how groups can empty populated spaces as a form of terror and "deterritorialization" and, as such, challenge the territory-based understandings of citizenship and state (2009). Her work is based on the conflict in Mozambique and her data is composed of interviews with survivors. Terror(ism), for critical geographers, is not just experienced but lived. Its link with space (as well as its use to de-link individuals from particular spaces) is possible grounds for further research. In all of these examples, critical geography – a focus on territorialization and deterritorialization, a concern with the violent meaning-making of particular spaces and the processes by which modern wars de-territorialize (and delete) peoples – becomes important. Further CTS research can focus on these themes.

- **Visualization**: critical geography-oriented approaches to terrorism make sites and issues visible. Here, visualization does not just mean mapping in the conventional sense but making visible those issues and actors who are often ignored in the "war on terror." It can also mean how particular bodies (e.g., Muslims in the USA) become "visualized" as they are kept under observation by the state. Comaroff's notion of Guantánamo as a "space of contradiction" draws on "political geography for understanding the war on terror" (2007: 381). He draws attention to the "legal, spatial and institutional" (2007: 387) contradictions, which visualize certain aspects of the space of Guantánamo while making invisible others. Thus, further research could focus on (a) visualizing spaces and peoples who are often "invisible" in mainstream terrorism scholarship; and (b) studying techniques which make (some) bodies and spaces visible.
- **Flows and movements**: Geographers concentrate on flows and movements and, as such, issues such as "terrorist financing," migration, movement of people who are under surveillance, and movements of those who are considered safe all form possible research topics.

History

From a critical perspective, historians can study events labeled terrorism in order to note how meanings of terrorism and states' reactions to it have shifted over time. Gerard Chaliand and Arnaud Blin in *The History of Terrorism: From Antiquity to Al Qaeda* (2007) outline historical "cases" of terrorism but also point out how perceptions of terrorism and counterterrorism have shifted.

Terrorism research drawing from history can also use methods of oral historiography as well as Foucauldian genealogical approaches. Critical historiography moves from a focus on individuals to a focus on social groups and the "making" of particular actors, such as "female suicide bombers" within processes of capitalism and globalization. Methodologically, critical historians examine events and actions which have been labeled terrorist and others which have not and ask about the sociopolitical processes which produce these different meanings. They are also wary of general theories (Gage 2011: 80) and, as such, concentrate attention on processes and mechanisms, rather than trying to develop a universal "theory" of terrorist action. CTS based on history can utilize similar methods (genealogy, oral histories, etc.) and also topics (collective identity-formation, sociological history, etc.).

Groups considered terrorist today have often had a long history, of involvement in anti-colonial movements and in resisting oppression. Historians, by pointing out processes of imperialism and oppression – draw attention to how terrorism is not just a new form of political violence or even something that is opposed to "the West." Questions of change – calling for political, economic, social change and using physical violence to do so – are other concerns that historians raise and critical terrorism scholars can focus on.

Questions of how to study terrorism are often at the forefront of critical historical analysis. As one US historian puts it:

> Almost a decade out from 9/11, most US historians remain hard-pressed to explain what terrorism is, how and when it began, or what its impact has been. There is little consensus about how best to approach the subject or even whether to address it at all. This is partly because the issue poses knotty political questions: How do we talk about terrorism without reinforcing the "war on terror " or lapsing into hopeless presentism? It also brings serious methodological problems: Is terrorism a word to be traced through centuries of semantic permutation? Is it an epithet to be applied to forms of violence we do not like? Is it a concept to be defined, however loosely, and followed through time?
>
> (Gage 2011: 74)[2]

Box 3.1 Terrorism in the USA: a historian speaks

"Scholars have noted that Americans in the mid-nineteenth century used 'terrorism' to describe a variety of activities, from strikes and boycotts to the institution of slavery and the terror of the Civil War. It was not until the late nineteenth century, however, that the words 'terrorism' and 'terrorist' were applied to a discrete form of violence, something to be inspected, claimed, and studied in its own right. After he attempted to assassinate the industrialist Henry Clay Frick in 1892, the anarchist Alexander Berkman boldly – and plausibly – claimed that he had committed 'the first terrorist act in America.' Viewed from a twenty-first-century perspective, Berkman's statement seems questionable. It does not account for many episodes of violence that have since been classified as possible examples of terrorism, from the brutalities (on all sides) of colonial-era Indian conflicts to the lynchings and other murders perpetrated by the Reconstruction-era Ku Klux Klan. Nor does Berkman's act resemble the form of violence currently dominating the news: organized, anonymous, international attacks aimed at large groups of civilians. Berkman, however, had a particular tradition in mind when he adopted the 'terrorist' label. To him (and to the first generation of social scientists to study the phenomenon), terrorism was a well-theorized revolutionary tactic consisting of targeted, individual attacks against symbols of government and capital. The terms 'terrorism' and 'terrorist', in that view, were descriptive rather than pejorative, part of a revolutionary ethos birthed in the Russian revolt against the tsar and subsequently dispersed around the globe."

(Gage 2011: 75–76)

"Like the idea of 'newness', assertions about terrorism's absence, or its foreign nature, have long served political agendas. In the late nineteenth century, elite commentators often explained anarchist violence as a European importation, suggesting that class and revolutionary conflict were antithetical to the American experience. Today, political leaders use the words 'terrorism' and 'terrorist' almost exclusively to refer to international networks and threats. By contrast, native-born white Americans who commit acts of political violence are usually treated as misguided individuals. Taking a historical view of terrorism begins to break down these accepted binaries. Terrorism, history tells us, has come both from without and from within, and it has emerged in a variety of political contexts. The historical approach also underscores the connections between the highly varied political actors who have, at one time or another, adopted some variant of terrorism as a tactic of vengeance or political gain. Seen from a historical perspective, terrorism has almost never emerged in a political vacuum. Whether in Harpers Ferry or Oklahoma City or downtown New York, dramatic acts of violence have tended to erupt in the context of much broader political and social conflicts. Those larger conversations – about slavery, plutocracy, or U.S. tyranny – give such acts of violence their communicative power."

(Gage 2011: 92)

Rhetoric and Cultural Studies

One way to approach terrorism through a media studies/rhetoric lens is to examine it as a form of language and communication. By doing so, representations of terrorism can then be analyzed in acts of (physical) violence but also in visual depictions, art and popular culture, speeches, novels and books (writing), and so on. Here, the representations of terrorism and how they are produced in different cultures are one possible way to study terrorism. While media studies examines representations of terrorism in general, rhetoric focuses more specifically on speech and talks of and about terrorism and terrorists. One can examine rhetoric as "masking" an underlying reality or as constituting interests and identities.

A focus on rhetoric and the use of language draws attention to how terms like "terrorist," "insurgent," "revolutionary," "radical Islamist" all have evaluation embedded within them. Calling people terrorist (as, for example, the 2012 claims by the Syrian government that it is fighting against terrorism; or the 2001–2006 claims by the Nepali government that "Maoist terrorists" were destabilizing the state and threatening the people) automatically allows for particular actions (use of military violence, suspension of laws, etc.). At the same time, such language also denies agency and silences (some) people (terrorists) and their demands. It makes their calls for change illegitimate without attempting to understand the social, political and historical conditions under which such demands may have emerged and resonated.

In an example of how media analysis can proceed, Hammon and Barnfield (2011) analyze how the "war on terror" has been made sense of within (mostly US) popular culture. They provide examples of how the Twin Towers were erased from big name films and TV shows in the aftermath of September 11, 2001, and how scenes with airplanes in danger were also deleted. The collection of articles includes some focusing on news media (the BBC in this case). Other media scholars have analyzed films and TV shows ranging from war films such as *Redacted* and *Hurt Locker* to fantasy like *The Dark Knight* and TV shows including *24* and *Spooks*.

Cultural studies critically questions particular representations of terrorism and counterterrorism, focusing on the production of difference. R. Jackson et al. describe the "cultural construction of terrorism" (2012: 50–71), focusing mostly on the United States.

Further research could examine how other cultural contexts (and media) have constructed terrorism and the different popular understandings of terrorism therein. In "Cultural Productions of 9/11," various media – video games, novels, plays, movies – are studied for different representations of "9/11" and how it has been narrated in (mostly Western) popular culture (Schaberg and Thompson 2011). The exceptionality of "9/11" and how, often, its invocation closes off avenues for discussions of other issues, threats, other "9/11s" elsewhere, are a common theme in these essays. These cultural studies-based examples utilize different forms of textual and visual ethnography (see Chapter 6 and Chapter 7) as well as discourse analysis (see Chapter 9) as their research methods. As such, adopting an interdisciplinary focus to CTS provides examples of research methods that are less commonly used in terrorism studies, and, by doing so, assists researchers by indicating how such methods have been and can be used to study terrorism.

Literature

From a literature standpoint, studying terrorism is often connected with its depictions in texts and pictures. There are obvious "payouts" of studying nonfiction or memoir-based accounts of terrorism; for example, to note how decisions were made by both terrorists and those who countered them, feelings and perceptions of terrorists and counterterrorists, under-standing how people (e.g., suicide bombers) justified their actions, and so on. For fiction, however, the "payouts" may seem less obvious. Here, we outline three ways in which literature in the form of fiction can and has contributed to critical research on terrorism:

1.   providing and questioning visions for the future;
2.   explorations of human experiences;
3   depictions of change.

Providing and Questioning Visions for the Future

Fiction, in the form of novels, drama or poems, allows for an exploration of various possibilities for the future. In this, it often gives voice to utopian or dystopian futures and creates worlds wherein various terrorist-related practices (whether terrorist violence or counterterrorist practices such as increased surveillance and enhanced interrogation) play out. For example, science-fiction author William Gibson's *Pattern Recognition* refers to the September 11, 2001, attacks while building a narrative of shifting identities in a networked world.

In the realm of thrillers, James W. Huston (*The Shadows of Power, Flash Point, Secret Justice*), Alex Berenson (*The Silent Man*), Vince Flynn (*Extreme Measures*), and various video games-related book tie-ins by Tom Clancy all deal with terrorism. While it may be a stretch to call these "literature," they are popular fiction which are sold in more places (airports, supermarkets, etc.) than the more "serious" novels and are likely to have been read by and inform the cultural repertoire of many English-speaking people. The common theme in these novels is that the West (or, as is most often, the USA) is under attack by terrorists and the novel's hero (often a military official or even the president; often male) has to save the USA (and, by extension, the world). In these books, the "future narrative" is of the USA and the West as under threat but ultimately, guided by its (militarized and masculine) leaders, capable of defeating the "terrorist enemy."

In this list of generic thrillers, Frederick Forsyth's *The Afghan* is a slight anomaly as its major character takes on the identity of an al-Qaeda-affiliated individual. A critical approach to this novel would point out questions of identity and the blurred boundaries between "self" (the former SAS hero) and "other" (the Afghan terrorist). The notion that a white, former Special Forces officer can change places with an Afghan (and become "the Afghan") is something that is worth mulling over. That both the hero and the terrorist require a similar skillset is something that is also worth pointing out.

Explorations of Human Experiences

Drama, poetry, memoirs, fiction, and nonfiction also express an array of diverse human experiences. Silva (2010) analyzes gender and terrorism as presented in two Sri Lankan plays. Patrick Magee, a convicted IRA (Irish Republican Army) bomber, wrote *Gangsters or Guerrillas: Representations of Irish Republicans in "Troubles Fiction"* (2001). Sid Jacobson and Ernie Colon have written a graphic novel about the 9/11 Commission Report as well a more recent one entitled *After 9/11,* which outlines some of the drawbacks of US foreign policy in the post-9/11 period.

Depictions of Change

There are many examples of novels that depict how change occurs, is understood, and can be dealt with in the aftermath of terrorist incidents or in the context of a counterterrorist state. For example, regarding the "war on terror," *Extremely Loud and Incredibly Close* (Foer 2005) has recently been turned into a film, depicting how the lives of a family changed when the father died in the attacks on New York City. Don DeLillo's *Falling Man* (2007) focuses on someone who survived the attack and the effects of such an event on his life afterwards. The quieter aspects of change – in communities, in individuals, in nations and globally, in ideas – have also been narrated in literature. Brian Friel's *Translations* (1981) deals with and is part of a rich history of literature on terrorism in Ireland. Earlier works in the late nineteenth and early twentieth century examined anarchism, revolutionary violence, and anti-colonial violence as terrorist and form sources for critical research on the meaning-making of terrorism and terrorist.

Philosophy

Questions of human nature, ethics and universalism/non-universalism are some of the key concerns that a critical philosophical approach to terrorism can bring to CTS. After all, philosophers have been concerned with issues of violence and ethics for many years. Discussions by philosophers such as Ashish Nandy, Ulrich Beck, Judith Butler, etc., have questioned universalized meanings of terrorism and, instead, drawn attention to links between society and violence, imperialism and terrorism, the liberal state and its responses and so on.

In recent years, the discussions between Jacques Derrida and Jürgen Habermas in *Philosophy in a Time of Terror* (Borradori 2003) outline how two well-known European philosophers analyzed the events of September 11, 2001. The role of the philosopher is laid out by Derrida:

> Though I am incapable of knowing who today deserves the name philosopher … I would be tempted to call philosophers those who, in the future, reflect in a responsible fashion on these [their interviewer's] questions and demand accountability from

those in charge of public discourse, those responsible for the language and institutions of international law.

(2003: 106)

Habermas outlines his experience of September 11, 2001, to relate them to questions of what could and could not be said in the aftermath of the event in the USA:

> The impressive American liberality toward foreigners, the charm of the eager, sometimes also self-consciously accepting embrace – this noble openhearted mentality seemed to have given way to a slight mistrust. Would we, the ones who had not been present, now also stand by them unconditionally? Even those who hold an unquestionable *record,* as I do among my American friends, needed to be cautious with regard to criticism.

(2003: 26)

Derrida, along with Habermas, is critical of the concept of terrorism and its widespread usage. Methodologically, Derrida utilizes deconstruction to question the accepted meanings of terrorist (and the related oppositional concept of "counterterrorist"). For him, naming September 11, 2001, terrorism is to dilute it of its horror. Habermas, while also critical of the "war on terror" label for providing legitimacy to terrorism seems to consider "September 11" a new type of event which took place in the eyes of the world's media. In the end, these are European philosophers and there is a thread of liberal cosmopolitanism running through both philosophers' musings, despite their differences. Both are in favor of (European) Enlightenment ideals and note that fundamentalism is antithetical to cosmopolitanism and Enlightenment.

Box 3.2 Habermas and Derrida on "tolerance" and "hospitality"

Habermas on tolerance: He understands that tolerance is problematic in that the concept possesses "[in] itself the kernel of intolerance" (2003: 41). Habermas counters this scenario by explaining how a constitutional democracy does not involve a single person or group tolerating another: "On the basis of the citizens' equal rights and reciprocal respect for each other, nobody possesses the privilege of setting the boundaries of tolerance from the viewpoint of their own preferences and value-orientations" (2003: 41). Anticipating Derrida's critique of tolerance, Habermas notes, "straight deconstruction of the concept of tolerance falls into a trap, since the constitutional state contradicts precisely the premise from which the paternalistic sense of the traditional concept of 'tolerance' derives" (2003: 41).

Derrida on hospitality: "Tolerance remains a scrutinized hospitality, always under surveillance, parsimonious and protective of its sovereignty" (2003: 128) ... "Pure and unconditional hospitality, hospitality *itself,* opens or is in advance open to someone who is neither expected nor invited, to whomever arrives as an absolutely foreign *visitor,* as a new *arrival,* nonidentifiable and unforeseeable, in short, wholly other" (2003: 17) ... "an unconditional hospitality is, to be sure, practically impossible to live; one cannot in any case, and by definition, organize it. Whatever happens, happens, whoever comes, comes (*ça qui arrive arrive*), and that, in the end, is the only event worth of this name [of hospitality]" (2003: 129).

Both Habermas and Derrida wonder if September 11, 2001, marked a turning point in history. A related question here could be to ask: *whose* history? After all, for many non-Americans and even Americans themselves, their daily lives did not change much with the declaration of the "war on terror" while for others (e.g., people located in Afghanistan and Iraq; (some) US citizens, etc.), lives changed drastically.

Another philosopher who has meditated upon the consequences of the "war on terror" is Judith Butler. She has examined issues of ethics as well as conditions of liberalism and sovereignty in her recent (post-September 11, 2001) work. In *Frames of War: When Is Life Grievable?* (2009), Butler directs attention to the double standards of representations of violence in the "war on terror." Her concerns with the "victims" of the "war on terror" are outlined in various chapters of the book, including one in which poems written by detainees at Guantánamo Bay are presented.

A New CTS? Methodological and Geographical Plurality

(Inter)disciplining CTS, therefore, includes drawing upon non-IR disciplines and how they have studied terrorism. This is useful because not only does such a "borrowing" draw attention to the paucity of research approaches that are common in traditional TS in IR but also supports the development of a vocabulary of critical research methodologies. Such a vocabulary can be useful when talking to researchers from non-IR disciplines as well as when making claims about using non-traditional critical approaches to study terrorism in IR. As briefly outlined above, critical study of terrorism from non-IR disciplines is still "scientific," in the sense of being systematic, public and focused on producing worldly knowledge, as P. Jackson (2011: 189) puts it. This means the possibility of methodological plurality – not just using different research methods but utilizing different ontological and epistemological standpoints for conducting research – is enhanced with these examples from different disciplines. Researchers interested in utilizing autoethnography, for example, do not have to despair because of the lack of that particular research method in TS; instead, they can (and should) expand their searches and horizons into other disciplines in which autoethnography is a fairly common technique for doing research.

In addition to methodological plurality and the exploration of diverse approaches to the study of terrorism in non-IR disciplines, CTS could also further develop non-Western empirical scholarship. So far, much of CTS has involved research on the global North or on preoccupations of the global North in the South (e.g., terrorist practices of Northern states in the South; US-assisted counterterrorism in the Philippines, etc.). Additional research from the perspective *of* the South and non-Western concerns and standpoints could inform CTS and bring forth new questions and diverse ways of studying and understanding terrorism.

Questions to consider

- Pick a non-IR discipline not reviewed here. How is research about terrorism conducted therein? What counts as evidence?
- What are some differences between Derrida and Habermas? Pick another philosopher and compare their ways of understanding violence and the human condition with that of Derrida and Habermas.

- Provide some examples of non-English literature that deals with terrorism. How do they make sense of their world(s)?
- Using Box 3.1 as an example, outline a brief historical analysis of terrorism in a context outside of the US.
- What are some key features of current CTS? Write how you would further develop one of these features.
- Do you find the concept of "making visible" useful for critical terrorism research? What might a terrorism-related research project that centralizes visuality look like?

Notes

1 http://www.geog.ubc.ca/research/political_geography.html/c.
2 Of interest to researchers, Gage (2011: fn 2) has a list of historical (mostly US-centric) research on terrorism.

Further Reading

Dixit, P. and Stump, J. (2011), "A Response to Smith and Jones: It's Not as Bad as It Seems; or, Five Ways to Move Critical Terrorism Studies Forward," *Studies in Conflict and Terrorism,* 34 (6): 501–511.

Gage, B. (2011), "Terrorism and the American Experience: A State of the Field," *The Journal of American History*, 98 (1): 73–94.

Hammond, P. and Barnfield, G. (2011), "Introduction: The War on Terror in News and Popular Culture," *Journal of War and Culture Studies*, 4 (2): 155–161. This is a special issue on the War on Terror and culture.

Jackson, R., Breen Smyth, M., and Gunning, J. (Eds.) (2009), *Critical Terrorism Studies: A New Research Agenda*, London and New York: Routledge.

Jackson, R., Breen Smyth, M., Gunning, J., and Jarvis, L. (Eds.) (2012), *Terrorism: A Critical Introduction*, Basingstoke: Palgrave Macmillan.

Tickner, A. and Waever, O. (Eds.) (2009), *International Relations Scholarship Around the World*, London and New York: Routledge.

Weblinks

For more from Derrida on terrorism, see http://www.press.uchicago.edu/books/derrida/derrida911. html.

For a list of theorists, readings, lectures and general discussion on violence, please see "Histories of violence" web site: http://www.historiesofviolence.com.

Different facets of surveillance, including its study theoretically and empirically, are available at the surveillance studies network: http://www.surveillance-studies.net.

Reconstruction, special issue on "Cultural productions of 9/11", vol. 11, no. 2, http://reconstruction. eserver.org/112/contents112.shtml, outlines some ways in which "9/11" has been represented and understood in popular culture.

For more fiction titles and media comments on them, please see http://www.nationalreview.com/ blogs/print/227560 and http://www.theatlantic.com/entertainment/archive/2011/06/wheres-the-great-novel-about-the-war-on-terror/240233.

The selection of texts for the Literature section of this chapter relied mainly on the books referred to in these media stories.

Part II
Methods for Doing Critical Terrorism Studies

4   Terrorism and Critical Theory

Introduction

This chapter works to clarify key methodological concepts for a CTS that draws from the Frankfurt School's CT. While CT is not a unified body of thought (Alway 1995: 2), we try to chart a path that stays "true" to CT roots and concepts, which clearly has not always been the case with the current formulation of CTS, as Joseph has critically noted (2011). In particular, we briefly sketch out the historical background of CT, clarify the meaning of "critical" in CT, discuss the unique methodological angle from which this mode of studying terrorism operates, describe some of the key concepts CT brings to the table, and then we indicate a potential research strategy that such an approach could pursue.

Historical Background

The Institute for Social Research (ISR) was established in Frankfurt, Germany, in 1923. Growing from a study group, the "Frankfurt School," as it became known, was the first Marxist-oriented research organization affiliated with a German university. During this early period, ISR members primarily focused on empirical, historical, and practical issues related to the labor movement following the Russian Revolution (Bronner 2011: 9).

   In 1930, Max Horkheimer took over the ISR. He gathered around him some of the most important thinkers of the time (e.g., Leo Lowenthal, Friedrich Pollock, Erich Fromm, Herbert Marcuse, Theodor Adorno, and others), reorganized the ISR around a synthesis of philosophy, social theory, and research, and distanced the Institute from the crude, deterministic Marxism of the day (Kellner 1990: 14–15). The first project of this reorientation focused on the situation of white-collar working-class people in Germany (Kellner 1990: 15), with a particular emphasis on better understanding and explaining how the labor process becomes mystified, or reified, and appears not to be a "purposeful construction of willful human beings" (Agger 1991: 108). This reification of the labor process leads people to experience their lives as products of immutable social conditions, Frankfurt School members argued, which is a kind of domination wherein people "internalize certain values and norms that induce them to participate effectively in the division of productive and reproductive labor" (Agger 1991: 108). As a result of reification, white-collar workers saw the world as rational and necessary and were unable to imagine that all changes are possible in an advanced technological society. Thus, continuing to draw from Marxist roots, Horkheimer emphasized that

ISR had a political intent aimed at modifying the concrete conditions that dominated people and made them suffer. This emancipatory aim was not grounded in general principles, but was thoroughly historical and contextual and dependent on the people in question and their particular sufferings (Kellner 1990: 19).

Following the triumph of Hitler and the Nazi regime in Germany, the majority of ISR members immigrated to the USA. The seat of the Frankfurt School resettled at Columbia University in New York City. In 1937, the phrase "Critical Theory" was coined. CT was juxtaposed against positivism, which focused on the measurement of variables and the testing of hypotheses about a presumably objective world. CT argued that positivism promoted habits of mind that reinforced the status quo by viewing social facts as immutable limitations on human freedom. CT promoted habits of mind opposite that of positivism, seeing social facts as "pieces of history that can be changed" in the future (Agger 1991: 109). However, positivist-informed studies in US social sciences continued to overshadow CT and related neo-Gramscian, post-Marxist, feminist, and postcolonial derivatives that were slowly making headway into a number of academic disciplines.

CT came onto the IR scene during the 1980s. As part of a series of challenges to the dominance of realism, liberalism, and the interparadigm debates, Robert Cox (1981, 1987), Mark Hoffman (1987), and Andrew Linklater (1990) were key to developing an alternative approach to the study of world politics. TS, as we have discussed in earlier chapters, was a comparatively young and developing field of study that was generally outside of IR debates and still dominated by positivist-informed approaches. CT had little connection to TS until after September 11, 2001, when some scholars at the University of Wales, Aberystwyth, began suggesting a more critical approach to terrorism was warranted. Since then, CT, what CT means, and its relationship to CTS have been a major source of debate and interest.

The "Critical" in Critical Theory

A Ballooning Number of Meanings

In 2006, the Center for the Study of Radicalization and Contemporary Political Violence and the University of Wales. Aberystwyth, jointly sponsored a conference called: "Is it Time for a Critical Terrorism Studies?" (Jackson 2007a: 225–226). Since then, a number of researchers have drawn from CT and begun to develop the notion of "critical" and what it means in regards to the study of terrorism. Reading through some of this CT-inspired CTS literature, we argue that "critical" has come to have a wide range of meanings. For instance, Marie Breen Smyth's discussion of a "critical" research agenda is indicative of the ambiguity. She wrote that a "critical" approach should "advance universal human security" and not just state security; "critical" scholars should avoid aligning their selves with the state and they should work alongside policy-makers in an effort to speak "truth to power so that the impact of the work and its prospects for effecting change are maximized"; "critical" scholars should also use valid and reliable data; "critical" analyses should reflect the complexity of power relations and not simply allocate blame to one or another actor; "critical" approaches should contextualize their analyses in local and global levels; "critical" studies of terrorism should not be ahistorical, but should recognize that "the political use of terror is a consistent historical pattern"; "critical" scholars should avoid "exceptionalizing the experience of any society," historical period of set of events; "critical" studies should also be "committed to the incorporation" of gender analysis; "critical" scholars should defend the intellectual integrity of their research and relations to their informants while realistically evaluating risks and legal environment; finally, "critical" approaches should engage with "communities of interest" (Smyth 2007: 262–263). Similarly, in a symposium on CTS, Smyth, along with a number of other key figures developing CTS, argued in a jointly written article that a "critical" approach to terrorism would include:

> a research orientation that is willing to challenge dominant knowledge and under-standings of terrorism, is sensitive to the politics of labeling in the terrorism field, is transparent about its own values and political standpoints, adheres to a set of responsible research ethics, and is committed to a broadly defined notion of emancipation.
>
> (Smyth et al. 2008: 2)

There are other examples in the literature (for example, see Gunning 2007a; Joseph 2009; Toros and Gunning 2009) that demonstrate the ballooning number of meanings of "critical" associated with doing CTS.

Our main point is that for CT-inspired CTS the meaning of "critical" has ballooned into an ambiguous mass of suggestions that pose more of a hindrance to the development of CTS than a benefit. There are two basic reasons for our concern and both are adapted from Patrick Jackson's similar criticisms directed at CT approaches in IR (2011: 184). One reason is that the diversity of meanings of "critical" provides no clearly distinct warrants for empirical claims. CT, in that sense, is an epistemological hodgepodge in the context of IR and CTS. We argue that a CTS that draws from CT should have a clearly distinguishable epistemic warrant that differentiates it from neo-positivist and critical realist methodologies. In this chapter, we argue that *reflexivity* is the central epistemic warrant that a CTS research project inspired by CT should have. The second reason that the ballooning number of meanings of "critical" is more of a problem than a solution is that the lack of a clarified meaning of "critical" deprives subsequent CTS researchers working from a CT perspective from simply adopting the established categories and presuming that those categories constitute a "critical" research approach to terrorism. Once the meaning of "critical" for a CTS drawing from CT is centered on an intersubjective ontology, reflexivist epistemological warrant and a practical political intent to transform some people's situation relating to terrorism, then we argue that a more defensible research program can develop.

A Narrower Meaning to "Critical"

Joseph (2009, 2011), Toros and Gunning (2009), and Richard Jackson (2011) have all suggested that philosophical ontology is a useful place to start the discussion of what "critical" means for a CTS drawing from CT. Philosophical ontology, or how we observers wager that we are hooked up to the world, is the logical starting point for any analysis "since we cannot make defensible claims about what exists until the basis on which we are doing so has been clarified" (P. Jackson 2011: 28; Patomaki and Wight 2000: 215). Along with Patrick T. Jackson, we argue that two basic wagers are at play in the philosophical ontology debate (Stump and Dixit 2012). In terms of CTS, the wagers might be broken down like this. On one hand, Joseph, Toros and Gunning, and

Box 4.1 Ontological wagers

Two Philosophical Ontologies

Wager 1: observer and observed, or subject and object, are distinctly separate – critical realism.

Wager 2: observer and observed, or subject and object, are deeply interconnected – reflexivism.

Jackson have all taken a *critical realist* ontological stance, which is another way of saying that they have wagered that the researcher and the world are, ultimately, separate. As Joseph put it, "reality" is "mind-independent" (2011: 26). On the other hand, in contrast to their critical realist stance, we argue that a CTS that draws from CT should make a different wager. Instead of maintaining that there is a rigid "distinction between object and subject" (Toros and Gunning 2009: 92), we argue that the researcher and the world are *interconnected* (P. Jackson 2011: 35–36) in a "dialectic in which objective conditions help constitute the subject, while the subject in turn helps constitute the objective" historical context (Kellner 1990: 18).

The relevance of these two different wagers when it comes to a CTS that draws from CT is important to better understand. Below, we discuss the differences in more depth.

What is at stake in making these two different wagers? The argument that a CTS that draws from CT should adopt a philosophical realist stance, we argue, is misguided. This is seen no clearer than when we look at the status and aim of knowledge and critique for a critical realist. From a critical realist angle, as Joseph notes, "the ultimate test of critique is in relation to the ability [of the theory] to explain something 'out there'" (2009: 93), to go beyond the empirical identification of regularities and "identify the deeper, underlying nature of reality" (Joseph 2011: 26). In other words, for a critical realist methodology, a valid knowledge claim offers the "best approximation to the world" (Jackson 2011: 198). In terms of terrorism, this methodology entails accurately describing the reality of terrorism as an objectively existing socio-economic relation of capitalism that interacts with discourses of terrorism (Joseph 2009, 2011).

In sharp contrast, for CT, a valid knowledge claim is connected to the everyday categories used by particular groups in society, explains their condition to them, and induces the group in question to reflect on their conditions and act (Guess 1987: 2). In other words, compared to critical realists who aim to offer the best approximation to the world "out there," a CTS that draws from CT would see knowledge as a "device for increasing self-awareness" of some groups of people (Jackson 2011: 198). For instance, when Horkheimer and Adorno write that:

> The culture industry endlessly cheats its consumers out of what it endlessly promises. The promissory note of pleasure issued by plot and packaging is indefinitely prolonged: the promise, which actually comprises the whole show, disdainfully intimates that there is nothing more to come, that the diner must be satisfied with reading the menu ... the culture industry does not sublimate: it suppresses. By constantly exhibiting the object of desire, the breasts beneath the sweater, the

naked torso of the sporting hero, it merely goads the unsublimated anticipation of pleasure, which through the habit of denial has long since been mutilated as masochism.

(Horkheimer and Adorno 1969: 111)

We argue that such claims are neither falsifiable hypotheses as neopositivists might assert nor are they the approximation of a deeper, underlying reality, as critical realists might claim (P. Jackson 2011: 176). Rather, Horkheimer and Adorno are offering a "provocative observation" (P. Jackson 2011: 176) about the workings of mass culture and deferred gratification and it addresses a particular audience: workers engaged in repetitive and joyless tasks.

The intellectual observation relates a piece of everyday social knowledge – "present denial brings future benefits" – to its function in reproducing a particular kind of social order, and as such engages in a dialectical process of helping the people who hold that piece of social knowledge to reflect critically on its overall value.

(P. Jackson 2011: 176)

In terms of the topic at hand, which we discuss in greater detail below, this entails identifying a specific audience that is related to terrorism and/or counterterrorism, elaborating on that audience's criticisms of terrorism and counterterrorism, explicating how their activities function to legitimate the oppression that defines their everyday lives, and finally by trying to induce that audience to progress beyond that condition of unfreedom.

In short, we are arguing that the two different philosophical wagers discussed above enable two very different claims about the status and aim of knowledge generation. A CTS that draws from CT should do more than simply offer better or worse approximations of the "objective" world that may or may not intend to be emancipatory.[1] Rather, CT-inspired knowledge should *always* aim to change the world because for a "reflexivist, knowing the world and changing the world are inseparable" (Jackson 2011: 160). More specifically, a CTS that draws from CT should embrace the claim that critical theories have a unique "standing as guides for human action" because they aim to produce reflective agents who can determine "what their true interests are" and because "they are inherently emancipatory" (Guess 1987: 1–2).

For the researcher, CT entails doing "critical activity" that is oppositional and is "involved in a struggle for social change and unification of theory and practice" (Kellner 1990: 22). It means, in other words, acting as an intellectual agent of revolutionary practice (P. Jackson 2011: 174) by challenging and trying to modify "a particular conception of the world" and the "line of moral conduct" that conception entails (Gramsci 1971: 9). So, as a Critical Theorist, intellectuals have a "duty as scholars and activists" (Toros and Gunning 2009: 104) to align their selves with particular groups of people. They do this not necessarily by sharing the living conditions of the oppressed or by protesting in the streets against the conditions (Bauer 2009: 132–136), but by seizing onto, highlighting, elaborating, and clarifying the tensions and contradictions that are already active in the oppressed groups' lives (Bruff 2010; P. Jackson 2011: 175). Table 4.1 illustrates this distinction in clearer terms.

Table 4.1 How ontology and epistemology are connected

Methodology	Ontology	Epistemology
critical realism	distinctly separate subject-object	best approximation to objective world
reflexivism	deeply interconnected subject-object	tool for inducing self-reflection of individuals and groups

Key Concepts

Ethical Commitment: A Terror-Free World and the Agents of Change Who Can Make It Happen

To say that the researcher of terrorism should actively align their selves with a particular group could invite a great deal of criticism; such was the point of much of Jones and Smith's rebukes (2009), for example. Critical Theorists studying terrorism are not alone in this matter. As we discuss in more depth in Chapter 6, ethnographers who study terrorist groups must be particularly attuned to and cautious about managing relations between the authorities and the terrorist group because the researcher's personal security and the security of their subjects are at stake. Critical Theorists, however, generally do not use interviewing and observational data-gathering methods, as we discuss later in this chapter. Concerns are still raised, however, as Richard Jackson's comment attests: "Contrary to the views of some critics, CTS is not an anti-state or anti-Western project, a discourse of complacency or an appeasement of tyranny" (2007c: 250).

Nevertheless, a CTS that draws from CT takes an explicit normative commitment. In fact, the normative commitment of this kind of CTS is similar to that espoused by peace research and conflict resolution studies (Jackson 2007c: 250). In a narrower sense, the commitment is concerned with the "most vulnerable" members of the community (McDonald 2007: 254). More broadly, though, the normative commitment of a CT-inspired CTS is "a vigorous anti-terror project based on fundamental human rights and values ... social justice, equality and an end to structural and physical violence and discrimination" (Jackson 2007c: 250). The ultimate goal for a CT-inspired CTS is "the creation of those political, social and economic conditions under which political goals can be legitimately and effectively pursued without recourse to terrorism" (Toros and Gunning 2009: 100).

As a practical matter pertaining to research conduct and because a CT with political intent entails the identification and addressing of an audience, the question remains: on *whose* situation should the researcher bring CT to bear? Marx was concerned with the proletariat, but a focus on the situation of the proletariat is probably untenable for CTS. CT has long rejected the proletariat as the proper audience and, in doing so, they have expanded the possible "agents of change" to include: "critical thinkers, artists, students, and other marginalized social groups" (Alway 1995: 131). Instead of just workers in a capitalistic system, in other words, all of these groups are engaged in the labor of producing and reproducing the social world through the course of their everyday actions.[2] This unreflective labor reifies the products of their work, which makes the product appear to the actor as independent of their work, as having a life of its own apart from the producer. Terrorism, in this sense, can be seen as a reified social relation – a product of a certain constellation of actors (Joseph 2011: 34) – and so can counterterrorism. At the same time, these actors, through reflection induced by a CT, can be a source of transformation; they can become aware of their work in producing and reproducing terrorism and counterterrorism and act otherwise in an effort to change the exploitative mechanisms. In regards to the topic of terrorism and in line with the expanded number of relevant actors, we suggest four potential situations and their attendant agents that a CT-inspired CTS project could consider.

Researchers, for instance, might want to focus on "moderate voices" (McDonald 2007: 254) across a spectrum of everyday life related to terrorism. One moderate voice might include those citizens and organizations criticizing violent counterterrorist operations and calling on their government to develop a dialogue with militant groups they oppose (McDonald 2007: 254). For example, a study may examine nongovernmental organizations (e.g., the American Medical Association, the National Religious Campaign against Torture, the American Civil Liberties Union, Witness against Torture, etc.) that are opposed to the policies surrounding the US government's extrajudicial prison in Guantánamo Bay, Cuba. Such a study may try to foreground the dialectical relationship between knowledge and its conditions. The specific emphasis might be on how these voices operated under historically established social conditions generated by the media and elite actors that rendered them politically marginal and ineffectual when speaking against the violent counterterrorist response employed by the US government after September 11, 2001.

A second possible audience for CT-inspired studies are the governments and their various agencies and individuals that formulate and implement counterterrorism policies (Toros and Gunning 2009: 101). While the governmental agency itself may be anti-emancipatory, individuals working to transform the organization from inside could be the focus of CTS. Toros and Gunning point to some relevant examples. Robert Lambert, for instance, was the head of the London Metropolitan Police's Muslim Contact Unit. He developed relationships with Islamic groups in the United Kingdom, even though some groups were widely seen as radical (Toros and Gunning 2009: 101). Another example of people working to progress a counterterrorist government agency beyond anti-emancipatory violence would be the British intelligence agents during the 1980s who advocated contacts and talks between the British government and the IRA. Their efforts helped bring about the 1998 Good Friday Agreement (Toros and Gunning 2009: 101–102). The general point here is that government agencies and the individuals who work inside them should not be written off as beyond the bounds of a CT-inspired CTS. A CTS that can identify and elaborate on contradictions and limitations inherent to the counterterrorist policies can possibly induce change from the inside out.

Third, those carrying out acts of terrorism (state or group) are an important audience that a CT-inspired study could engage (Toros and Gunning 2009: 101). Indeed, the acts of violent terrorism may be seen by the group carrying them out as an emancipatory action, but the possibility of transformation to forms of nonviolent politics should be actively sought (Toros and Gunning 2009, 101). Gunning has indicated that through political participation, for instance, Hamas has transformed from a more "absolutist" position on issues related to women's rights to an acceptance of "power-sharing" with more leftist groups and grassroots political activists (2004: 253). A CT-inspired study could focus on important individual actors within the militant groups, especially those like Ismail Abu Shannab, a Hamas leader in Gaza who was central to the progressive internal changes occurring in that organization (Gunning 2007b: 236–237, cited in Toros and Gunning 2009: 101).

Box 4.2 Fundamentals of CT's ethical commitment

1. An anti-terror, pro-human rights position
2. Applied to some specific audience that might include:

    a. Marginal voices
    b. Government agencies
    c. Terrorist groups
    d. Attentive citizens

Fourth, instead of the marginal voices protesting the government's use of violent counterterrorist policies, an important focus of a CT-inspired CTS might be the attentive citizens who quietly sit at the center of the political system. For instance, in the USA, most citizens do not protest but are attentive to the use of violent counterterrorist policies by the government. CTS could directly address this audience. A study could highlight the contradictions and tensions that emerge between the lofty language of "freedom" and "democracy" on one hand and, on the other hand, between the web of media myths that obscure security policies that undermine civil liberties and obscure elite cliques of policy-makers and corporations that determine those policies (e.g., Herman 1982; Herman and O'Sullivan 1989). Working to make these attentive audiences at the center of the USA and other Western states aware of the contradictions should be a central strategy for a CTS drawing from CT.

Emancipation

Matt McDonald (2007, 2009) and others (Jackson 2007c; Toros and Gunning 2009; Joseph 2011) have argued that emancipation should be a central concept for CTS. Indeed, as we have suggested above, the concept of emancipation is closely related to CT's normative commitment. The normative commitment to a terror-free world and to one of the groups of people discussed in the above section who can make that world happen, in other words, is a commitment to the development of a CT that can be used by the group in question to effectively emancipate their selves from some enslaving and coercive knowledge and its social conditions. But what, in more precise terms, does emancipation mean?

There is no one universally accepted definition of emancipation for CT or CTS. Emancipation can be distinguished from utopianism because it is not about the achievement of goals that are outside of "humanity's reach" (Toros and Gunning 2009: 100). Nor is emancipation about achieving a contradiction-free, perfect state of affairs (Held 1980: 178). Rather, at base, emancipation should be about "feasible alternatives that grow out of the here and now" (Toros and Gunning 2009: 100). Such a view of emancipation, which contains a normative vision of a better world, logically entails a particular ontological wager regarding the nature of concepts in history. In contrast to the "the notion of a (broadly) immutable status quo so dominant in traditional terrorism studies" (Toros and Gunning 2009: 99), a CT-inspired CTS bets "that the actually existing empirical world is *not* simply 'one damn thing after another' but that instead history is, in a very real sense, *going somewhere* – and it is going somewhere that the researcher, through the act of producing reflexive knowledge, can contribute to" (Jackson 2011: 165).

Emancipation, thus, should be about a specifically formulated CT that aims to induce some sort of situational progress among some group of people associated with the violence of terrorism or counterterrorism. CT does not guarantee progress, but is dependent on "the productive and reproductive practices of historically acting subjects" (Held 1980: 178). CT does not predict progress but aims "to enlighten agents about how they ought rationally to act to realize their own best interests" (Guess 1987: 77). Thus, the particular content of situational progress is not generalizable across cases or known *a priori*; what it "actually entails" is a matter that "can only be truly engaged with when studying specific cases" (Toros and Gunning 2009: 102).

In general, though, emancipation implies a *process* of "social transition" from one actually existing set of social conditions and knowledges to a more enlightened state of existence (Guess 1987: 58). A transition from a more closed, exclusive, monological conversational space where engagement with one's opponents is limited to nonexistent, for instance, to a more open and less exclusive "space for dialogue and deliberation" where "crucial questions, experiences and practices neglected in dominant accounts of security and terrorism" can be voiced (McDonald 2007: 253) would constitute one possible emancipatory social transition. That understanding of a transformative process where space is opened up for marginal voices, however, should not be seen by researchers as the only possible form of progress. How progress is constituted will depend on the context and audience at hand.

More schematically, though, a model of the emancipatory process might resemble this: in the initial state of existence, the people in question live unfree insofar as their "ideological world-picture" makes the coercive social institutions that shapes their lives appear to be legitimate and inevitable (Guess 1987: 58). For example, take the passage of the Uniting and Strengthening America by Providing Appropriate Tools Required to Intercept and Obstruct Terrorism Act (USA PATRIOT Act). Many US leaders and policy-makers publicly justified as required and inevitable the various domestic and foreign counterterror measures the law put into place. Indeed, only one Senator, Russ Feingold, opposed the Bill during the initial vote in 2001. President George W. Bush initially signed the USA PATRIOT Act into law and then nearly a decade later, and with solid Congressional support, President Barack H. Obama signed a four-year extension of the law in 2011. Similarly, public-opinion surveys conducted throughout the 2000s by the Pew Research Center indicate that a plurality of Americans continue to see the law as a "necessary tool that helps government fight terrorists" (2011). In other words, the ideological world picture espoused by many American leaders and the public in general makes the law and the coercive counterterrorist measures it entails (increased domestic surveillance, curtailment of free speech, limitations on freedom to assemble, etc.) appear to be legitimate and necessary for US national security.

In effect, then, because Americans' distorted world picture is so intimately connected to their unfree condition, the emancipatory transition entails a dual process. On one hand, the distorted worldview of the group in question must be clarified. As we have argued above, this is precisely the role of the intellectual for a CT-inspired approach to CTS. The CT-inspired intellectual who is committed to some oppressed group, like attentive Americans, should be trying to make knowledge that clarifies and elaborates on the contradictions and obstructions that sustain the unfree conditions, and they should indicate the key actors and possible routes of action that could be used to overcome that oppression. On the other hand, emancipation also entails that the group in question is freed from or progressed beyond their initial social conditions, which in the example above would entail that American leaders and the public more generally freely accept the critique and act to repeal or curtail the law. So, not only is a distorted world picture clarified but the process of clarifying one's world picture must also induce the audience in question to act to overcome the oppressive counterterrorist institutions. In short, the emancipatory transition entails both processes (world picture clarification and progressing beyond coercive conditions).

The world picture that the individual and the collective may hold, in other words, is a kind of self-imposed delusion that makes certain features of social, political, and economic life appear necessary, objective, and unchangeable. Becoming conscious of the *appearance* of necessity and immutability, we argue, is the threshold of emancipatory change. In the end state, one's world picture has been altered and unfree conditions are no longer imposed on one's self. The people in question, rooted in their specific situational and historical contexts, are effectively emancipated.

Critique: Immanent and Functional

CT, in important ways discussed above, is about the critique of existing patterns of domination and progressing beyond that situation. How does one go about this process when it comes to terrorism? We argue that two modes of critique, immanent and functional, are the most relevant. We discuss each in more depth.

Box 4.3 Two modes of critique

Immanent – the identification and elaboration of discrepant features of social life for some group of people, which can then possibly be worked into an emancipatory political strategy.

Functional – the explication of how some features of social life function to reproduce domination and unfree conditions.

Immanent critique is the first mode of analysis and it entails three steps:

1. observing situations;
2. identifying features of life within those situations that have emancipatory potential;
3. putting into practice the political tactics needed to develop those possibilities.

Observing a situation means gathering data. As we indicate in other chapters throughout the text, types of data can be broken into interviews, participant observations, and documents (texts and visuals). Scholars working from a CT perspective could engage in participant observation and write up fieldnotes. Yet fieldwork from a CT angle is rarely carried out, which means that there are many potential situations in the present that are ripe for such an approach. Generally, though, data for CT means *documents*. Habermas's immanent critiques focused on the philosophical treatises of Greek and German authors. More closely related to the topic at hand, Richard Jackson's immanent critique of TS and the scholars that operate in that milieu, for instance, observed "more than 100 academic monographs, articles in core TS and IR journals, papers presented at major international conferences, and reports and websites from TS think tanks and research institutions" (2009a: 68). In short, observing some situation in which some group of people are operating under social conditions and knowledges that make them unfree entails that a corpus of documents be gathered and studied closely. Usually the corpus of documents is rich enough or complete when new documents fail to generate additional insights or concepts relevant to that study.

The next step in immanent critique is to locate or identify features of that situation that have emancipatory potential. Some of the more important features of life active in particular circumstances that have emancipatory potential would be, for instance, contradictions between words and deeds and silences that exclude relevant voices and experiences. Following Marx, Horkheimer argued that the bourgeois order emphasized the universal values of "'justice, equality, and freedom'" (quoted in Held 1980: 183). However, these values were effectively "negated in practice" because workers were alienated from their labor and dominated by the system they helped generate through their work. There was little justice, little freedom, and great inequality, which enslaved workers to the machines they labored over and threatened them with "every kind of suffering" (Horkheimer, quoted in Held 1980: 183–184). These conditions for the working sharply contradicted the values espoused by the bourgeois leaders and, therefore, were seen by Horkheimer as having emancipatory potential. In regards to terrorism and immanent critique, Jackson has convincingly argued that "what is accepted as well-founded 'knowledge' in terrorism studies is, in fact, highly debatable and unstable" (2009a: 74). For instance, it is commonplace to conceptualize terrorism as an objectively definable phenomenon that is strictly non-state violence directed at governments. Jackson demonstrates that defining terrorism as an objective phenomenon is "highly questionable" and that "states have killed, tortured, and terrorized on a truly vast scale over the past few decades" and that a great many states continue to terrorize domestic and foreign populations (2009a: 75). The point is that the definitions and commonly employed conceptualizations of terrorism are open to challenge and hold the potential for change. Showing people how definitions and conceptualizations exclude or hide the possibility of state violence is central to the transformation of knowledges and conditions away from the violent, terrorizing social conditions that shape their lives.

Once features of life that have emancipatory potential are identified, the final step of immanent critique involves working through and trying to implement the political tactics and strategies needed to actually progress beyond the current unfree situation. For workers in early twentieth-century America, for instance, this meant picketing, striking, and unionizing in the name of a just wage, less inequality, and more freedom. For TS, as Jackson indicates, this entails challenging the "self-perpetuating set of knowledge-generating practices" that "tends to accept dominant 'myths' about terrorism without strong empirical investigation" and even after "empirical research disproves" the long-held beliefs (2009a: 80–81). More specifically, this means challenging the important and influential think tanks, like the RAND Corporation, which have close relations with the US Air Force and the American military more generally, when it comes to the knowledge they generate about terrorism (Jackson 2009a: 81). In different unfree situations, the documents collected, the features of life that have emancipatory potential, and the particular political strategies employed to change the situation, will vary greatly.

Beyond immanent critique is functional critique. This mode of critique centers on the explication of how some situational feature of life for some group of people, like a particular definition or the language of justice or terrorism used by government officials, consequentially functions to stabilize and legitimize domination. The features of some situation that stabilize and legitimize domination can be used instrumentally by important elites and institutions to "structure the primary subject positions, accepted knowledge, common sense, and legitimate policy responses to the actors and events being described; exclude and de-legitimize alternative forms of knowledge and practice; naturalize a particular political and social order; and construct and sustain a hegemonic 'regime of truth'" (Jackson 2009a: 69). However, the features of life that stabilize and legitimize domination are not limited to instrumental uses by elites and institutions. Non-elites, through mundane language, actions, and photographic representations of people, places, and events, for instance, effectively stabilize and legitimize domination (Shapiro 1988). In short, across a wide variety of situations, elites and non-elites intentionally and unintentionally contribute to the unfree circumstances that dominate their lives. The goal of this second mode of critique is to "expose the political functions and ideological consequences of the particular narratives, practices, and forms of representation enunciated within the dominant terrorism studies discourse" (Jackson 2009a: 76) and within other situations completely outside academia, such as those discussed earlier in this chapter like marginal community voices and government agencies.

Turning back to the critique of the TS literature, Jeroen Gunning has argued that the prevailing way of studying terrorism is centered on "problem solving" (2007a). Problem solving, as Robert Cox pointed out, "takes the world as it finds it," including current actors and their social, economic, and political relations, and then works to make these various actors and relations work more smoothly and efficiently (1987: 208). Thus, to the extent that TS is centered on problem solving, the literature functions to reproduce the legitimacy of the state as the most important actor in world politics and functions to mask the state's implication "in the very 'problem' of terrorism itself" (Jackson 2009a: 77). Furthermore, this literature functions to legitimate state violence carried out against groups and delegitimate non-state, group violence carried out against the state by providing an "authoritative academic justification for using what may actually be [state] terroristic forms of violence against their opponents and citizens" (Jackson 2009a: 78). By presenting group terrorism as a "catastrophic threat to Western society," the TS literature also functions to support and legitimate the "economic interests" of certain actors, such as "private security firms, defense industries, and pharmaceutical companies" that have garnered multimillion dollar contracts to secure airports, public spaces, government buildings, and public health from terrorism (Jackson 2009a: 79). Explicating the function of certain institutions and practices in stabilizing and legitimating violent terrorism and counterterrorism is the point of this mode of critique.

Potential Research Strategy

How, then, can one design their research project? In general, research design can be schematically broken down into a series of practical steps:

This still takes "terror" as a category

1. We begin our study with a commitment to a terror-free world or to a world in which conditions are such that political goals can be accomplished without a resort to terror.
2. We identify a situation and its attendant audience which is related to terrorism and/or counterterrorism. For the purpose of this example, we will focus on the situation of attentive Americans.

3. We pose an answerable research question that would set the stage for immanent and functional critiques, such as, "Are there identifiable discrepancies between Americans' stated values of 'freedom' and 'democracy' on one hand and domestic counterterror programs on the other?" on "How do Americans and the media institutions, experts, and policy-makers on which they depend contribute to the legitimation of these domestic counterterror programs?"

4. We identify and gather the data needed to answer our research questions. Documents, as we mentioned, are generally the primary sources of needed information. They might include print, online, and digital news, policy papers, laws, contracts, and official speeches.

5. We closely analyze the data by looking for contradictions and silences where, for instance, freedom and democratic politics in America are negated and undermined by the implementation of domestic counterterror surveillance policies. Furthermore, we closely analyze the data with a specific focus on explicating how the actions of ordinary Americans, the media, experts, and policy-makers effectively function to legitimate these domestic counterterror surveillance programs or to mask their consequences from Americans.

6. We work out the political implications of our findings, especially in terms of the tactics and strategies appropriate to challenging this oppression. We attempt to persuade attentive Americans through public lectures, editorials, or other outlets to reflect on their situation, agree that their condition is increasingly unfree, and to take collective counteraction to progress beyond their conditions. When the audience in question freely agrees and acts to change their unfreedom, then the CT is considered adequate.

Questions to consider

- What is the history of the Frankfurt School's CT and when did CT become connected to CTS?
- What does "critical" mean for CT and how does that meaning relate to CTS?
- What does emancipation mean for CT and how does that meaning relate to CTS?
- What are some potential audiences that a CT can be used to emancipate?
- What is the political aim of a reflexive epistemology?
- What are the two modes of critique CTS can employ when drawing from a CT perspective?

Notes

1 We say "intend" here because Joseph argues, wrongly in our view, that critique for CT may or may not "intend" to be emancipatory (2011: 36). We argue that for CT knowledge production is always emancipatory or, at least, always aims to be emancipatory.

2 Joseph is rightly critical of much of the CTS literature for its lack of emphasis on the work of production. Joseph, however, too narrowly understands production as physical labor associated with capitalism. He indicates that language and communication cannot be productive (2011: 30). We disagree with this and argue that production is important, but production should be broadly understood to include all human activity – everyday physical labor and communication.

Further Reading

Booth, K. (1991), "Security and Emancipation," *Review of International Studies*, 17 (4): 313–328.

Guess, R. (1987), *The Idea of a Critical Theory: Habermas and the Frankfurt School*, Cambridge: Cambridge University Press.

McDonald, M. (2007), "Emancipation and Critical Terrorism Studies," *European Political Science*, 6: 252–259.

Toros, H. and Gunning, J. (2009), "Exploring a Critical Theory Approach to Terrorism Studies," in R. Jackson, M. Breen Smyth, and J. Gunning (Eds.), *Critical Terrorism Studies: A New Research Agenda*, London and New York: Routledge, pp. 87–108.

Weblinks

See www.marxists.org for an extensive Internet archive with a variety of topics, authors, and selections of texts related to Critical Theory.

Dialectical Marxism is the website of Bertell Ollman at New York University. It features his writings and the Class Struggle Board Game: http://www.nyu.edu/projects/ollman.

The University of Iowa's Department of Communications Studies also has an extensive set of resources called Rhetorical and Cultural Studies: Critical Theory. See http://www.uiowa.edu/~commstud/resources/critical_authors.html.

Dr. Malinda S. Smith at the University of Alberta also maintains an extensive set of resources called Critical Theory on the Web. See http://www.arts.ualberta.ca/~courses/PoliticalScience/661B1/resources.htm.

5 Postcolonial and Feminist Approaches to Terrorism

Introduction

These research approaches draw attention to the less visible sites and peoples involved in the study of terrorism. Experiences of terror and violence are not just at the national or transnational level but also at everyday levels, a view of terror that postcolonial and feminist scholars have proposed and theorized. Debates about what terrorism is and how to counter it usually ignore that terrorism is experienced differently by different races, genders, and classes across the world. Postcolonialism and feminism also direct attention to the role of standpoint in meaning-making. What counts as "knowledge" and "truth" is based on which standpoint the researcher is analyzing from (see Table 5.1). Postcolonial theorists indicate this centrality of race and imperial power in constituting dominant meanings about particular acts and actions. Generally, postcolonial and feminist analysis is about how the "other" is conceptualized and related to postcolonial feminist scholarship points out the raced and gendered practices that structure and constrain self–other relations in IR.

There is no one specific research method attached to feminist and postcolonial approaches. For example, in IR, a scholar may use a feminist approach along with network analysis or a postcolonial understanding of discourse (e.g., Inayatullah and Blaney 2004; Chowdhry and Ling 2010; Nayak and Selbin 2010). Thus, it is best to think of feminism and postcolonialism as ways of interrogating the study of IR (and IR itself). Indeed, both these approaches utilize research approaches such as ethnography (Chapter 6 and Chapter 7) and discourse analysis (Chapter 8). Both feminism and postcolonialism have taken a deeper hold in disciplines such as sociology, cultural studies, and literature than in IR. In this chapter, we shall focus on the application of postcolonial and feminist approaches to security studies, specifically terrorism, and provide an overview of existing research on security and terrorism that has used these approaches.

This chapter is organized as follows: the next two sections provide brief outlines of feminism and postcolonialism in the study of terrorism. The section that follows describes postcolonial feminism, which is sometimes also called "Third World feminism," and its possible application to TS. After that, examples of research using feminism, postcolonialism, and postcolonial feminism are presented and research designs outlined. The Conclusion reviews some of the approaches presented in the chapter and discusses questions of ethics.

Table 5.1 Some common themes and goals in feminist and postcolonial analyses

Assumptions	Issues to consider	Goals
Race and gender as central to analysis	Outline different ways of relating to others	Excavating subaltern knowledges
Historical social processes form categories of "colonized", "women", "men", etc	Questioning conventional research methodologies and designs	Interrogating dominant meanings
No one Truth-truth depends on the standpoint of the researcher	Who can speak (usually Western/white/males) and who is silenced (usually non-white/ non-Western/females)	Indicating the raced and gendered structures of power and knowledge

Feminism and Terrorism Studies: An Overview

Despite the rapid expansion of feminist security scholarship recently and the related output of terrorism-related scholarship in general, feminist research on terrorism is still limited. However, there have been some exceptions (e.g., Enloe 2010; Wibben 2011; Sylvester and Parashar 2009; Masters 2009; Hawthorne and Winter 2003; Hunt and Rygiel 2006). Even without an explicit focus on terrorism, Feminist Security Studies (FSS) is a growing subfield in IR, and its proponents have advocated a change in how we understand "security."

The question of redefining security and understanding security differently is a key one for feminist security scholars. Laura Sjoberg points out,

> Feminists have suggested that one of the key contributions of scholarship looking for women and gender in global politics to thinking about war and security is seeing them as fundamentally differently defined than the "common sense" understandings which pervade contemporary security scholarship. In "common sense" understandings, security is about the threat, use, and control of military force, and war is a time-delimited but sustained violent conflict between two states, which starts and ends as/when those states decide it does.
>
> Instead, feminisms have seen security policies as performed in/on women's bodies, and personal security at the margins/periphery as every bit as important as (and often threatened by) state security/ies at the center/core of the international system. Feminists have provided evidence that gendered logics and war logics are co-constituted.
>
> (Sjoberg: 2011)

Terrorism researchers adopting a feminist approach should, therefore, work towards transforming TS by researching how security and terrorism are differently defined and understood once gender is taken seriously. A priority of this research approach is to refocus attention on what counts as "normal" or "secure" in the first place. Annick Wibben, in *Feminist Security Studies: A Narrative Approach*, writes, "because feminist theorizing starts from women's experiences of everyday life, it has to accommodate the varied contexts of women's lives while also remaining attuned to the contextual nature of 'normality'" (Wibben 2011: 1–2). Feminist terrorism scholars could centralize women's lived experiences while questioning seemingly commonsensical understandings of "normal."

Wibben uses September 11, 2001, as an example to show how "9/11" did not change the "normality" of many people. Wibben refers to quotes by US women in which they describe how their "normality" after the events of September 11 prioritizes different concerns (health of family members, unemployment, etc.). Within such a conceptualization of normality, everyday life continues, and notions of 9/11 as having led to a catastrophic change (which is how the event is represented in much of conventional terrorism scholarship as well as media reports and official statements) make little sense (Wibben 2011: 2–4). Wibben claims feminist security scholars emphasize continuities and changes – war and conflict are not crises or deviations from the norm of everyday life but, rather, everyday life itself is filled with conflicts and negotiations, different types of insecurities. She writes, "As discourses about security make stark distinctions between peace and wartime and emphasize certain events (e.g., the events of September 11, 2001) as ushering in a new era, feminists locate them within the struggles of everyday life and on a continuum that spans peace and wartime" (2011: 25). This questioning of normality and exception is something that can be an example for those doing feminist analyses of terrorism.

In outlining ways to question commonsensical notions of security and to question the subfield of security studies itself, feminist analysis of security centralizes experiences of women. Feminist security scholars direct attention to women's relations with each other, with other genders, races, nations, and with institutions and processes of world politics. In this, feminist analysis is often relational; asking, "Where are the women?" is not about just adding women to a particular research concern but (a) asking what does an analysis which centralizes women's experiences tell us about that particular question or issue that would otherwise remain unheard and unresearched? And (b) examining the role of women in relation to other processes, institutions, genders, that they interact with. Thus, feminist analysis is about making visible sites of (in)security which usually remain outside of conventional terrorism scholarship. In general, feminist analysis is concerned with empowerment and emancipation. Wibben claims feminist methodological commitments include an "emancipatory agenda" (2011: 112).

Overall, feminist analyses would aim to *transform* TS, *make visible* sites where women's experiences are located and *relate* these to nation, class, and gender while calling for *empowerment.* It is not about adding women to a research concern but pointing out that this "adding women" or, more appropriately, centralizing women's experiences transforms what IR (and security/TS) mean in the first place. So, feminist security scholars do not spend much time discussing what "added value" feminist scholarship brings to security studies. Instead, FSS scholars concentrate on how "security studies" and "security" have different meanings once practices and processes which produce particular identities for women (e.g., mothers and wives of terrorists, suicide bombers, policy-makers, etc.) are centralized in analysis (see Table 5.2).

Postcolonialism and Terrorism Studies: An Overview

Postcolonialism … correlates with struggle, subversion, the nation, the region, resistance to the global status quo – whether that be capitalist-driven colonialism or contemporary neo-imperial globalization … [It] reveals the continuing impositions of colonialism. It does so, however, in order to subvert them.

(Gregory, quoted in Boehmer and Morton 2010: 143)

Table 5.2 Some concepts of feminism and their possible uses in research on terrorism

Concept	Use	Examples in studying terrorism
Patriarchy	Social system in which the male is centralized and privileged.	"Women terrorists" are seen as products of a gendered social system and their agency is subsumed into a larger patriarchal framework. Research may question this identity of women.
Male gaze*	Centralizes processes of representations wherein the (heterosexual) male gaze's point of view is foregrounded. Indicates an unequal power relationship and the objectification of females (and other genders).	Research may include analysis of visual culture wherein representations of terrorism are presented. The focus on women as objects – whether as suicide bombers compelled by race, social norms, religion, "hopelessness"; martyrs; – and the invisibility of women in crafting narratives about themselves. Examples include: Sjoberg, Shepherd, Wibben, Cloud, Tickner, Weber 2011, and essays in R. Riley et al. 2008.
Empowerment and emancipation	Often presented as goals for feminist analysis, these are contested terms. Emancipation can mean allowing space for women to present their standpoint when analyzing terrorism.	Wibben 2011
Transversal politics	The view that standpoints should be taken into account when discussing particular situations and that difference with equality is possible.	Yuval-Davis 2010
Intersectionality	Methodology where race, class, gender, ethnicity, sexuality, age, are seen as interlocking factors in contributing to systems of domination and subordination (Berger and Guidroz 2009a: 1).	Postcolonial feminism. See examples in text and also Berger and Guidroz (2009a: 61–80)
Masculinization and feminization	Associated with value judgments in which masculine traits are praised and seen as desirable while feminine traits (and feminization) are seen as weak.	Usually in representations of terrorists as masculinized and a "bunch of young guys" while females are seen as manipulated by the patriarchal society or men. Important in terms of agency as feminization leads to a lack of agency.

* Let the dinosaurs explain it! http://www.qwantz.com/index.php?comic=859.

If this is the goal for postcolonial theory, there has been less inroad of postcolonial approaches in TS or even in security studies in general (unlike feminist scholarship). Considering most of the world is implicated in colonial practices, whether as colonizers or as colonized, and ideas and understandings of IR and security studies have been informed by colonialism, it is quite surprising how little interest there has been in the use of postcolonial theory in studying terrorism. Even those postcolonial theorists who are sometimes cited in IR have been undertheorized. It seems Fanon, Spivak, Bhabha, Said, Chatterjee, etc. are only relevant in "marginalized" settings, away from the mainstream of IR.

This has two main implications for critical research on terrorism: one, there is a vast potential for reviewing these and other postcolonial theorists in order to see how their understanding of violence helps us study and understand terrorism and political violence today. After all, many of these theorists (and theories) emerged from times of violence – whether direct experience of the end of colonialism, the emergence of new nation-states or the development of new forms of political and socioeconomic orders. Many of these theorists have written extensively about forms of violence, different understandings and experiences of violence as well as how governments control violence to manage populations. This is the first possible arena for the inclusion of postcolonial theories in critical terrorism scholarship: new and diverse ways of understanding violence and violent actors, especially those labeled terrorist, drawing from the works of postcolonial scholars.

The second possible research agenda is to identify a series of themes from the scholarship of postcolonial theorists and to apply that to the study of terrorism. What does postcolonial scholarship provide that other critical approaches to the study of terrorism do not? What are the benefits of adopting a postcolonial stance? Similar to feminism, rather than being a specific theory, postcolonalism is an orientation that allows us to critique existing ways of explaining terrorism and point towards an alternative approach which centralizes "race" as a category of analysis and focuses on de-colonization. This approach makes visible the rules, norms, and language which have emerged from practices of colonialism and become implicated in what we consider "IR" or "TS." As such, postcolonial theorists argue that mainstream explanations of world politics in general and terrorism in particular have underlying biases due to their emergence from a colonial and imperial past. While feminists point out the gendered nature of the world privileges masculine traits, postcolonial theorists draw our attention to how raced colonial practices have created dependency, division, and inequalities in different parts of the world.

Here are five areas that a postcolonial analysis of terrorism could focus on:

1. interrogating historical continuities;
2. the role of the state in violence;
3. redrawing boundaries;
4. visualizing relations with others;
5. methodology: language and power.

Interrogating Historical Continuities

(Dis)continuities between current terrorists and past anti-state actors: Many current terrorists are groups who resisted colonial occupation. They were part of the fight against colonization and were active during protests to seek independence. Some possible cases to study here are Malaysia, the Philippines, and Ireland. A postcolonial approach to such groups interrogates their identity as terrorist by outlining practices of oppression and inequalities that have historically marginalized such groups. For example, in the Philippines, the Muslim Moros have been at the margins of political order, often left outside of the central Spanish colonial control (Frake 1998). When the Philippines became independent and Mindanao and the southern Philippines became part of the new nation-state, concerns about discrimination by the majority Catholic population continued.

Of course, a study of political violence in the Philippines needs to consider the dual colonial role of Spain and the USA in creating alliances and divisions amongst the Filipino population. The USA was involved in quelling the Huk rebellion (noted in many counterinsurgency texts as a successful counterinsurgency operation). Another "success" was the British efforts in what was then Malaya. Thus, a postcolonial approach, examining intersections of state power, ethnicities, religions, and with a critical geographical focus may yield different outcomes, rather than framing the Moro Islamic Liberation Front (MILF) (or the Moros in general) as a terrorist group affiliated with al-Qaeda, as much of post-9/11 terrorism scholarship does.

The question of modernity and responses to it is another common theme in postcolonial scholarship. Boehmer provides a postcolonial interpretation of terrorism as a response to the violent modernity imposed by colonizations:

> "Terror" here denotes the attempt by the colonized to seize hold of technical mastery and control in a situation, that of colonialism, where modernity is routinely introduced in violent forms (through land seizures, labor laws, and the like) ... this apparently alternative reading of terror allows us to examine its occurrence in the reciprocally violent historical contexts of colonialism and global neocolonialism rather than of the ahistorical "war on terror" in which terror is viewed simply as savage and irrational, an irruption of the primitive.
>
> (Boehmer and Morton 2010: 147)

This is something a postcolonial research project on terrorism could explore.

The Role of the State in Violence

Similar to feminists, postcolonial theorists draw attention to how the emergence of the nation-state was tied in with violence, often against its own peoples. This is connected to how the state or "the center" acted during colonial times. For example, in India, the British coopted numerous ethnic groups into fighting for the colonial state. Later, these forces would fight against other Asian/colonized peoples. In creating this security force, it was the state that trained these different ethnic groups to use violent means (such as guns and ammunition) effectively.

In terms of practice, the notion that a state could act against "its" people is also something that postcolonial analysts are continuously aware of. A postcolonial analysis of violence draws attention to the usage of violence and the legitimation of such usage. It questions conventional accounts of terrorism in which the state's use of violence is seen as commonsensical and legitimate while non-state actors' use of violence is (often) labeled terrorist. By asking who uses violence and how such usage is justified, postcolonial approaches do not take for granted the state's use of violence.

Redrawing Boundaries

In contexts such as the Middle East (e.g., Israel and Palestine, both of which are entities that emerged from and are products of colonial practices) and in India, colonial practices reinscribed difference as dangerous. In many colonial spaces, the arbitrary establishment of political boundaries created some states and erased others while ignoring pre-existing ethnic and national boundaries. For example, Winichakul (1994) discusses the physical boundary-making of Siam (Thailand) while Mitchell (1991) focuses on colonialism in Egypt.

But what does this have to do with terrorism? First of all, attention to colonial practices in drawing and redrawing political (and social) borders allows for a deeper understanding of how differences amongst races have been produced and maintained over time. It draws attention to how particular races were described as "dangerous," a description that informed policies and practices towards them. Postcolonial analysis would argue it is not tribal allegiances or religions that are explanations of terrorist violence; it could be oppression and historical powerlessless, experiences which occurred during (political) colonization and continued even after the establishment of new nation-states. An example here could be the concept of "martial races" that the British promoted in India. Furthermore, a postcolonial approach draws attention to the socially constructed nature of many social divisions and categories. For example, in many colonial societies censuses and the practice of census-taking made people aware of their ethnicity/race and forced them to choose a particular racial identity for themselves, rather than allowing for a more fluid identity-formation (Hobson, n.d.).

Visualizing Relations with Others

The question of how to deal with difference/others is central to postcolonial analysis. Postcolonial theorists point towards a multiplicity of relations with "the other," ranging from conflict to hybridity and multiculturalism (see Table 5.3).

In terms of multiplicity of relations, on the one hand, postcolonial theory draws attention to how some spaces and peoples remain "neo-colonized." For example, the concept of "the Muslim world" or "the West" divides the world into easily identifiable blocs and separates them from each other. It ignores that "the West" contains Muslims within its geographical (and conceptual) space and also ignores that "the Muslim world" is not a monolithic bloc. On a related note, postcolonial approaches perform a dual task of reminding us of the continuities between colonial processes and practices while cautioning us about notions of "global" communities of postcolonial thought or peoples. In other words, postcolonial scholars point out the way the world is structured today – e.g., in terms of the Global North and the Global South or the Westphalian state system – is based on colonially imposed ideas and imperialist socioeconomic exploitation. But, postcolonial theorists also caution against lumping people from different regions and with different colonial histories into one monolithic "postcolonial" entity. Instead, by focusing on the diverse everyday experiences of peoples and spaces in different parts of the world while reminding us that "colonial" processes did not end with the end of political colonization, postcolonial theorists open up TS to new avenues and questions in research.

Table 5.3 Some postcolonial concepts and their possible uses in research on terrorism

Concept	Use	Examples in studying terrorism
Orientalism	One of the most common concepts in postcolonial studies. Refers to a system of thought in which others are represented from the point of view of the imperial (European) power. It is also an example where the general meaning of the word was re-defined by Edward Said.	It can be argued much of conventional terrorism scholarship, especially regarding "Islamist terrorism" is Orientalist. Pointing out Orientalism (e.g. Tickell 2010) and imperialist meaning-making is a goal of postcolonial analysis.
Hybridity	Instead of looking at the colonizers and the colonized as distinctly different groups, analysis based on hybridity examines the connections and links amongst the two in terms of joint creation of meanings and the formations of new identities. Can be cultural as well as linguistic.	Hybridity-based research could look at how "states" and "terrorists" (e.g.) co-constitute meanings of danger and violence during particular events. It is also useful to study societies where the mixture of various cultures has produced a hybrid new form of identity (or why such identity is lacking, leading to increased divisions and distrust of minorities in some places.)
Going native	Often used derogatorily to describe the loss of "neutrality" of the colonizer. Ignores that an outside-culture perspective is never possible in much of critically-informed research.	This would be best applicable at a methodological level where "going native" could be reclaimed to explain a focus on reflexivity and sensitivity to context when studying terrorism.
Exoticism	"Literally translated as that which is introduced from or originating in a foreign (especially tropical) country or as something which is attractively strange or remarkably unusual." [Imperial Archive, see weblinks]	Useful when studying (for example) Islam and its relationship with Christianity or other traditions in which Islam is often seen as "strange" and "unknowable" and yet discussions about its "peacefulness" are also common. Other possible research avenues could include studying how particular discourses (e.g. British) represent groups and peoples (e.g. segments of the Irish) both as romantic and literary but also as inherently violent.
Domination and privilege	Pretty much self-evident. Postcolonial theorists interrogate hierarchy as well as privilege of certain spaces, places, peoples and meanings.	Looking at how historical patterns of domination and privilege have produced spaces and peoples who suffer from such dominations and (may) resist, often violently. For example, Boehmer and Morton 2010.
Dichotomies	Asking, Who benefits? Who pays? as well as the binary identity formations (male/female; state/terrorist, etc.) that exist in world politics.	Using a critical political economy perspective to study "terrorism." Examples are research which examines how the "Global North" or particular governments benefit, both financially and in terms of maintaining authority, from terrorism. For example, Research on State Terror

Table 5.3 (continued)

Concept	Use	Examples in studying terrorism
Contrapuntality	Yet another term popularized by Said, it is used to refer to a method of analysis in which connections amongst seemingly-disparate issues, spaces, peoples are highlighted.	e.g. Leela Gandhi.
Complicit postcolonialism	Often used to describe postcolonial theorists (and theories) which accommodate colonial practices of meaning-making. Contrasted with oppositional postcolonialism, which rejects practices and ways of making sense deemed "colonial."	Two ways of examining the relationship between postcolonialism and colonialism.
Subaltern	Areas and peoples who are outside of the core power dynamics in the international system. Used generally to refer to colonized peoples and spaces.*	Studying violence and "terrorism" from the perspective of the subaltern. Foregrounding the experiences of the subaltern when researching and communicating terrorism. Additionally, a subaltern focus can lead to subverting the mainstream (hegemonic) ways of studying terrorism.
Worlding	"describes the way in which colonized space is brought into the 'world', that is, made to exist as part of a world essentially constructed by Euro-centrism" (Ashcroft et al. 1998: 241)	Gayatri Spivak theorized and discusses worlding. For our purposes, postcolonial scholars can point out examples of "worlding" in terrorism scholarship in which events and actors are placed within a Euro-centric hegemonic counterterrorism discourse. Researchers can also conduct subversive "worlding" in which the spaces occupied by imperial presence, (e.g. the US in the Philippines post-9/11) can be outlined and examined. Here, the agency of the occupied spaces and peoples is given priority as their ways of understanding US (for example) presence is studied.

* Spivak has a different and more specific definition: "*subaltern* is not just a classy word for oppressed, for Other, for somebody who's not getting a piece of the pie. ... In postcolonial terms, everything that has limited or no access to the cultural imperialism is subaltern—a space of difference. Now who would say that's just the oppressed? The working class is oppressed. It's not subaltern" (de Kock 1992).

Methodology: Language and Power

Finally, postcolonial theory draws attention to the colonial norms underlying language use in IR and terrorism scholarship. Some postcolonial theorists argue that the language used when narrating mainstream IR carries with it imperial norms and practices. The dominant language in narrating IR and explaining terrorism is English. It is not just English but a particular format of English in which tales about IR need to be told. Deviations from this may be tagged "non-scholarly" or (worse!) "anecdotal." Research projects have to follow a specified outline which, again, is derived from colonial understandings of what counts as "research" and how it should be presented in order to be accepted as such. The written word is prioritized. This discounts oral histories and physical enactments as modes of presenting IR research. Postcolonialism thus draws attention not only to how people experience terrorism differently and make sense of terrorism differently but also how narration itself (and what counts as narrative) might be different across contexts. By drawing attention to questions of language and power, postcolonial theory gives researchers the option to either co-opt the dominant language (English) or to reject it.

Postcolonial Feminism and Terrorism: An Overview

While postcolonial theorists and feminists separately centralize effects of colonial and gendered processes, postcolonial feminists focus on gendered processes as related to colonial practices. For postcolonial feminists, "colonial" may mean practices of political, social, economic colonization or colonization in the form of language and ideas, as discussed above. Postcolonial feminists draw attention to historical contexts where feminists from colonizing countries were often complicit in practices of colonization; they also draw attention to colonial and postcolonial spaces and peoples wherein females are often further marginalized than males. Scholars have written that postcolonial feminists especially experience "double colonization." This means they have been oppressed by patriarchal as well as colonial norms and practices. Women in postcolonial contexts have to maneuver through a world characterized by colonial practices (e.g., social orders in which certain ethnic groups and races are deemed inferior or prone to violence) and also patriarchal viewpoints (e.g., a woman's role is at home).

Postcolonial feminists remind us that the category of "the colonized" ignores issues of gender and class. They call for a centralization of gender *and* race when talking about "colonized peoples." At the same time, postcolonial feminists discuss the diversity of experiences during colonization – different colonized women were represented (and made sense of) in different ways and by different colonizers. "Double colonization" thus refers to how women suffered from colonial practices but also experienced discrimination because they are women. McLeod makes this clear: "double colonization" indicates "the ways in which women have *simultaneously* experienced the oppression of colonialism and patriarchy" (2010: 175). Postcolonial feminists also point out that there is a tension between "First World feminism" and "Third World feminism" especially as many First World feminists have been complicit in the colonial processes which have led to patterns of dominance and oppression for "Global South women." At the same time, however, there is also gender discrimination *within* "Global South" communities. Postcolonial feminists draw attention to these interlinked patterns of dominance, oppression, and resistance.

In IR, postcolonial feminism has taken on the task of questioning gendered norms of (often male) mainstream postcolonial theorists while reminding us of the interconnections between gender and race. In order to think about potential research projects utilizing a postcolonial feminist approach, it is worth quoting Chowdhry and Ling (2010) at length here:

> For postcolonial feminism in international relations [PFIR], three major components are involved in analyzing world politics: culture, politics, and material structures.

By culture, PFIR refers to conventional markers of difference (e.g., race/ethnicity, gender/sexuality, class/caste, nationality/location, language/dialect) which are conveyed and constructed through various venues of representation, ranging from the textual (e.g., literature, newspapers, reports, advertisements, manuals) to the performative (e.g., theater, dance, film, radio, television) to domains of life and work (e.g., field, school, office, factory, hotel, brothel, household). Politics is a site where we struggle over and negotiate legacies of conflict (e.g., settler vs native, civilized vs savage, masculinized vs feminized) as well as entwinement (e.g., patriarchy, hierarchy, mimicry, simulacra, hybridity), derived from historical encounters between colonizers and the colonized. And material structures accrue physically and institutionally from the imposition of Westphalian interstate commerce and capitalism at every level (e.g., global, regional, national, local), affecting all aspects of life including the family and the individual, but in conjunction with prior modes, means, and relations of production (e.g., agricultural, pastoral, nomadic, maritime, trade and barter) to produce the mixed and interactive contexts we operate in today.

Research Designs: Feminism, Postcolonialism, and Postcolonial Feminism

In terms of research designs, postcolonialism, feminism, and postcolonial feminism all share similar sensibilities of transforming what counts as knowledge of terrorism. A reflexive orientation to research is advocated. All these ways of doing research centralize subject positions usually considered "marginal" in IR (see Table 5.1). That being said, there are some specific topics that each approach can focus on (see Tables 5.2, 5.3 and 5.4 for an examples of possible research programs).

The rest of this section will elaborate upon what each approach can contribute to the study of terrorism, rather than providing a generalized research design that fits all. First, we start with feminism.

Feminist Analysis of Terrorism

Feminist research on terrorism can ask about women's experiences during particular terrorist events, such as Wibben's work on 9/11. By centralizing experiences of women whose everyday lives did not change with the event, Wibben (2011) draws our attention to what is usually left out when studying security and terrorism – experiences of (some) people and their meanings of (in)security. Similarly, Shepherd (2006), Cloud (2004) and Puar (2008), and Khan (2008), among others examine how gendered narratives on "war on terrorism" have emerged and helped justify particular policies (e.g., the US invasions of Afghanistan and Iraq), but also how there is a discrepancy between how American and non-American women are represented. At the same time, these scholars indicate how the women themselves – Jessica Lynch or Lynndie England or women in Iraq and Afghanistan – do not often get a chance to have their voices heard and their stories told.

But what do feminist analysts of terrorism do? McLeod quotes Belsey and Moore who claim that a feminist reader "is enlisted in the process of changing the gender relations which prevail in our society, and she regards the practice of reading as one of the sites in the struggle for change" (McLeod 2010: 173). In the task of "changing the gender relations," feminists read texts (or world events) to note gendered representations.

Table 5.4 Research designs on suicide bombing from feminist, postcolonial and postcolonial feminist methodologies

	Feminism	Postcolonialism	Postcolonial feminism
Research questions	How do women suicide bombers make sense of their actions? [vs conventional narrative of women who commit violence being "abnormal" or "bad." See Sjoberg and Gentry 2011 for a more detailed overview of a feminist program on suicide bombing.]	How is suicide terrorism understood in mainstream/conventional terrorism scholarship?	How are female suicide "terrorists" made sense of?
To clarify	Maintain focus on the women themselves or how they are viewed by others or both.	Specify who or what demarcates the "mainstream."	Specify by whom [who is the population whose meanings are being explained?]
			Same as the other two.
Data	Statistics about "suicide bombing"; interviews with women bombers/other women/general population; representations of suicide bombings in film, photographs and media.	Statistics; documents; visuals; who is talked or written about as "suicide bombers" or "suicide terrorists." Colonial archives.	
Data gathering	Interviews: specify which population and then conduct interviews. Goal would be to elicit how violence (suicide bombing) is made meaningful.	Interviews: could interview writers/journalists/terrorism researchers to ask how they describe the subjects of suicide bombing. Conventional methods often do not study whether oppression may have contributed to people feeling suicide bombing is the only way to talk/communicate.	Similar to the postcolonial approach but the goal here is to explicate how "double colonization" may be occurring in the study of female suicide bombers.
	– archives/texts: note how suicide bombing is framed in documents (both textual and visual). Who is given importance? What are the reasons given for the act? How are women presented in comparison to men?	– archives/colonial documents: note what is left out. Usually, narratives utilize the colonizers' perspectives and voices rather than those of the colonized.	– in analysis, note raced and gendered representations by interviewees and in texts, including postcolonial texts (e.g Chowdhry 2007).
	– participant observation: this works mainly if the population is the general public or policy-makers or researchers, rather than suicide bombers as successful suicide bombers are unlikely to be accessible for the researcher to observe.	– autoethnography: the researcher could utilize herself as a mode of gathering data especially if the research population is (other) researchers and terrorism scholars. Here, reactions to the researcher's race and gender form part of the data gathered.	

Table 5.4 (continued)

	Feminism	Postcolonialism	Postcolonial feminism
Presuppositions/ possible outcomes	Women's narratives are presented within a masculinized worldview and women's actions are filtered through the male gaze such that their agency is denied.	Suicide "terrorism" is a raced term in that it is often linked with racial and geographical markers; a binary opposition is constructed between "us" (usually white Europeans and Americans) and "them" (usually non-white, "backwards" or "barbaric" and thus prone to possibly blowing themselves up); colonial legacies are often ignored or silenced in much of the existing research on suicide bombings. That oppression may have led to suicide bombing as the only way to talk/communicate is not often the focus of discussion in conventional research on suicide bombings.	Postcolonial female narratives about violence are silenced by colonial and masculinized institutional structures. – modes of expression may be different not just from colonized meaning-making practices but also from "First World feminist" ways of communicating knowledge.

Wibben clarifies this: "Part of the feminist research agenda is, therefore, to examine how gender has infused our very ways of thinking. We see the world through gendered lenses – our own experiences of gender shape the way we think about and represent world politics" (Wibben 2011: 17). She adds that IR has a "male bias." For example, a concern with terrorism is often equated with a state-centric and a male-centric view of the world, one in which the act of terrorism is countered by military means and which is made sense of by (often male) policy-makers. Wibben writes, "To reduce such [male] bias, feminists ask that scholars become aware of the context in which the research is conducted by asking two basic questions: what is the location of the researcher in relation to the subject of research and how are the subjects of research selected?" (2011: 18).

These questions in TS would clarify the methodological choices of the researcher and their relationship with the researched – what we have called for elsewhere (Stump and Dixit 2012). Thus, a feminist analysis begins with a research question which is informed by the notion that our representations of the world and our knowledge of it are gendered and, often, from a masculine standpoint. The research then proceeds to outline the effects of this gendered world – in our case, a gendered understanding of terrorism and counterterrorism.

Some examples of feminist research on terrorism include Hunt and Rygiel (2006) *(En)gendering the War on Terror*. Essays in it examine the "war on terror" through a gender lens, with chapters on postcolonial feminism (Zine), "Embedded feminism" (Hunt), the construction of rescuers and victims and tracing connections between the representations of Muslim women in Europe and in the "war on terror." Similarly, Hawthorne and Winter's *After Shock: September 11, 2001: Global Feminist Perspectives* (2003) includes narratives on race, class, gender, and personal reactions to the event from a wide range of people and in differing formats (including poems and letters). In much of this scholarship, the dominant meaning of "9/11," that it was an exceptional event, is questioned and alternative meanings of (in)security are provided. Sjoberg and Gentry in *Mothers, Monsters, Whores* (2007) examine the varied identities of women in the "war on terror."

Discussing the "war on terror," Hunt and Rygiel write, "Feminist analyses of this (en)gendered war ["on terror"] disrupt and make visible the masculinized, militarized, racialized, sexualized, and classed dynamics through which the war operates and which often go unnoticed, ignored or hidden by official representations of war" (2006: 3).

Sylvester and Parashar (2009) are one of the few to bring gender analysis to CTS. They provide an overview of some ways in which feminist analysis can contribute to TS. Their method of using the *Mahabharata* (a Hindu epic) as a metaphor for exploring some of the concerns of gender and terrorism itself speaks to how a feminist methodology questions conventional ways of doing and presenting research. By linking the questions they raise and explore to a well-known (but not "academic") text, Sylvester and Parashar illustrate the ubiquity of silencing of women's actions and words as well as how such practices of silencing have not changed despite the thousand-year-plus time between the *Mahabharata* and today's terrorism scholars. They raise questions of who can (and cannot) speak when discussing women's roles in terrorism and counterterrorism.

As indicated earlier, feminist methodology is often standpoint analysis, seeking to empower women across nations, races, and classes with the aim of transforming world politics. Standpoint analysis means being aware of the differing and often divergent positions of researchers with regards to how they view and communicate terrorism. As Steans clarifies, "[S]tandpoint theorists insisted that knowledge claims were not 'objective' but were always 'situated'" (2006: 136).

In terms of how feminist analysis proceeds, we have mentioned here that feminist research can take many forms including statistical analysis, social networks and case studies. However, much of feminist analyses use interpretive approaches. Laura Shepherd writes, "the value in telling a different story is in the telling, in illustrating the ways in which these stories are constructed and could be constructed differently" (2008: 5). In a foundational text for feminist IR, Tickner (1992) outlines how world politics is masculinized such that women's experiences are seen as inauthentic. Thus, asking "Where are the women?" is not just to add them or to essentialize their actions as "of women" but to talk of how this masculinized world which ignores women's voices and experiences is socially constructed and maintained.

On a similar note, Shepherd explains her research, "This research investigates the discursive construction of Resolution 1325 through the identification of practices of (re)production, (re)presentation and (re)legitimization in the document itself with specific reference to articulations of gender, violence, security and the international" (2008: 26). For Shepherd, then, the research question is how a particular text and practices related to it construct particular identities for women in relation to other social forces. Her methodology is discourse analysis. By bringing attention to the experiences of women in relation to other genders and institutions, feminist security scholars question this system of patriarchy and transform our understanding of security.

To sum up, critical feminist analyses of bombing centralize women's experiences and question the silencing of women in mainstream terrorism scholarship. As such, they draw attention to gendered practices which often legitimate particular policies. They do so in order to emphasize reflexivity and standpoint in research, to change the gendered structures of security practices (including meanings of terrorism and counterterrorism) and to transform the meaning of terrorism.

Postcolonial Analysis of Terrorism

Postcolonialism centralizes connections and disjunctures amongst colonial and post-colonial modes of knowledge production. Postcolonial theorists studying terrorism examine how colonial modes of being and ways of seeing the world have infused how and what we know about world politics today. A key issue in research is "the other" (or others) in which a concern with those conceptualized as different is prioritized. Research can then include how social actors and meanings are conceptualized as "other" in the first place as well as how to relate with these "others". Edward Said, Frantz Fanon, Homi K. Bhabha, Gayatri Spivak, and Ashish Nandy (among others) are the postcolonial theorists referred to most often in IR, and some of the main concepts are outlined in Table 5.3.

A significant part of postcolonial scholarship uses historical analysis to question established practices and knowledge. For example, Barkawi and Laffey critique the Eurocentricism of security studies and argue, "understanding security relations, past and present, requires acknowledging the mutual constitution of Europe and the non-European world and their joint role in making history" (2006: 330). Here, their call, similar to that of feminists, is for security studies (and IR) to acknowledge its (Eurocentric) standpoint and to open up the field to new ways of doing research. Regarding terrorism, Barkawi and Laffey argue it is difficult to understand al-Qaeda's actions and its meanings amongst its supporters without a postcolonial viewpoint.

Similarly, scholars from outside IR have studied nations, identities, formation of ethnicities and races, and political economy and development-related issues via a postcolonial approach. While there has been limited application of postcolonial theory in studying terrorism, an example is Tickell (2010). Tickell interrogates conventional terrorism scholarship's understanding of the *thuggee* of India as prototypical terrorists. Tickell writes, "'il/legible' bodies from very different eras are brought together in a search for the origins of terrorist violence and, in the process, suppositions are made about cultural difference, the truth claims of colonial archives, and the cultural-historical location of so-called 'religious terrorism' that are deeply troubling" (2010: 180). He goes on to criticize terrorism scholars (e.g., David Rapaport and Bruce Hoffman) who have used thugs as examples of terrorism. By comparing his (and postcolonialism's in general) use of history with that of David Rapaport, Tickell clarifies: "Thus, Rapaport's essay is not only significant because of its use of colonial history within its own field; it also represents the methodological opposite of the postcolonial – finding an atavistic origin for terrorism in colonial descriptions of indigenous violence, where postcolonial theorists might interrogate the 'epistemic' violence inherent in the description itself" (2010: 182). Here, a difference between a conventional approach and a postcolonial one is clearly laid out.

Tickell's historical analysis – examining primary sources and colonial texts about the thugs (or *thuggee*) – outlines how the "'discovery'/policing" of *thuggee* assisted in maintaining and legitimating colonial sovereignty. By describing the thugs as a violent cult, the British colonizers were able to justify policing, create ethnic boundaries that rewarded locals who provided information about the *thuggee* and link violence to local religion (the *thuggee* were described as fanatical devotees of the Hindu goddess Kali). Popular culture – there were many books published in which the *thuggee* were villains – helped constitute and spread this understanding of the *thuggee* among their (mostly British, literate) readership. Tickell's historical analysis indicates there is no certainty over how many people were killed by the *thuggee* and how long they were in operation and yet the view of them as fanatical mass murderers has continued over time. Tickell thus outlines the problems with taking for granted colonial (dominant) accounts of the *thuggee* and such accounts being uncritically reproduced by current scholars: "Rapaport's 'Fear and Trembling' essay would be less significant had it not subsequently become a supporting pillar in TS readings of 'religious terrorism'" (2010: 188).

Here, a postcolonial analysis is useful in interrogating what has become a foundational essay in "religious terrorism" – Rapaport's – and outlining how Rapaport's sources (texts and meanings produced by the colonial power) are inadequate for an understanding of the *thuggee*. Tickell's work performs two tasks of postcolonial analysis of terrorism: (1) it utilizes historical documents and texts to understand how meanings of *thuggee* – the dangerous subject – were produced. (2) It also draws attention to silences within our discipline of IR and its myopia regarding research in other disciplines. Tickell claims there is extensive historical scholarship on *thuggee,* most of which contradicts Rapaport's understanding of them (2010: 189). Rapaport ignores this scholarship in his writing as do other terrorism scholars who refer to Rapaport's essay. Tickell's work also indicates silences in the study of the terrorist *thuggee* – "the thugs … can be interpreted both as subsidiary social and economic byproducts of colonial expansion into central India and as vital self-consolidating figures in the exception-based juridical preservation of colonial sovereignty" (Tickell 2010: 196 n8). And, yet, in conventional TS, this understanding of the *thuggee* is subsumed in favor of their representation as prototypical terrorists.

By interrogating the dominant understanding of *thuggee,* Tickell's work is transformative as taking it (and similar postcolonial analysis) seriously would draw attention to how the state's use of violence is implicated in its representations of others – the *thuggee* in this case – as dangerous and as terrorist.

Using historical analysis, postcolonial theory looks at iteration and repetition as moments when new meanings can be produced. One possible research topic regarding postcolonialism and terrorism would be to study how colonial representations and tropes are repeated in discussions of "the terrorist" or terrorism today. By unpacking the raced representations of who is considered terrorist in the twenty-first century, connections with past colonial strategies and representations of the colonized can be noted. Here, historical analysis is not just to question contemporary understandings of terrorism but also to outline how colonial tropes and representations have permeated our contemporary understandings of terrorism. The analytical tools of iteration and repetition could be methods for data analysis.

Discussing postcolonialism in relation to the French Empire, Grovogui writes, "Here postcolonial criticisms originate from a longstanding anticolonialism that owes its character to its ambivalence toward Enlightenment ideas, its associated modes of inquiry and the political project of colonial *assimilation*" (quoted in Chowdhry and Nair 2002: 36). While Grovugui is making this claim to distinguish the emergence of (French) postcolonial criticisms from South Asian subaltern postcolonality, his description of postcolonialism as emerging from anticolonial resistance ideas and comprising of an ambivalence towards dominant or mainstream ways of knowing holds for postcolonial research in general.

To sum up, postcolonial research designs are about critiquing existing ways of studying and knowing the world. They outline connections and disconnections to colonial ways of knowing and direct researchers' attentions to raced tropes and concepts that are still utilized today. Postcolonial research interrogates different ways of relations to "others" and critiques racism and oppression in structures of power and knowledge; structures that often help establish meanings of what (and who) are considered terrorist. Postcolonial analysis excavates silenced voices and narratives. Historical analysis, textual ethnography and contrapuntal reading of dominant (mainstream) texts are some common research methods that are used.

Postcolonial Feminism in Terrorism Research

As indicated earlier, postcolonial feminists question the focus on (often masculine) race by postcolonial scholars as well as the emphasis placed on concerns of the "Global North" women on the part of many feminists. Instead, postcolonial feminist research studies the role of "Global South" women in relation to other classes and institutions. For example, a postcolonial feminist research project could study the social construction of gender differences in colonial and anti-colonial contexts. Another possible research topic could be an analysis of the changing representations of women in colonial and post/anti-colonial discourses (McLeod 2010: 172). With regards to terrorism, researchers could question whether colonial and other dominant discourses interact with colonized men and women in the same way. On a related note, postcolonial feminists could ask how women (and men) made sense of colonialism, violence, anti-colonialism, nation, nationalism, and terrorism differently. As Silva points out, women have remained at the margins in narratives of violence and terrorism (2010).

While TS has been noticeably lacking with regards to postcolonial feminist analysis of terrorism, there have been some efforts towards this in the general IR arena. Two recent edited collections – R. Riley et al.'s *Feminism and War: Confronting US Imperialism* (2008) and R. Riley and Naeem Inayatullah's *Interrogating Imperialism: Conversations on Gender, Race, and War* (2006) – have a series of essays critiquing imperial and raced ideas and practices that perpetuate today. In both, the focus is on a wide range of approaches to critiquing the continued effects of imperial power but *Feminism and War* concentrates specifically on feminist critiques of US imperialism. For example, Shigematsu's chapter is a dialogue between former US military officials and Shigematsu, a "scholar-activist" (2008: 93). Written in the form of a conversation, the chapter provides an illustration of a postcolonial feminist methodology (narrativization and oral histories) which does not fit in perfectly with conventional notions of "research design" in IR. Other essays in the volume examine responses to US foreign policy, especially in the post-September 11, 2001 period. Part III is about Afghan and Iraqi women and their positioning (and role) in these wars that they did not ask for. Colonized notions of "rescuing" women and its limits are explored by Khan; there is an interrogation of "how the essentializing and dichotomizing discourse of orientalism has justified, facilitated and shaped torture at Abu Ghraib" (2008: 179) by Nusair; while Hyndman asks "Whose bodies count?" Following in a similar fashion, Fisher (2008) gives us snippets illustrating differing notions of "freedom" in different contexts, thus questioning (and making us question) what is freedom. She has three main questions:

1. Does freedom emerge through opportunity plus education?
2. Do our desires lead us to greater freedom?
3. Is freedom made possible by our connections with others – and which others?

Her answers to these questions are explorations and vignettes which could lead to further reflection. In writing about postcolonial women's experiences of violence and terrorism, then, the research design and also the outcome of the research may (and often do) look different to what we usually expect from mainstream or conventional approaches to terrorism.

On a related note, *Interrogating Imperialism*'s essays expand "imperialism's" definition from the USA to a more generalized imperialism with essays expressing ambivalence about women's "solidarity" in different contexts. Armstrong and Prashad study the USA and South Africa, especially how US foreign policy towards Africa expressed its own military aims and goals for controlling oil rather than reflecting upon past involvement in oppression (2006: 155). In an essay about studying terrorism, Monisha Das Gupta asks "Bewildered? Women's Studies and the War on Terror." She begins her essay by reflecting on "my apprehensions about my safety as an Indian citizen working in the United States" (2006: 129) when war in Afghanistan was imminent. In this one sentence, Gupta draws attention to: (a) how so much of conventional terrorism scholarship assumes the standpoint and perspective – and meaning-making – of the center (i.e. the "West" or the USA), and (b) how, in today's global world, individuals in the USA can and do have personal concerns about family and friends in areas which are near (or actually have been) designated "target" areas.

As such, the beginning of Gupta's essay serves as a timely reminder for reflexivity being at the forefront of postcolonial and feminist research. She remains critical of "Women's Studies" and claims, "Women's Studies continues to be an imperial site implicated in the American state's long history of empire building" (2006: 130). Indeed, she argues, Women's Studies' attention to race, class, and gender has actually been detrimental to interrogating imperialism since a race-, class- and gender-based paradigm separates the domestic from the international and prevents researchers from being aware of "domestic" sites where race, class, gender, and imperialism have intersected (2006: 130). Gupta, in company with other postcolonial and feminist authors described here, connects her own experiences with that of the topic she is investigating – the interconnections between international and domestic, which are often missing in Women's Studies research on terrorism (2006: 134–135). Part of Gupta's critique is methodological and pedagogical as she points out courses on colonialism, globalization, neoimperialism, and the like, are often taught by "third-world scholars," a practice she finds problematic as it separates the domestic "faculty members who teach about domestic issues no longer need to learn and teach about international issues" (2006: 135) and international while categorizing colonialism, neoimperialism, etc., as a problem not faced by "domestic" politics (and the "domestic" faculty who teach them) (2006: 135).[1] For postcolonial methodology, this is an important piece as it attempts to "decolonize" current ways of knowing and studying terrorism. Thus, there are three major points to be made here regarding postcolonial feminist research designs:

1. The domestic/international divide is not just problematic for the study of imperialism and counterterrorism but also in terms of how "we" teach students about these topics.
2. The "we" – researchers and teachers – is itself opened up to question and the "offshoring" (Gupta 2006: 135) of topics such as feminism, imperialism, and colonialism to "third world bodies" is noted as problematic.
3. Commonalities, if understood as the suspension of power relations, may never be possible between "third world" (or postcolonial) feminists and "Women's Studies."

Theoretically, too, postcolonial feminists ask, "where are the women?" to note the structures of power and gendered and raced hierarchies that often relegate women to the sidelines and to silence. This is especially the case in IR, where Said, Nandy, and, to a lesser extent Bhabha, are better known than female theorists, of which Spivak often gets relegated to "feminism and gender" classes. In other words, it is Spivak's female identity that is usually prioritized in syllabi on IR theory rather than her postcolonial credentials. On a similar note, Carole Boyce Davies wonders where female postcolonial theorists are and adds, "it seems so far that the discourses of post-coloniality are not, at this point in history, overly populated by 'postcolonial women'" (McLeod 2010: 180).

Postcolonial feminism's research strategies bridge feminism and postcolonialism. For example, Chandra Mohanty was one of the earliest postcolonial feminist theorists to critique how "First World" feminists homogenized "Third World" feminists. In her influential essay "Under Western Eyes," she writes,

> While feminist writing in the U.S. is still marginalized (except from the point of view of women of color addressing privileged White women), Western feminist writing on women in the third world must be considered in the context of the global hegemony of Western scholarship – i.e. the production, publication, distribution, and consumption of information and ideas. Marginal or not, this writing has political effects and implications beyond the immediate feminist or disciplinary audience. One such significant effect of the dominant "representations" of Western feminism is its conflation with imperialism in the eyes of particular third world women. Hence the urgent need to examine the *political* implications of *analytic* strategies and principles.
>
> (1988: 336)

This is a methodological critique that Mohanty makes, as she points out some analytical shortcomings in how mainstream feminism has co-opted other types of feminism and represented others in ways that only make sense within the dominant framework. As such, this indicates an important caution to researchers – a critique of attempts to create and talk of a "universal womanhood" (McLeod 2010: 188–189). It also outlines that feminist and postcolonial research is politically motivated and often seen as an intervention or a corrective to masculinized hegemonic ways of doing and communicating research.

Another example of postcolonial feminist research is from Gayatri Spivak who theorizes the subordinate position and subsequent silencing of the "subaltern." Spivak's work, especially in her famous essay, "Can the Subaltern Speak?" theorizes on the position of postcolonial women. To the question of whether the subaltern (woman) can speak, Spivak answers no. Well, not within the current interpretive framework in which her voice is either silenced or forced to speak in a way that is alien to her. So, even if her voice is "excavated," her words and narratives are made to fit within a worldview and knowledge-making practices which are *not* of her making. As McLeod (2010) emphasizes,

> Any attempt to retrieve her [subaltern woman's] voice will disfigure her speech. So, she [Spivak] concludes, Intellectuals must instead critique those discourses which claim to rescue the "authentic" voices of the subaltern as female from their mute condition, and address their complicity in the production of subalterneity. Simply inserting subaltern women into representation is a cosmetic exercise as long as the *system* of representation endorses discredited models of essential, centred subjectivity.

On a similar note, postcolonial feminism in IR asks a series of questions drawing attention to connections between the past and the present in terms of representations of women, the "Global South," and colonial and anti-colonial meaning-making. To sum up, here are Chowdhry and Ling's words as they clarify the research context of Postcolonial Feminism in International Relations (PFIR):

> PFIR combines postcolonial and feminist insights to ask: How does the stratum of elite power (e.g., the boardroom–bedroom–war room complex) interlock with subterranean layers of colonization (e.g., the "servants' quarters," the "sweat shop," the "red light district," the "opium den," the "Casbah") to produce our contemporary world politics? How do these intersections of race, gender, sex, and

class inform matrices of power in world politics? Furthermore, how do we account for elite and subaltern agency and resistance to the hegemonic sphere of world politics?

(McLeod 2010)

Conclusion: Ethical Concerns

The choice of a feminist, postcolonial or postcolonial feminist approach to research itself is an exercise of ethics in that each of these approaches critiques entrenched ways of understanding terrorism. In addition, ethical concerns also arise in the foundational common goal of all these three approaches: how to relate to difference and theorizing about relationships with "the other." This concern with those outside of the researcher's self is an ethical exercise in which "our" ways of studying and understanding difference are foregrounded and "our" practices of "self-making" (or identity-formation) are questioned.

   In terms of engagement, postcolonial and feminist researchers propose a series of possible encounters with those considered other (Table 5.5). For example, Yuval-Davis calls for a "transversal politics" which is in-between the universalism of the Left and "identity politics" (2010). This notion of transversal politics takes as foundational the view that research is always "unfinished," since it emerges from a particular standpoint. On a related note, a concern for others is tied in with an awareness and possibility of dialoguing with those considered different. This, too, is part of an ethical research process. Yuval-Davis is concerned with the seeming "authenticity" of people who claim to speak for their constituency, an authenticity that she disputes based on the unfinished nature of standpoint theorizing. A similar caution is provided by other postcolonial feminist scholars such as Mohanty and Spivak. As McLeod writes,

> Spivak has consistently advocated that critics must always look to the specifics of their own positions and recognize the political, cultural and institutional contexts in which they work. The space from which we speak is always on the move, crisscrossed by the conflicting and shifting discourses of things like our social class, education, gender, sexuality and ethnicity. It is very difficult to assume that the critic can ever speak "on behalf" of anybody, because the position of both the critic and their "object" is never securely fixed.

(2010: 186)

Table 5.5 Some ways of relating with "difference"

Possible relationships with others	Theorists
Multiplicity	Chowdhry and Ling
Subjugated knowledges	Foucault
Subaltern	Guha and Spivak
Negritude	Aimé Césaire; criticized by Édouard Glissant and his subsequent Creolite movement
Transversal politics	Yuval-Davis
Critical relationality	Boyce Davies

Carole Boyce Davies' definition of *critical relationality* and her use of "going a piece of the way with them" when discussing how she relates to Western theory (quoted in McLeod 2010: 198–199) could form part of this ethical engagement with the other that feminists and postcolonial scholars call for. Inayatullah and Blaney perform a similar task for IR as they too call for a re-reading of dominant discourses in order to note contradictions and cracks in so-called mainstream understandings of IR.

On a practical note, feminist study of gender relations and postcolonial study of race indicate how particular raced (e.g., Tickell) and gendered (e.g., Shepherd, Hyndman) discourses produce legitimacy for colonial powers or masculine authority figures (sentence adapted from Shepherd 2006). Hence, by outlining the concepts and representational practices of particular groups of people, feminists and postcolonial scholars interrogate the dominant framework of how "we" make sense of IR, security and terrorism. In doing so, they undermine the legitimacy and the authority of such seemingly commonsensical representations. This is an ethical task that postcolonial and feminist researchers have taken up.

Research Strategy

As postcolonialism, feminism, and postcolonial feminism are research approaches rather than specific methods, research designs utilizing these approaches can adopt the research strategies outlined in Chapter 4 and Chapters 6–10, depending on how the research wants to proceed. Generally, postcolonial and feminist research asks these main questions:

1. "How does X deal with others?" where X usually refers to a mainstream historical tradition or scholar (e.g., Rapaport, TS) and "others" may be particular groups of people (e.g., colonized, minorities, women).
2. "Where are the women/minorities?" Similar to the first question, asking "Where are the women?" or "Where are minorities?" then draws attention to the raced and gendered structures of power and knowledge that comprise world politics.

Research Methods

As indicated above, research methods can range from CT to ethnography to discourse analysis and network analysis. It is the political goals of postcolonial research (to excavate oppressed and raced meanings) and feminist research (to give voice to silenced women and outline the effects of a patriarchal knowledge production system) that distinguish feminist, postcolonial and postcolonial feminist analyses.

Data

This, too, can range from documents (speech, written, visual) to physical enactments (people's daily actions) and oral histories. Usually, postcolonial analysis attempts to "make visible" seemingly hidden and often forgotten aspects of history and, thus, utilizes historical analysis.

Analysis

Tables 5.2 and 5.3 outline some of the analytical concepts that have been and can be used to analyze postcolonial and feminist research on terrorism. Examples of authors who have used those concepts are also included. Table 5.4 outlines what a research project on suicide bombing would look like from feminist, postcolonial and postcolonial feminist research approaches.

Questions to consider

- What are the key features of feminist and postcolonial approaches to terrorism?
- What would terrorism research from a feminist or postcolonial perspective emphasize?
- What are some critiques that postcolonial feminists make of postcolonialism and feminism? Do you find these critiques valid? Why or why not?
- Using Tickell's analysis of the *thuggee* as a guideline, do a brief critical historical analysis of a group that have been labeled a terrorist or prototerrorist. What would your data be? Where would you find your data?
- List some spaces and peoples that have been marginalized and silenced in conventional terrorism scholarship. What does that tell us about our knowledge of terrorism?
- How does standpoint analysis and reflexivity inform postcolonial and feminist research?
- Feminists and postcolonial scholars seek to transform IR. In our case, feminist and postcolonial research on terrorism would seek to transform TS. What would this transformed TS look like?

Note

1 Gupta's section subtitled, "Terrain of Gender and War: Post-9/11 Feminist Inquiry" gives an overview of feminist analyses of terrorism that informs and adds to IR-related analyses. See Gupta (2006: 145–148) for more.

Further Reading

Ackerly, B. A., Stern, M., and True, J. (Eds.) (2006), *Feminist Methodologies for International Relations*, Cambridge: Cambridge University Press.

Ashcroft, B., Griffiths, G., and Tiffin, H. (Eds.) (2005), *The Post-Colonial Studies Reader*, London and New York: Routledge.

Barkawi, T. (2010), "Empire and Order in International Relations," in R. A. Denemark (Ed.), *The International Studies Encyclopedia*, Oxford: Blackwell Publishing.

Boehmer, E. and Morton, S. (Eds.) (2010), *Terror and the Postcolonial*, Oxford: Wiley-Blackwell.

Chowdhry, G. and Ling, L. H. M. (2010), 'Race(ing) International Relations: A Critical Overview of Postcolonial Feminism in International Relations," in R. A. Denemark (Ed.), *The International Studies Encyclopedia*, Oxford: Blackwell Publishing.

Darby, P. (2009), "Recasting Western Knowledges About (Postcolonial) Security," in D. Grenfell (Ed.), *Rethinking Insecurity, War and Violence: Beyond Savage Globalization?* London and New York: Routledge, pp. 71–85.

Heeg, J. (2010), "Feminist Ontologies, Epistemologies, Methodologies, and Methods in International Relations," in R. A. Denemark (Ed.), *The International Studies Encyclopedia*, Oxford: Blackwell Publishing.

Hobson, K., n.d., "Ethnographic Mapping and the Construction of the British Census in India," http://www.britishempire.co.uk/article/castesystem.htm (accessed August 3, 2012).

Inayatullah, N. and Blaney, D. (2004), *International Relations and the Problem of Difference*, London and New York: Routledge.

McLeod, J. (2010), *Beginning Postcolonialism*, Manchester: Manchester University Press.

Shepherd, L. J. (2010), "Feminist Security Studies," in R. A. Denemark (Ed.), *The International Studies Encyclopedia*, Oxford: Blackwell Publishing.

Shilliam, R. (Ed.) (2010), *Non-Western Thought and International Relations*, London and New York: Routledge.

Sjoberg, L. and Martin, J. (2010), 'Feminist Security Theorizing," in R. A. Denemark (Ed.), *The International Studies Encyclopedia*, Oxford: Blackwell Publishing.

Spivak, G. C. (1994), "Can the Subaltern Speak?" in P. Williams and L. Chrisman (Eds.), *Colonial Discourse and Post-Colonial Theory*, New York: Columbia University Press, pp. 66–111.

Steans, J. (2008), "Telling Stories About Women and Gender in the War on Terror," *Global Society*, 21 (1): 159–176.

Sylvester, C. and Parashar, S. (2009), "The Contemporary 'Mahabharata' and the Many Draupadis: Bringing Gender to Critical Terrorism Studies," in R. Jackson, J. Gunning, and M. B. Smyth (Eds.), *Critical Terrorism Studies: A New Research Agenda*, London and New York: Routledge.

Yuval-Davis, N. (2009), "What Is 'Transversal Politics'?" *Soundings*, 12 (summer).

Weblinks

Some main concepts used in postcolonial studies can be found at http://www.qub.ac.uk/schools/SchoolofEnglish/imperial/key-concepts/key-concepts.htm and "The Imperial Archive: Key Concepts in Postcolonial Studies", http://www.qub.ac.uk/imperial/key-concepts/key-concepts.htm.

Chandra Mohanty, author of the influential essay on postcolonial feminism, "Under Western Eyes: Feminist Scholarship and Colonial Discourses," has a website at http://as-cascade.syr.edu/profiles/pages/mohanty-chandratalpade.html.

Laura Sjoberg discusses feminist approaches to war and security at: "Feminist IR 101, Post #6, War and Security (in Practice), 10 March 2011": http://duckofminerva.blogspot.com/2011/03/feminist-ir-101-post-6-war-and-security.html.

On "Orientalism": http://www.english.emory.edu/Bahri/Orientalism.html.

"Introduction to postcolonial studies: a comprehensive list of scholars and major issues and concepts": http://www.english.emory.edu/Bahri/Intro.html lists some well-known researchers and concepts of postcolonial theory.

6 Ethnography of the Terrorist Subject

Introduction

Ethnography is a word used to refer to a particular set of *methods* (participant observation and interviewing), a *methodology* that aims to make sense of how a population of people attach meanings to their social and political environment, and to the finished, written *product* of that research (Jackson 2008: 91; Gusterson 2009: 94; Schatz 2009: 5). Our focus in this chapter is less on the finished product and more on the methods and methodology associated with ethnography.

What do we mean by methodology and method? The two are often conflated. By methodology we mean the commitments or presuppositions that enable and support any logically consistent line of inquiry (Yanow and Schwartz-Shea 2006; Jackson 2008). Once a methodologically consistent stance has been taken, then the different methods of *data gathering* and *data analysis* are tactical matters that should be evaluated in terms of the skill of their application.

Ethnographers put human meanings and socially constructed arrangements at the heart of their analysis. They take seriously the voices and practices of people in their everyday contexts. To this end, ethnography is a more or less systematic effort to make sense of "the other" who is no longer treated by the researcher as an object but a subject, a producer of social meaning. Social meaning can be seen as "the constellation of symbolic relations instituted among and lived by people within a given social group" (Auge 1998: xvi). Given the frequency and significance of the terrorist label being applied by governments and neopositivist-oriented academics to a variety of groups over the past forty years, we argue that it is important to study the meaning making practices (linguistic and embodied) of groups labeled terrorist. To be sure, the label terrorist does not capture all of the fluid complexity of life on the ground because, as Harmonie Toros aptly points out, actions deemed terrorist represent only a fraction of their daily conduct, which could include running schools, development programs, court systems, and so on (2008: 282). Yet this is one of the main points of ethnography: to more precisely describe the complex, fluid, lived symbolic relations that constitute the daily life of terrorists and to confront the abstract, removed claims about terrorists that make up the vast majority of the literature.

Ethnography is understood as

Methodology: presuppositions that inform a logically consistent perspective. Ethnographic methodology presupposes an interpretive orientation where the meanings generated by particular communities of people are the focus of analysis.

Methods: the techniques used to access a community's meanings (e.g., data), with an emphasis on participant observation and interviewing, and the techniques used to study that data.

Product: a written ethnography, which consists of a more or less analytical and systematic combination of rich descriptions, reflections, and corroborated conjectures about some group or groups of people.

Identifying a Community, Gaining Access, and Developing Rapport

Doing ethnography entails a particular interpretive methodological sensibility that abandons the goal of accounting for the world "'as it really is in itself'" (Jackson 2008: 91) and embraces the goal of making sense of the meanings that some group of people attach to their surroundings.

One of the first steps that an ethnographer must make is to identify a group of people to study. This can range widely. In relation to individuals or groups labeled terrorist, this is complicated further. As Joseba Zulaika and William A. Douglass note about the taboo surrounding such individuals and groups: "Contact with them is polluting; dialogue is pointless since terrorists are, by definition, outside the pale of reason" (1996: x). Yet, like Zulaika (1988), Begona Aretxaga (1997), Cynthia Keppley Mahmood (1996, 2001), Jeffrey Sluka (1989, 1990), Harmonie Toros (2008), Abufarha (2009), and others, ethnographic studies of such groupings most likely entail working in the field.[1]

Researchers taking up such a challenge should choose from any number of militias or protest organizations from around the world that are commonly labeled terrorist by their members or by authorities, news sources, academics, and/or people in everyday contexts. There are a number of examples: Animal Liberation Front, Earth Liberation Front, Aryan Nation, Ku Klux Klan, Jewish Defense League, Continuity IRA, Hamas, Hezbollah, World Tamil Movement, United Self-Defense Forces of Columbia, African National Congress, ETA (Basque Homeland and Freedom) and so on. There are many other possibilities. What is important is that members of these groups will most likely share understandings, language, and policy courses related to past, present, and future political arrangements. Furthermore, their views will probably differ significantly from other groups' understandings, language, and policy courses related to past, present, and future political situations. And, as a matter to be determined by close observation and interviewing, individuals and groups labeled terrorist are more fluid in their composition and actions than the unqualified label suggests.

Once a terrorist group is identified by the researcher, then the practical issue of gaining entrance to that group moves to the foreground. Gaining entrance to non-militant groups, such as magician healers in Ethiopia or US nuclear weapons scientists or crack dealers in New York City's Spanish Harlem, can be trying in the best of circumstances (see Young 1975; Gusterson 1996; Bourgois 1996). Gaining entrance into militant groups such as Hamas or the Ku Klux Klan can, in some circumstances, be nearly impossible because of factors such as race, class, gender, dialect, education level, nationality, or other possible characteristics. An African-American man, for instance, has little chance of gaining entrance into the Ku Klux Klan or the Aryan Nation to do research. Similarly, whereas a letter from a US government official may aid one in gaining entrance into the small community of US military families (Harrell 2003), it may well destroy any chance of gaining entrance into Hamas. So what in particular works for gaining entrance into one group may be disastrous for gaining entrance into another group. At base, an ethnographer must be practical, flexible, and creative when trying to gain entrance into some group labeled a terrorist organization.

When trying to gain entrance into some group, a researcher should be able to tell a story about what they are doing, and it must make sense to the audience at hand. "You have to anticipate being questioned by the people whom you study," Erving Goffman says frankly, "so you engage in providing a story that will hold up should the facts be brought to their attention" (2001: 155). In regards to the ethnography of terrorism, because of the risk of counterterrorist agencies infiltrating the group in question and the group's effort to prevent that from happening, the story one provides directly relates to the researcher's safety. Word choice in relaying the story is important, so Anne Speckhard tries to adopt the most "neutral words" that she can find or she uses "the words used in the community" under study because she does not want to convey belligerence or close-mindedness (2009: 209). The function of the researcher's story is to prevent or limit suspicion and to convince the subjects of their study that they are who they say they are and not a spy or intelligence agent. The problem of what language to use is precisely the problem that Jeffrey A. Sluka encountered when he studied the IRA in Belfast (1990: 118). While Sluka conducted his fieldwork without incident, other researchers working in similar areas had very different experiences. A researcher studying the IRA in Andersontown, for instance, was intimidated enough to leave the field when several hooded men forced him into a car and hours later let him out unharmed (Sluka 1990: 117). Another researcher working in Donegal, for instance, was outspoken about his service in US Army intelligence during the Korean War. Apparently, he was unable to sufficiently convince the community that he was not an intelligence agent, which is indicated most clearly by the fact that he was shot in the chest one night when someone knocked on his door (Sluka 1990: 117). Doing ethnographic research on groups labeled terrorist, in short, entails having a convincing story composed of contextually appropriate words that accounts for who you are and what you are doing and makes sense to the audience.

At the same time that the researcher should have a convincing story to tell curious subjects, it is important to constantly monitor the stories told about you the researcher (Sluka 1990: 122). In interacting with community members, regularly note how they describe you to their acquaintances, how they introduce you to new people, and what their body language indicates in regards to your presence. How people define you will change over time, especially as your stay in the field lengthens. But what is important is that you are not commonly described in terms that mark you as an outsider, as a risk to the individuals or group members that you are studying or as a person to take advantage of or to abuse. Having an appropriate standing among the community that you are studying is important. Monitoring the stories people tell about you and being sensitive to changes in those stories are one way to make sense of that standing.

The researcher's story by itself is useless unless the researcher has someone to tell it to. In that vein, the researcher should try to ally themselves with a gatekeeper to the group, to find someone who can vouch for the researcher and who can help them straddle the threshold between group-outsider and group-insider. When Sluka was conducting fieldwork in Belfast, his first successful contact was a Catholic priest who was active in the local residents' association. Sluka told the priest his story, swore that he was not a spy, showed him his passport, provided letters from the university that attested that Sluka was indeed a researcher, and told the priest that if he called the university they would confirm his identity. Still, it "was nearly impossible" to convince the priest (Sluka 1990: 118). Once the priest was convinced and would vouch for Sluka, however, other members of the community followed.

Harmonie Toros studied the MILF in the Philippines. She was able to access information in relatively safe environments such as the gender and conflict workshops sponsored by the Mindanao Commission on Women (Toros 2008: 286). At the same time, Toros was put into some very dangerous situations, especially in terms of kidnapping and death. In her own words:

> I was petrified in my weeks of fieldwork in the Philippines – scared as I haven't been since childhood. I was scared of lawless groups, of disease-bearing mosquitoes, of harmless giant cockroaches. I was scared of not coming home. I was so scared that a few times even my shadow gave me fright.
>
> (Toros 2008: 288)

She makes clear that in many instances her personal security was out of her hands and in the hands of rebels, soldiers, NGOs (nongovernmental organizations), and so on, who knew the social, political, and geographic situation far better than she (Toros 2008: 287). These people helped bridge the divide between insiders and outsiders in a dangerous context. For instance, a retired military officer allowed her to join him on an overland trip to Cotabato City where she could interview militants. It was a trip and access to data that, without the retired military officer helping her move, would not have happened because the risk was too great. This brings the point home: having a story and someone to tell it to who can help you gain entrance is practically an essential aspect of doing this kind of research.

In other dangerous contexts, such as when ethnographers are studying crack dealers in urban settings, Terry Williams described his strategy for finding someone to tell his story to:

> Initially I prefer to be taken into a crack house or dealing location by someone who is known there. They vouch that I'm OK and no cop. When initially approaching a crack house without someone to introduce me, I'll claim to be sent by someone they may know, like Robby, KeeKay, or someone else with a common street name. When I get inside, I may explain that I'm writing a book on crack houses (or another topic). I usually have a copy of a book I've written to show people. This approach goes a long way toward convincing skeptical persons that I'm an author and serious about my intentions.
>
> (Quoted in Williams et al. 1992: 346)

The point is that a convincing story is necessary and so is finding someone to tell that story to. That person or group of persons is central to establishing the legitimacy of the researcher in that context.

Meeting someone who can vouch for the researcher and help bring them across the threshold is a challenge in the best of circumstances and even more difficult in trying to study groups labeled terrorist. Meeting someone and convincing them of your research endeavors entails having a story and, just as importantly, it entails being in the appropriate places at the appropriate times, wearing the appropriate clothing, and associating with the appropriate people. When Sluka was studying the IRA, he worked to counteract any impressions others might have that he was a spy. He did this by, among other things, not associating with the police or soldiers and actively trying to associate with as many members of the community as he could (Sluka 1990: 119). Anne Speckhard notes that being in the appropriate place is very important when studying militants. In contexts where the populace is less supportive of terrorist actions and there are stronger counterterrorist measures taken, it is far more difficult to identify groups and gain access. Similarly, in places like Palestine, Iraq, Pakistan, Kashmir, and Indonesia there are ample opportunities to study militants (Speckhard 2009: 205). Appropriate dress is also important. Speckhard says that when she was interviewing militants in Gaza, for instance, she wore a headscarf; likewise, in an Iraqi prison she wore a burka; and in the slums of Casa Blanca, Morocco, she wore common Moroccan clothing (Speckhard 2009: 210). The point is that as a researcher trying to make a connection with a gate-keeper to some group, the whole performative package matters: the story one relays, where they tell it, how they are dressed when they tell it, and who one associates with before and during the research are all very important to the process of gaining entrance and establishing a fruitful rapport.

Box 6.1 The process of doing ethnography

1. Identify a group commonly labeled "terrorist."
2. Carefully consider the possibilities, limitations, and risks of studying the group.
3. Do preliminary research as a means of gaining knowledge about appropriate language and dress.
4. Attempt to make contact with and gain entrance into that group usually through some person who can cross the threshold from an outsider to an insider.
5. Attempt to build a rapport with members of the group and access relevant information over time.

Accessing Data

Participant observation was, for an older generation of ethnographers, the heart and soul of the research enterprise. Participant observation continues to be a central tool in accessing data, but it is not the only tool. Drawing from Dvora Yanow's (2000) excellent discussion of accessing data for interpretive and ethnographic studies, we outline three basic techniques for gathering information and the sources of that information.

But first, what is the ontological and epistemological status of that information? For researchers working from a neopositivist methodological perspective, it is assumed that it is necessary and possible to gather data from a point external to the data itself, and to make objective, value-free assessments of that data (Yanow 2000: 5). For example, when the language of policy-makers is examined, researchers often make a comparison between "the words of legislation and the projected or implemented actions in the field, under the assumption that policy words can and should have univocal, unambiguous meanings that can and should be channeled to and directly apperceived by implementers and policy relevant publics" (Yanow 2000: 5–6). As indicated earlier in this chapter, interpretive methodologies are centrally focused on how different communities of people make sense of and attach meaning to the ongoing events around them. Consequently, ethnographers make alternative ontological and epistemological assumptions regarding the information they access and their connections to it. Nor is it possible for an ethnographer to stand outside the issue they study or the data they access, or to divorce oneself from the values and meanings associated with the issue, the data, or the analyst's own values and meaningful interpretations. The researcher is part and parcel of the situation under study. Knowledge is produced, in this regard, through experience and interpretation. Or as Clifford Geertz casually put it: "what we call our data are really our own constructions of other people's constructions of what they and their compatriots are up to" (1973: 9).

The meanings that some group of people attaches to events and their surroundings can be accessed through three basic sources of information:

1. written sources;
2. oral sources
3. observed and experiential sources.

(Yanow 2000: 37–38)

The data that a researcher is accessing, in other words, is the said and done, which includes the words, artifacts, and actions made by relevant actors. Generally speaking, the ethnographer purposefully selects, records, notes, and copies these sources of information and then sets about systematically studying them.

Documents

An ethnographer may seek out written documents. Depending on the issue one is studying, these can include a wide variety of texts: news articles and other news media, transcripts of speeches or radio or television broadcasts, advertisements, reports, legislation and other enactments, graffiti, notes, journals, communiqués, photographs, flags and other symbolic props, and so on. These documents, especially for a textual ethnography, can be the centerpiece of the study. Robin Erica Wagner-Pacifici, for instance, conducted a textual ethnography of the 1978 kidnapping of the Italian politician, Aldo Moro, by the Red Brigades. Her datum consisted of "spoken, written, photographed, and filmed" documents generated at that time (Wagner-Pacifici 1986: ix). Wagner-Pacifici was trying to understand "the discourse of terrorism – the ways in which some actions are defined as terrorist, and the ways in which terrorism is publicly represented" in the "mass mediated surround" (1986: ix). For fieldworkers, however, documents are only part of the data. Documents enable researchers to identify key actors that warrant interviews, they enable researchers to refine the meaningful boundaries of the community under study, they enable researchers to corroborate or refute the researcher's working assumptions regarding the group, and the documents enable researchers to gather background information on the topic under study.

Documents are often combined with interviews as a means of accessing the meanings that some community of people attaches to their surroundings and to events. Interviewing is a method of accessing data that entails the researcher has made contact with members of the community under study and achieved a rapport and level of trust that will enable them to talk. As argued above, appropriate dress, word selection, demeanor, and so on are very important and relate directly to the researcher's safety, so care must be taken to cover all one's bases.

Interviews

Generally, we can conceptualize three different kinds of interview strategies: structured, semi-structured, and unstructured conversational interviews. Structured interviews are basically surveys, which means that there is little variation in how the interviewer asks the questions to the interviewees and there are pre-given, or close-ended answer sets interviewees can choose from and that can easily be coded and measured. For instance, a survey question might look like this: "Do you agree, disagree, or are indifferent to the use of the phrase, 'Global War on Terror,' to describe current US national security policies relating to 9/11?" The interviewee has basically three options to choose from when answering the survey question, which severely limits their ability to talk at length and construct a sense-making perspective out of available cultural artifacts. As a result, political ethnographers, generally speaking, do not conduct surveys; their focus is on semi-structured and unstructured approaches to interviewing. While it is not the goal of this chapter or this book to go into great detail regarding interview techniques, because there are texts that already do that (see Georges and Jones 1980; Holstein and Gubrium 1995; Rubin and Rubin 2004), it is important to look more closely at these two types of interviewing strategies.

Semi-structured interviewing strategies are looser in their organization compared to surveys. There may be a definite set of interview questions that are asked by the interviewer to most all respondents, but the possible answers are open-ended, which means that respondents can answer however they choose. For instance, an ethnographer carrying out a semi-structured interview may put the following kinds of questions to an interviewee:

- Could you describe who you/your group are fighting against?
- Could you describe why you/your group are fighting?
- Can you give an example of "X"?
- Could you elaborate on what you mean by "X"?
- What is "X"?

These kinds of questions open the door for the interviewee to speak at length. To be clear, the goal of semi-structured interviews for ethnographers, in contrast to structured interviews' goal of variable measurement, is to get at the meanings people associate with particular people, organizations, events, and so forth. The aim is not to get at the "real" motivations driving some group to act nor is it to get an accurate description of some event, but to prompt the interviewee to talk at length, to construct a sense-making narrative out of the commonplace cultural categories that that person (as part of a interpretive community) uses in the course of their everyday lives. These narratives and cultural categories and how they are used to define particular circumstances and events are, for the ethnographer, the data that is studied.

The final interview strategy is an unstructured conversational approach. It is unstructured because there are no pre-given sets of questions to ask interviewees and all the responses are open-ended. It is an active, emergent interviewing technique. Usually this type of interviewing occurs during the course of hanging out in the context and amidst the community of people under study. A conversational interview can be the most unpredictable. It can veer off topics relevant to the researcher; it may get emotional for the interviewee and/or interviewer; it may be tense or boring or joking; it

---

Box 6.2 Three basic interview strategies

1. Structured (surveys) – Close-ended questions that yield easily measurable responses and administered in consistent format to all interviewees.
2. Semi-structured – Open-ended questions that are administered in a more or less consistent format to all interviewees. But the interviewer should place greater emphasis on using conversational prompts that enable the interviewee to develop their response further, which allows the researcher to access the culturally available resources employed by the interviewee to make sense of the situation.
3. Unstructured – Conversational interactions with no particular format, set of questions, or interview goals; less predictable. Like semi-structured interviews, unstructured interviews are tools that enable the researcher to access the culturally available resources employed by the interviewee to make sense of the situation.

---

may smoothly flow along or run into an impasse (Soss 2006: 135). Like conversations in general, unstructured interviews are navigated on the spot and include not just words but body language and gestures, silences that signal meaning, changes in tone and creative word selection, laughter, lies, manipulation, "self-serving frames, and dissemblance," all of which are data that can be noted and which must be grappled with by the researcher in the course of conversation (Soss 2006: 135).

Given that the interviewees' responses can range widely in semi- and unstructured interviews, the issue of recording devices emerges. Generally, there are two views on the matter: do use recording devices or do not use recording devices. Arguments against using recording devices usually center on questions of trust: the person being interviewed may become nervous or fearful about the use of a recording device, which is especially the case when dealing with groups or persons labeled terrorists who may already be concerned about someone studying them. When Yamuna Sangarasivam was studying the Tamil Tigers in Sri Lanka, for instance, she did not use a recording device because her interviewees "feared identification and arrest." Indeed, the "visible presence of a tape recorder or a notebook and pen in the contexts of everyday conversation" was "highly problematic" because interviewees were "cautious about how and where their voices are heard." Had the recorded interviews or notes been confiscated, the Sri Lankan military would have arrested Sangarasivam and the people she studied (Sangarasivam 2001: 97). Several interviewees in Northern Ireland had similar concerns about their recorded words and who would have access to them (Sluka 1989; Aretxaga 1997). This is similar for politicians and elite officials who do not want their words recorded because they fear their statements may be used against them (Peabody et al. 1990: 453). Another argument against recording devices is that they may distract the interviewer from the task at hand or disrupt the rapport and flow of the encounter. Another reason is that interviewers can train themselves to make quick jottings of key phrases and words, brief interview outlines, and they can recall important aspects of the interview from memory. At the same time, a recording device can be very useful. It can free the interviewer from worrying about note taking, outlining, or recalling the interview from memory and, therefore, make the interview move along more smoothly. Similarly, the recording device offers precision. If the researcher is analyzing the interview data very closely, such as with ethnomethodological techniques, then exactly what was said and how it was said are very important. Recorded interviews can also corroborate claims made by the researcher or by other interviewees. In general, then, the ethnographer must make the best decision they can with the circumstances on hand when choosing to use or not use a recording device for interviews.

Observations and Experiences

The final way that ethnographers can access data is through extended periods of time observing the community and experiencing what the community goes through on a daily basis. This is not easy, to be sure. Fieldworkers, for the most part, are not given a tool belt of methods for dealing with circumstances that may arise when studying groups labeled terrorists. Sangarasivam, for instance, when she studied the Tamil Tigers in Sri Lanka, was detained and interrogated by the Sri Lankan military police on twenty-five different occasions over the course of two years as well as being subjected to body searches and having her belongings and residence searched (Sangarasivam 2001: 97). Nevertheless, this can be what observing and experiencing everyday life are about for an ethnographer studying groups labeled terrorist. As Erving Goffman put it:

> [b]y subjecting yourself, your own body and your own personality, and your own social situation, to the set of contingencies that play upon a set of individuals, so that you can physically and ecologically penetrate their circle of response to their social situation, or their work situation, or their ethnic situation, or whatever. So that you are close to them while they are responding to what life does to them. I feel that the way this is done is to not, of course, just listen to what they talk about, but to pick up on their minor grunts and groans as they respond to their situation. When you do that, it seems to me, the standard technique is to try to subject yourself, hopefully, to their life circumstances, which means that although, in fact, you can leave at anytime, you act as if you can't and you try to accept all of the desirable and undesirable things that are a feature of their life.
>
> (Goffman 2001: 154–155)

Gathering data in this manner has many benefits. Hugh Gusterson notes three:

1. Sustained contact with some person or community is key to developing a trusting relationship and open rapport.
2. The data gathering through direct observation and experience is richer than only learning about certain communities through documents because it allows for a richer, more varied data set.
3. Observing and experiencing the everyday life circumstances of the interpretive community that one is studying are a particularly effective way to get at the often messy and contingent practices that constitute everyday life, which contrasts with the more formal accounts that a researcher may find in documents or hear espoused in interviews (Gusterson 2009: 100).

Inscriptions

Whether you are conducting a textual ethnography or going to the field, note-taking is an important practice that all researchers do. To be clear, fieldnoting is not simply a matter of determining the "true" and "accurate" course of events, but an effort to "reveal the multiple truths apparent in others' lives" (Emerson et al. 1995: 3). In other words, there are multiple possible descriptions of "the same" situation and it is not up to the ethnographer to determine which is "true" and which is "false." Just the opposite, the aim of fieldnote-taking is to inscribe experiences and observations made by the researcher while immersed in some context or amongst a wealth of documents. It "involves active processes of interpretation and sense-making: noting and writing down some things as 'significant,' noting but ignoring others as 'not significant,' and even missing other possibly significant things altogether" (Emerson et al. 1995: 8).

But when are notes taken? For a textual ethnography, note-taking can be done at any time. Immersed in documents, the researcher reads and notes words and phrases deemed significant. For fieldworkers, note taking is a bit more complicated. Goffman says that the "first day you'll see more than you'll ever see again … [a]nd you'll see things that you won't see again. So, the first day you should take notes all the time" (Goffman 2001: 157).

As we mentioned above, however, when conducting interviews and in some observational circumstances, it may be the case that you cannot record what the interviewee says or you cannot immediately inscribe what you observe. The point is that you should "find corners in the day when you can take notes" (Goffman 2001: 157) and safely exploit those times and places to get the data you need. In the case of interviews, for instance, inscriptions of the interview are often made immediately following the event. Notes may be taken on the body language, gestures, and facial expressions made by the interviewee, as well as notes regarding what the interviewee actually said. In terms of observations, you may be able to openly take notes. On other occasions, however, you may have to engage in what Goffman calls

> fake off-phase note taking. That is, don't write your notes on the act you're observing because then people will know what it is you're recording. Try to discipline yourself to write your notes before an act has begun, or after it has started so that people won't be able to detect from when you start taking notes and when you stop taking notes what act you're taking notes about.
>
> (Goffman 2001: 158)

The point is that note-taking is an important activity for ethnographic work. Your observations, your data, your notes, and your findings are inseparable from each other; they are all part of the process of research and analysis.

Once available documents are collected, interviews conducted, observations made, and experiences had, typically a set of notes are yielded. What do you do with those notes once they are generated? How are they organized? To be sure, there is no one answer to these queries. Generally, though, this is when a process of directed, intensive analysis starts, which is distinct from analyzing during the process of data gathering (Yanow 2000: 32). The researcher reads and rereads her notes, develops codes, writes up longer memos, and pulls together an analytic narrative. Some researchers do this by putting key codes and information on index cards and filing them away in retrievable systems. Some organize their notes around individual biographies of important actors whom they've interviewed or observed; others take scissors and cut out key quotes from documents or interviews and organize them in manila folders; still others depend on computer

Table 6.1 Accessing data

Methods of Accessing Data	Sources of Data	Kinds of Data Yielded
Observation & experience Meetings Talk, body language	Meetings	Talk, body
	Seminars Daily routines Extraordinary acts	Use of objects Interactions
Interviewing	Family, friends, acquaintances	Talk and body language
Documents records	Fliers, memos, letters Poems, journals, newspapers Graffiti	Written words Descriptions Historical

programs, such as Atlas.ti, to help organize their information. Table 6.1 summarizes the sources and methods of data gathering.

Ethical Issues

There are ethical tensions associated with ethnographic research. Addressing some of the issues are formal ethical standards that the American Political Science Association and the American Anthropological Association and other professional organizations have established regarding research on human subjects. In order to protect human subjects from the potential for harm, universities have also established institutional review boards to vet research proposals. In turn, these boards are a required part of the grant process for government agencies such as the National Institutes of Health. A curious reader can easily find these standards online, and there are blogs that devote a considerable amount of discussion time to these issues. Our goal, however, is not to discuss these formal standards.

In particular, we discuss some ethical issues and tensions that may arise in the course of doing ethnography of groups labeled terrorist. In particular, we identify and elaborate on three key ethical relationships:

1. researcher to self;
2. researcher to subjects and bystanders;
3. researcher to colleagues.

One important ethical tension may exist between your own personal conduct and between the activities of the group in question. In trying to build up and sustain a trusting rapport with the subjects of your research, you may be invited to partake in illegal, immoral, and/or dangerous activities. For instance, when studying Basque political violence, Joseba Zulaika was informally asked on two different occasions to join the armed organization in their struggle. Zulaika, against "all common sense," indicated a "willingness to join" the group, but he "made clear" to them that he was "not interested in any nationalist agenda" or in "martyrdom." As circumstances changed, he was later told by group members that "they did not want me around" (1995: 207–208). When studying groups labeled terrorist the researcher must be prepared to make hard judgments regarding their own conduct and what they will or will not do for their ethnography. We are not encouraging the researcher to necessarily accept these invitations but, at the very least, to seriously consider and reconsider them and to make the best possible judgment given the circumstances at hand.

Researchers should be concerned not only for their own safety but also for the safety of the subjects of their study and for the safety of bystanders. It is conceivable that the information that you have gathered in relation to a group labeled terrorist, any written documents that you may have obtained or any interviews that you may have digitally stored or actions that you have observed and noted, can be used by counterterrorist government agencies to harm the group or its members. Yamuna Sangarasivam, as we indicated above, was put into this very situation when studying the Tamil Tigers in Sri Lanka. If Sangarasivam recorded her interviews and that information was obtained by the military police, who regularly searched her body and her belongings, the recorded words of the interviewees would have put them in "danger of arrest – and worse" (Sangarasivam 2001: 97). She avoided this situation by not recording the spoken words of Tamil Tigers or the words of those noncombatants who were impacted by fighting between the Sri Lankan military and the Tamil Tigers. It is important, in other words, to not tip off the authorities about the group that you are researching. Similarly, when Anne Speckhard studies militants who carry out coordinated violent actions, she tries to avoid learning about "operational details" of attacks because it puts her into an ethically difficult and potentially dangerous position. Not only is there an "ethical duty to warn the victims and to do everything possible to thwart the attack" but, Speckhard says, there is also the risk that a "researcher can be seen as a threat once an interview containing operational details has been given" (Speckhard 2009: 201). She, like Sangarasivam and other ethnographers, tries to ease this ethical tension by doing interviews as "anonymously as possible" and by making herself clear that operational details are "strictly off limits" (Speckhard 2009: 201). The point is that a researcher must be able to navigate ethically challenging invitations on one hand and, on the other hand, researchers have an ethical obligation to do no harm to the subjects under study and an obligation to not knowingly and intentionally allow harm to come to unaffiliated bystanders.

A final tension that we will note is associated with what Zulaika and Douglass describe as the "taboo" surrounding the act of talking with people called terrorists (1996: x). Empathy, an important aspect of doing ethnography for some researchers, with a person or group called terrorist is criticized as relativist and perhaps even dangerous (Jones and Smith 2009: 297–298, 301). And in concrete circumstances among academic colleagues, people who study groups labeled terrorist are sometimes treated as if they represent or speak for the group in question. The researcher may be expected to justify acts of violence carried out by the terrorist group, to defend their claims to impartiality and "objectivity," to be the punch line in office jokes, or to bear "tenuous" professional relations that are "fraught with" a sense of "fear and suspicion" regarding how one stands personally and politically (Sangarasivam 2001: 96–97, 99). In short, then, there is a potential ethical tension between the researchers of groups labeled terrorist and between their institutional home place and the colleagues they work with there. Navigating this tension, especially for an untenured professor, is worth consideration before and especially during the research process.

The ethical position of the ethnographer of terrorism is burdened with ethical issues and judgments that researchers in other areas will probably never encounter. Our goal here was to sketch out a useful framework for thinking about ethical relations for ethnographers and offer concrete sets of issues that researchers have encountered when conducting fieldwork on a group labeled terrorist.

Potential Research Design Strategy

In considering a potential research project that focuses on the terrorist subject, here are three suggested questions to ask as the research design is organized:

1. How many terrorist subjects does one wish to study? The answer can result in a single subject or one can go in a more comparative route that involves two or more subjects. Most often, but not always, ethnographic research focuses on a single terrorist subject. For instance, Cynthia Keppley Mahmood focused on a single terrorist subjectivity, the Sikh militants (1996). Sluka, however, focused on two terrorist subjectivities, the IRA and the Irish National Liberation Army (1990).
2. What temporal perspective will your study emphasize? The answer can result in a study that focuses on the present or a study that emphasizes the past. Toros' study of the MILF, for instance, focused primarily on the present (2008). Brian Axel's study of Sikh militants and the formation of the Sikh diaspora takes a historical perspective (2001).
3. Closely related to the temporal perspective taken by the study, what are the richest sources of data that can be gathered? A study focused on the historical development of diaspora, like Axel's book (2001), drew primarily from documents. However, a study based on the present state of affairs, such as Toros' study (2008), depended on observations and experiences, interviews, and documents.

In the following, Figure 6.1 illustrates how these questions look for a general research design.

Looking more closely at specific research projects, Figures 6.2, 6.3, and 6.4 show how they relate to this design strategy.

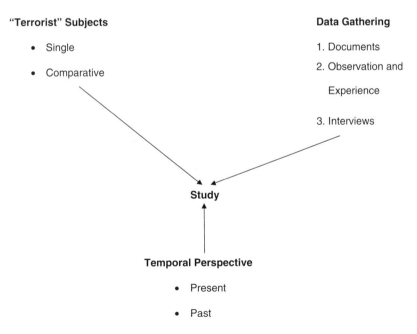

Figure 6.1 General research outline

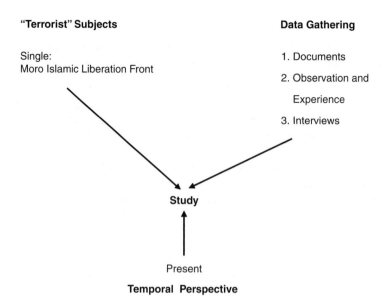

Figure 6.2 Research design for Harmonie Toros' study of the MILF

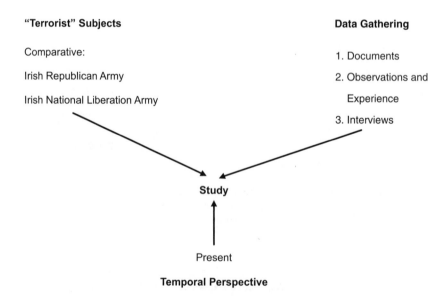

Figure 6.3 Research design for Jeffrey Sluka's study of the IRA

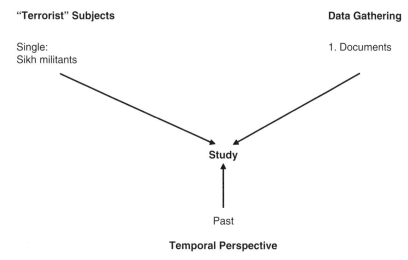

Figure 6.4 Research design for Brian Axel's study of the Sikh militants and diaspora

Questions to consider

- What are the three meanings of ethnography?
- What is the process of doing ethnography?
- What are the types of data that enable a researcher to access meanings generated by a subject?
- What are the types of methods used to gather data?
- What are the three types of interview strategies?
- What types of questions does an ethnographic interviewer ask? Why those types of questions?
- What does Goffman say about participant observation?
- What are three ethical relationships that the ethnographer must consider?

Note

1 I say most likely entails working in the field because ethnography does not necessarily entail fieldwork. Some researchers like Robin Eric Wagner-Pacifici (1986) have used what Patrick Thaddeus Jackson has called "textual ethnography" (2006a: 272) to study historical events. Textual ethnography does not entail fieldwork. Neither does David Altheide's Ethnographic Content Analysis (1987, 2004) entail fieldwork.

Further Reading

Abufarha, N. (2009), *The Making of a Human Bomb: An Ethnography of Palestinian Resistance*, Durham, NC: Duke University Press.

Holstein, J. A. and Gubrium, J. F. (1995), *The Active Interview*, Thousand Oaks, CA: Sage.

Mahmood, C. K. (2001), "Terrorism, Myth, and the Power of Ethnographic Praxis," *Journal of Contemporary Ethnography*, 30 (5): 520–545.

Sangarasivam, Y. (2001), "Researcher, Informant, 'Assassin,' Me," *The Geographical Review*, 91 (1/2): 95–104.

Sluka, J. A. (1990), "Participant Observation in Violent Social Contexts," *Human Organization*, 49 (2): 114–126.

Speckhard, A. (2009), "Research Challenges Involved in Field Research and Interviews Regarding the Militant Jihad, Extremism, and Suicide Terrorism," *Democracy and Security*, 5 (3): 199–222.

Weblinks

Ethnography.com at http://www.ethnography.com is a useful blog.

"100 Most Influential Ethnographies and Anthropological Texts" http://www.architectonictokyo. com/architokyo/100_of_the_Most_Influential_Ethnographies_and_Anthropology_Texts.html offers an overview of ethnographic methodologies, methods, and topics of study.

Anthropologists and War, *The Diane Rehm Show:* http://thedianerehmshow.org/shows/2007-10-10#13756 explores the relationship between the US-led war in Afghanistan and the role of anthropologists.

The Ethnography of Violence, The University of Pennsylvania Press: http://www.upenn.edu/pennpress/series/EPV.html lists books related to the ethnographic study of violence.

7 Making Sense of Terrorism and Counterterrorism

Introduction

In Chapter 6 we focused on the ethnography of the terrorist subject. Our concern was with identifying a community to study, gaining access to that community, developing rapport with members of the community, accessing data, and the ethical tensions that may arise when studying groups labeled terrorist.

What does ethnography mean, again?

Ethnography denotes the following items:

- **methodology** – an interpretive approach to the study of sociopolitical life that puts human meanings and socially constructed arrangements at the heart of their analysis;
- **method** – ethnographers take seriously the voices and practices of people in their everyday contexts. Ethnography is a more or less systematic effort to make sense of "the other" who is no longer treated by the researcher as an object, but as a subject, a producer of social meaning.
- **product** – a finished, written product.

Touching on similar issues, this chapter "flips" the ethnographic study of terrorism over. This means that we turn our gaze away from the terrorist subject, away from those who define themselves as terrorists or who are defined by policy-makers, media sources, and experts as terrorists. Our concern here centers on how to study a particular community or set of communities' interpretations of and responses to events or persons deemed terrorist. Community, as we use it here, very generally indicates a set of actors who relate to each other through shared vocabularies and actions – from a neighborhood or a business to the US Congress or a town council. We are interested in how different communities of people give meaning to and conduct themselves toward terrorism and counterterrorism in particular contexts. Given the broad range of contexts across which terrorism and counterterrorism are used to describe events, questions pursuing this research angle can vary widely, as the examples throughout the chapter show. The broad range of contexts, unfortunately, is met by a paucity of CTS research investigating these areas through an ethnographic lens. Apart from the value of more clearly marking out how to do this type of research, the chapter points to areas of sociopolitical life that are observably shaped by terrorism and sorely in need of systematic investigation.

Locating a Community: Policy-makers, Policy Implementers, and the Affected

All ethnographers must identify some community of people to study. Chapter 6 focused on the issues and problems surrounding the study of groups commonly described as terrorist. To help clarify and focus our discussion in this chapter, we turn to a useful suggestion made by Dvora Yanow (2000). She argues that interpretivists can conceptualize three basic communities to study:

1. *policy-makers*: actors in positions to make binding and enforceable counterterrorist policies such as elected officials, bureaucratic officers, and hired executives;
2. *policy implementers*: actors in positions to carry out and enforce counterterrorist policies such as soldiers, police officers, and citizen volunteers;
3. *affected individuals and communities*: actors affected, intentionally and unintentionally, by events deemed terrorism and by the implementation of particular counterterrorist policies.

Below, we will discuss each community more thoroughly and suggest some advice on how to gain access and how to develop a rapport within each context. This advice comes with a caveat, however: *there is no one right way to carry out these tasks.* As we insisted in Chapter 6, an ethnographer must be creative, persistent, and flexible when it comes to doing research in this mode.

First, let's look more closely at policy-makers. When studying how some community of people make sense of and respond to some event or group of people deemed terrorist, policy-makers are certainly an important possibility for a researcher to consider. John M. Murphy, for instance, closely examined President George W. Bush's speeches immediately following the violent death of over 3000 people on September 11, 2001. Murphy, using a kind of textual ethnography, focused on the specific rhetorical techniques Bush used to account for and describe that day's events. He argues that Bush rhetorically crafted the authority to define the public interpretation and the legitimate response, which was the "war on terror" (Murphy 2003). Through a kind of textual ethnography, this study focuses on how elite policy-makers in the USA made sense of and responded to the threat deemed terrorism.

There is ample room for more researchers examining a wider range of contexts and policy-makers outside of the executive. There is great potential for future researchers to conduct fieldwork in policy-making institutions such as the US Congress. Members of the US Congress have been studied using fieldwork methods such as participant observation and interviewing (Mayhew 1974; Fenno 1978; Weatherford 1985; Cook 1986) but not in relation to the topic of terrorism. As J. McIver Weatherford described, the US Congress can be seen as a set of "endless rituals" with little effect (1985: xii). How terrorism has changed relatively established Congressional rituals between Congress persons or Congress persons and their constituents, created new rituals, or been incorporated into other rituals remains to be investigated and is therefore an open possibility for future researchers.

One area, for instance, would be to study local policy-makers, such as city councils and mayor's offices or even state-level representatives. In Portland, Oregon, for instance, the city council has voted to join, separate from, and is currently debating rejoining the regional Joint Terrorism Task Force. Similarly, after the passage of the USA PATRIOT Act in October 2001, a number of municipalities, counties, and states passed resolutions that challenged the federal law on the grounds that it undermined civil liberties and sowed fear in ethnic and religious minorities. Explaining these ongoing processes in Portland and elsewhere around the USA are important components of this type of CTS. Terrorism is made sense of and responded to by communities of policy-makers across these sectors of life and should therefore be scrutinized.

Another research avenue is policy-makers outside government. For instance, one could examine a business, corporation, or NGO and focus on how policy-making executives have made sense of and responded to the danger of terrorism. There is a history of research on business executives and elites (e.g., Mills 1956; Domhoff 1967; Hirsch 1986; Useem 1979; Thomas 1993), but not in terms of terrorism. Companies as varied as McDonald's to Northrop Grumman have responded to the possibility of terrorism in a variety of different ways, from internal policies directed at employee conduct to changes in how the company advertises and relates to the public. All of these are relevant sites composed of important, regularly occurring interactions among policy-makers relating to terrorism. They too should be the focus of analysis.

So, in short, policy-making communities at all levels of political life in and outside of government are open empirical fields when it comes to studying how these communities of people have made sense of and responded to terrorism. Both textual ethnography and field ethnography are valid and valuable methods that one can use to accomplish this goal.

Another important group to study when examining how some community makes sense of and responds to events deemed terrorism are the bureaucratic policy implementers. By policy implementers we mean those individuals and agencies (e.g., police units, fire departments, soldiers, office workers, other emergency management personnel, and so on) that enact or carry out policies. Kerry B. Fosher (2009), for instance, closely studied the making of homeland security in Boston immediately following the airplanes slamming into New York City's Twin Towers on September 11, 2001. Primarily relying on participant observation, she conducted fieldwork for approximately two years in Boston. During this time, she interacted with local, state, and federal policy implementers, including members of the Federal Bureau of Investigation, city police and fire response officials, and citizens groups such as the Boston area lobstermen. All of these communities of people participated in the implementation of security programs around the city. Their practices and how they constructed and institutionalized homeland security in response to terrorism in the context of Boston were the empirical foci of her study.

This area of research is, generally speaking, also wide open. Federal bureaucracies have been the focus of ethnographic study before (Britan 1979), but not in relation to terrorism. Take the Department of Homeland Security, for example. One could examine policy implementers as they carry out their work in contexts across the USA. How do US Border Security agents along the US–Mexico border embody counterterrorist policies, for instance? That type of question would lead easily into a comparative study of US–Mexico and US–Canadian borders and how counterterrorism is given meaning and contextually embodied by border agents. Transportation Security Administration policy implementers represent another potential community and regional, national, and global transportation hubs (e.g., airports and bus depots) are the field sites where this particular dynamic of terrorism could be studied. Urban police and mass transit security communities in New York City, London, or Moscow, have become responsible for carrying out counterterrorist policies. Explaining how these agencies make sense of and respond to terrorism in the course of everyday events is an appropriate line of inquiry from this perspective.

So, bureaucracies at all levels of political life are important sites where terrorism is made sense of and responded to by policy implementers.

Finally, a third community of people that could be studied by ethnographers are those who are affected by terrorist-related happenings, including events deemed terrorist and counterterrorist. This is perhaps the richest and most active vein of research. For instance, Carolyn Nordstrom studied the Mozambican civil war in her excellent ethnography, *A Different Kind of War Story* (1997). As the fighting raged, Nordstrom avoided the capital city and conducted fieldwork in rural areas starting in 1988. Returning to the field on multiple occasions, she focused on noncombatants who were subjected to ongoing policies that destroyed the basic institutions of everyday life and effectively terrorized the people. In particular, Nordstrom studied how ordinary Mozambicans creatively made sense of and responded to the terror of warring factions attempting to control the state. She argued that instead of the Hobbesian war of everyman against everyman, affected community members operated according to a "strong code of ethics ... [that] was intricately linked with the constitution of self and world" when both were under attack (Nordstrom 1997: 13). "Survival" under conditions of what she calls "terror-warfare," involves human agency and the crafting of "a new universe of meaning and action" (Nordstrom 1997: 13). This study offers an exemplary illustration of the affected communities of state terror.

Similarly, relying on fieldwork, Egla Martinez Salazar studied Guatemalan women between 1999 and 2002. She focused on the ways that state terror was fashioned into a political culture of terror through educational techniques (Salazar 2008). Terror, as Salazar indicates, is not simply the state sanction and use of extraordinary violence, killing, rape, and genocide against some group of people. It also includes quite ordinary strategies such as a variety of racialized, classed, and gendered teaching-learning processes. These ongoing processes effectively limit, but do not eliminate, the possibility of affected communities resisting and transforming the unequal relations of power that work to define the meanings of their everyday lives. Focusing on this particular community and how state-directed educational policies institutionalize a culture of terror is another way that ethnographers can study affected peoples and how they make sense of and respond to certain policies.

Setha M. Low used ethnographic methods to study gated neighborhoods in New York and San Antonio, Texas. In particular, she was interested in explaining how members of these gated communities made sense of and responded to post-9/11 "terror talk." Low argues that these affected communities are, in response to the increased sense of insecurity, further fortifying their residential space (Low 2008). The "terror talk" legitimates various exclusionary practices that racialize the boundary between insiders and outsiders, between home and foreign spaces.

Jacob L. Stump (2009, 2010) also studied affected commuters. In particular, he was interested in how people made sense of terrorist and counterterrorist activities in the context of the Washington Area Metropolitan Authority transit system in Washington, DC. Conducting fieldwork for nearly three years in the subway system, Stump participated, observed, interviewed, and collected relevant documents in an attempt to explain how the pervasive sense of danger associated with the Washington Metro system shaped the flows of everyday commuter life. He argued that commuters' response to the various signs of terrorism (e.g., unattended book bags and "suspicious" appearing individuals) and counterterrorism (e.g., biochemical detectors and police with chemical protection masks) that litter the Washington Metro ranged widely. Some people performed a kind of lateral surveillance (riders watching each other for signs of terrorism) and other riders engaged in a kind of resistance (riders refusing to be searched by authorities and ignoring official announcements regarding terrorism).

In short, communities affected by terrorism and counterterrorism are an important component of a CTS. They can range from commuters affected by signs of terrorism and counterterrorism in the Washington Metro to the creative responses of Mozambicans working to survive the warring factions trying to capture the state government. Overall, a researcher can study how people make sense of terrorism by looking closely at the policy-makers, the policy implementers, and the affected communities. An ethnographer could focus on one community or a researcher could focus on how two or more communities interact in relation to terrorism. The possibilities are wide open.

Once you have identified the community or communities that will be the focus of the study, the next issue centers on gaining entrance or getting close enough to do ethnography. Studying policy-makers, policy implementers, and affected communities and how they relate to terrorism overlaps with the discussions in Chapter 6, but are also considerably different accomplishments. For instance, generally the researcher faces little risk of violence or intimidation when studying Congressional policy-makers and how they respond to terrorism, which contrasts sharply with the problems of gaining entrance into a terrorist group in order to observe and interview members carrying out their everyday activities. Yet the risks of intimidation, violence, and death that Nordstrom faced in the field during the Mozambican civil war are no less than those faced by ethnographers of the terrorist subject. In the next few paragraphs, our focus will be on fleshing out the different ways that researchers can gain entrance into a policy-making, policy-implementing, or affected community.

Regardless of which community you plan to study, the same basic point holds: what works for gaining entrance into *this* community may be disastrous in terms of gaining entrance into *that* community. Consequently, a useful rule of thumb is to be sensitive to the situation at hand, flexible, and creative when trying to gain entrance and building rapport.

Gaining Access to a Community and Developing Rapport

Gaining entrance into sites where elite policy-makers (in the government or in private enterprise) are at work is certainly a challenge. The ethnographer must find some sort of confidant or gatekeeper to make the transition from outsider to insider. When Weatherford studied the US Congress, he initially gained entrance by getting a job in the Senate and living two blocks from Capitol Hill among lobbyists and political aids (1985: xii). The job, not a particular person, functioned as the gatekeeper. Once inside the site, over the course of time like an anthropologist trying to study a remote tribe, Weatherford "worked and lived with the natives, learned to speak their language, eat their food, wear their clothes, and go through their rituals" (1985: xii). Along similar lines, Rachel Sady conducted a long-term and intensive participant observation of Democratic district leaders in Greenburgh, New York (Sady 1990). To gain entrance into this site and community, she initially served as an election inspector and then as a district leader. Once inside, she was able to observe, take notes, and interview local policy-makers with little difficulty. The key point for both Weatherford and Sady is that to gain entrance into and develop a rapport with the policy-making circle, they had to get a job or function in some role that was appropriate to that setting and that would legitimate their presence. Their job or function helped make the transition from outsider to insider, a process that made their study possible.

This is similar to elite policy-makers in private enterprise. Trying to study how a corporate board or set of executives are making sense of and responding to terrorism is a tough proposition. As Robert J. Thomas put it: "You cannot just walk into an office suite and expect to strike up a conversation or hang out and observe the scene" because there are a series of gatekeepers (e.g., public relations departments, official spokespersons, mid- and lower-level management) who are trained to keep an eye out for those that do not belong and to present the company line to the outside world (1993: 82). In one case, for instance, Thomas said that it took two years of phone calls, meetings with assistants, and networking to score some in-depth interviews with elite executives (1993: 83). When finally able to access elite policy-makers in private enterprise, similar to when studying the terrorist subject or Congress or local district leaders, being familiar with the language used in those settings, the appropriate clothing to wear, and the habits and rituals likely to encounter in their offices, is of utmost importance (Thomas 1993: 84–85; Hertz and Imber 1993). Indeed, the ethnographer's whole performative package, from their story and body language to their attire, can make or break the study of policy-makers.

Bureaucratic policy implementers, as we indicated earlier, are the second community one might study. Like studying policy-makers, gaining entrance into a circle of policy-implementers poses its own set of challenges. A bureaucracy is a goal-oriented formal organization. Those who work in that context are, generally speaking, well-educated people who have been exposed to a wide range of social science (Britan 1979: 213), which may help open doors for the researcher to do their work, as it did in Fosher's case (2009). At the same time, at worst, the ethnographer can be seen as a kind of active interferer that threatens the conduct of policy implementers (Britan 1979: 213). Avoiding the stigmatization as an interferer with bureaucratic policy implementation is important in the same way that avoiding the stigmatization as a spy is important when studying the terrorist subject: both can severely undermine one's ability to access the information required to do ethnography.

Clearly, however, the ethnographer is not always seen as a problem when studying policy implementers. Britan studied a large federal bureaucracy; his status as an employee of the National Academy of Science legitimated his role as an ethnographic researcher, as well as the fact that his research was of interest to the bureaucratic superiors (1979: 217). Similarly, Iver Neumann studied the Norwegian Ministry of Foreign Affairs (2007). Neumann gained entrance and legitimacy along the same route as Weatherford (1985); he got a job in the bureaucracy as a speech writer, which positioned him inside the circle of implementers that he was studying. This enabled Neumann to access the everyday activities that occur inside of a bureaucratic organization, such as water-cooler talk, attending meetings, and observing office routines. Fosher, who studied the implementation of homeland security in Boston immediately following the events on September 11, 2001, started with three key informants. From there, the informants helped her cross the threshold from outsider to insider; they helped her meet planners and first responders, got her into meetings, showed her operations and, eventually, put her to work constructing homeland security (2009: xv). Gaining entrance into some site as a means of studying some community of policy imple-menters entails having a story and playing roles (as a speech writer, aid, or planner, for instance) that makes sense to the gatekeepers and the community in that context.

Finally, gaining entrance into some community affected by events deemed terrorism is the last point of discussion. As we indicated earlier in this chapter, the potentially affected communities that one might study are wide-ranging: from commuters to neighbors to teachers to civil-war survivors. A letter from the Ministry of Health authorizing Nordstrom to travel around Mozambique was, by itself, apparently enough to gain access to many affected peoples and communities. Sometime she would get to the village immediately following a violent attack by one of the warring parties or she would arrive long after an attack or, in a few instances, she was present as an attack occurred. Either way, the people whom Nordstrom studied had worries far more sig-nificant than any concerns they might have had regarding her or her project. Showing the letter and relating her story about doing research most often were enough to gain entrance into some person's, family's, or village's life. Once inside, she observed and interviewed ordinary Mozambicans and analyzed how they were making sense of and responding to their experiences of terror.

Another example is Aretxaga's study of nationalist women in Northern Ireland and how they made sense of the ongoing political struggle there. She initially gained entrance primarily through her personal and professional connections, but this was not sufficient to gain entrance to all members of the affected community under study. Against the warnings of colleagues to stay out of certain areas, a friend and native of Belfast first showed Aretxaga around the area called the Falls, which helped her over-come her sense of "apprehension" (1997: ix). On top of that, she used the names sup-plied to her by colleagues and was able to meet and conduct multiple interviews with important nationalist women. Not everyone agreed, however. Given the political risk involved for some of the women and given that the issue has been extensively studied by academics, and even when members of the Sinn Féin political party helped arrange meetings, some women refused to be interviewed about their political histories and some even refused to meet with Aretxaga (1997: xi). Gaining entrance into com-munities of people affected by events deemed terrorism entails having an appropriate story and having the appropriate connections with informants who can help the researcher access the necessary information, but the story and the connections do not guarantee access.

At the same time, gaining entrance is much less of a practical problem for research-ers studying public spaces. Explaining the constitutive effects of publicly displayed symbols in Northern Ireland, for instance, did not entail that Santino gain entrance into any particular community. He could photograph publicly displayed murals or visit public shrines and memorials or watch a parade without telling a story or needing an informant. His book, while focusing on Northern Ireland, also "ranges freely over other times, places, and events" in Boston and London, for instance (Santino 2004: ix). This contrasts with Sluka and Aretxaga in their respective studies, which focused on specific communities of people in Northern Ireland. Aretxaga, for instance, focused on one specific district and Sluka focused on one particular ghetto.

Similarly, Stump's study of commuters' experiences in regards to signs of terrorism and counterterrorism in the Washington Metro did not entail he gain entrance into any particular community. Rather, for Stump, because participant observing and interviewing the wide range of Washington Metro riders played such an important role in the data gathering aspect of the study, establishing a moment of trust so that an interview could be accomplished amidst the noise and bustle of the subway station was important. Most commuters Stump spoke with were open to the interview, even apparently excited about the opportunity to speak, but a few were not. In general, Stump's strategy was the same: on subway platforms across the Washington Metro transit system, he approached people waiting for the train to arrive, introduced himself as a researcher with a particular university, indicated that he was studying the Washington Metro, and asked if they would be interested in answering a few questions about their experience on the Metro. Some responded with questions of their own about his intentions, his activities, his experience, his institutional affiliation, his degree, his professional goals, which is precisely when it is important to be able to convincingly tell stories that contribute to the building up of a shared sense of trust. The overall point is simple: Whether one is studying the terrorist subject or the community responding to events deemed terrorism, being prepared to tell a contextually appropriate story about who you are and what you are doing that holds up under closer scrutiny is very important for the ethnographic enterprise.

Potential Research Strategies

In considering a potential research project that focuses on those communities making sense of events deemed terrorism, here are some suggested questions to ask as the research design is organized:

- How many communities does one wish to study? The answer can result in a single community or one can go in a more comparative route that involves two or more communities. Most often, but not always, ethnographic research focuses on a single community. For instance, Fosher focused on a single community of policy implementers: those people constructing homeland security in Boston (2009). Low, however, compared a gated community in New York to a gated community in Texas (2008).
- What temporal perspective will your study emphasize? The answer can result in a study that focuses on the present or a study that emphasizes the past. Jackson's textual ethnography of presidential language and the justifications for torturing those deemed terrorist, for instance, focused on the past (2006, 2007c). Santino's study of public shrines, memorials, and parades focused on the past and the present (2001), while Stump's ethnographic research in the Washington Metro focused on the present (2009, 2010).
- Closely related to the temporal perspective taken by the study, what are the richest sources of data that can be gathered? A study focused on the past, like Jackson's (2006, 2007a, 2007c), may draw primarily from documents. Stump's study, however, was built on documents, interviews, and participant observations (2009, 2010).

Figures 7.1, 7.2, and 7.3 illustrate how these questions look for a research design in general and specific studies.

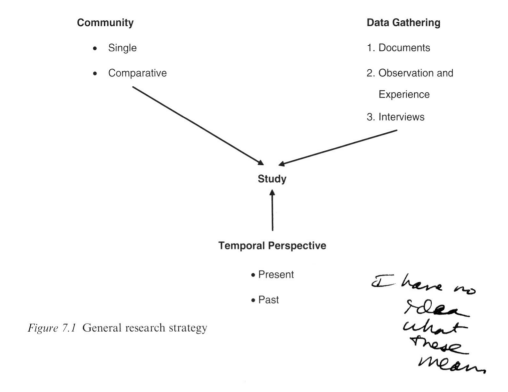

Community

- Single
- Comparative

Data Gathering

1. Documents
2. Observation and
   Experience
3. Interviews

Study

Temporal Perspective

• Present

• Past

I have no idea what these mean

Figure 7.1 General research strategy

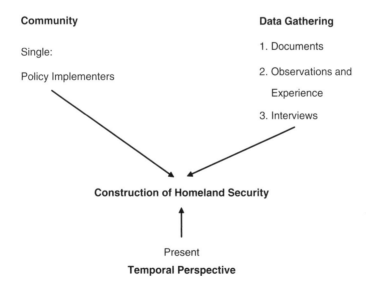

Community

Single:

Policy Implementers

Data Gathering

1. Documents
2. Observations and
   Experience
3. Interviews

Construction of Homeland Security

Present

Temporal Perspective

Figure 7.2 Research design for Kerry B. Fosher's study of the construction of homeland security in Boston

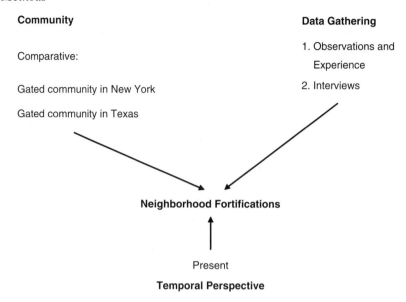

Figure 7.3 Research design for Setha Low's study of two gated communities

Questions to consider

- What are the three types of communities discussed in this chapter?
- What are some similarities and differences between entering into the communities discussed in this chapter compared to terrorist groups discussed in Chapter 6?

Further Reading

Fosher, K. B. (2009), *Under Construction: Making Homeland Security at the Local Level*, Chicago: University of Chicago Press.

Murphy, J. (2003), "'Our Mission and Our Moment': George W. Bush and September 11th," *Speech Communication*, 6 (4): 607–632.

Nordstrom, C. (1997), *A Different Kind of War Story*, Philadelphia, PA: University of Pennsylvania Press.

Low, S. M. (2008), "Fortification of Residential Neighborhoods and the New Emotions of Home," *Housing, Theory and Society*, 25 (1): 47–65.

8   Discourse Analysis and Terrorism Studies

Introduction

In recent times, the turn towards language and practice in IR has produced numerous discourse-oriented approaches to world politics. Though slower in making its way to security studies, there have been some well-known analyses of security as discourse, such as those by David Campbell, Karin Fierke, Jutta Weldes, and the Copenhagen School of security scholars. In TS, however, discourse analysis is relatively new. Therefore, this chapter has two main goals:

1. To outline some of the main understandings of "discourse" in IR and how some terrorism scholars have utilized discourse analysis in their research.
2. To indicate how discourse analysis, specifically poststructural or Foucauldian discourse analysis, has been used in security studies and to draw some lessons from it for terrorism scholarship.

The chapter will end by discussing some of the key aspects of designing a discourse-analytical research project on terrorism. In this, it takes up the challenge set forth by Magnus Ranstorp who wrote that there are very few studies done about the TS field to "account for what we know; how we know what we know; and what research questions we ought to focus on in terms of individual and collective research efforts" (Ranstorp 2009: 14). This chapter will attempt to describe what we know regarding terrorism as discourse, the type of research questions that are suitable for analysis under a discourse-analytical approach and the payoffs of studying terrorism as discourse.

Defining Discourse

There have been many meanings of the term "discourse" (see Box 8.1). Discourses, for Michel Foucault, are "composed of signs; but what they do is more than use these signs to designate things … it is this 'more' that we must reveal and describe" (Foucault 1972: 49). Foucault's views on discourse serve as reminders of two main assumptions about discourse:

1. Discourse is not natural and self-evident. It is something that the researcher herself determines based on empirical study. Thus, the identification of a discourse (or, more commonly a series of discourses) is itself part of the research process. Researchers are not presented with a series of discourses to analyze. Instead, they delimit discourses based on their research puzzle. For example, to study US national identity, a researcher may examine official discourses (Weldes 1999;

Campbell 1998a; Doty 1993) or popular discourses (media discourses, such as Croft 2006; Comics, as in Jenkins 2006; TV shows, as in Erickson 2007, 2008).

2. The second implication of Foucault's understanding of discourse for TS is that discourses do not refer to things outside of themselves but the meanings of issues and identities of social actors are themselves produced from *within* discourse. Discussing the USA, Stuart Croft writes:

> Discourses create and reflect identities, and thus they construct those who are our allies and those who are our enemies. When not in flux, they settle who "we" are, and who "they" are; what "we" stand for and what "they" mean to us. They construct the space for "our" legitimate activity, and the space for the behaviour we will (and will not) tolerate from "them."
>
> (2006: 1)

Hence, discourses are not ways to access the mental states or motivations of social actors (including so-called terrorists). It is worth repeating Foucault's understanding of discourse analysis here: "A task that consists of not – of no longer – treating discourses

---

Box 8.1 What is discourse and how can we study it?

While there are different ways in which "discourse" is defined and understood in the social sciences (see text), there are some common features. For example, with respect to "terrorism," official discourses in United States in the post-9/11 period have made it difficult, if not unthinkable, for people to comment on bombs/bombing in relation to aeroplanes and airports. Even a fairly innocuous activity such as fitting a vehicle with a propane gas tank in order to convert it into a "green" vehicle (Guilfoil 2011) is deemed dangerous by observers who link the ethnicity of van owners (Middle Eastern/Muslim) with the act (carrying a large gas tank into a van) and conceptualize them as potential "terrorists." Thus, discourses:

> [A]rticulate what is generally "sayable" or "thinkable" (that young men carrying a gas tank into a car are "terrorists") in relation to a given class of phenomena (terrorism) in any given cultural and historical context (post-9/11 USA). They articulate bodies of "knowledge," as well as authoritative producers of this knowledge (those who observe the act; police officers who responded; the government, etc.) that in turn constitute culturally and historically specific beliefs or "truths" about these phenomena (that young men of Middle Eastern appearance are likely dangerous). They articulate their "subjects' – the people that act within them or that they act upon (government, public, media personnel) – in such a manner that these subjects can be seen to, or even start to, personify or conform to these representations. And, finally, they articulate social structures that organize and regulate collective practice in a manner that is consistent with these representations (police force; legal system) ("Lecture 11", Antaki 2008; parenthesis added to provide examples)

Furthermore, "discourses are as much defined by what they *exclude* as by what they include. They simultaneously influence what is *not* sayable or *not* thinkable in a given cultural context ... " (ibid.). Thus, in the United States, Jared Loughner, a young (white) male who shoots a politician and had previously expressed dissent about her political views, is not considered "terrorist," while Abdulrahman al-Awlaki, a teenager who had not committed any acts of violence against civilians, is killed for being a terrorist.

On a more general note, Jonathan Potter in *Representing Reality* outlines different research methodologies' understandings of language (spoken, written, visual) and practices. He gives overviews of ethnomethodology, conversation analysis, semiology (a more structuralist tradition wherein metaphor analysis and frame analysis falls) and various ways of doing discourse analysis. The common theme to much of discourse analysis is its emphasis on studying ways in which we ourselves and our ways of knowing are socially constructed. In other words, discourse refers to ways in which we are located in the world (subject positions; subjectivities) and ways in which we understand the world (what can and cannot be said). At the same time, discourse produces bodies – whether individuals or states or other collectives – and creates a binary (or a hierarchical) set of relations between these bodies. Meanings are created and a hierarchy is established, again within particular discourses. R. Jackson (2005) outlines the binary opposition between "us" (the United States and its allies) and "them" (al-Qaeda, terrorists in general and those who support them). These formulations then establish a set of (im)possibilities for action. For example, the PATRIOT Act in the United States gives authorities greater power over arresting suspects and suspends some of the civil rights that US citizens previously had. However, these practices remained mostly unchallenged by the public because they were seen as necessary to "fight terrorism," a phrase that was (and still is) commonly used to justify particular actions.

In terms of types of discourse analysis, despite the recent increase in IR research utilizing this methodology, there is often a lack of clarity of which type of discourse analysis is being conducted. For a clear and comprehensive overview on discourse in IR, Milliken (1999) remains one of the best sources. We propose the following two ways in which discourse analysis can proceed:

a) Critical Discourse Analysis (CDA)

Critical Discourse Analysis draws upon the traditions of research in institutionalism and ideology. In this approach, ideologies and oppression (domination) underlie discourses and discourse analysis is a method to uncover these ideologies and structures of domination. A central focus in CDA is on emancipation. Scholars who utilize CDA are Ruth Wodak, Theo van Dijk, Norman Fairclough, Paul Chilton and, in CTS, Richard Jackson.

b) Poststructural/Foucauldian Discourse Analysis

As described in text, poststructural DA collapses the idealism/materialism divide, looks at "emancipation" and "ideology" as socially-constructed and contextually-understood and operates on the presupposition that discourses are unstable. Scholars who utilize poststructural DA in IR include Jutta Weldes, Patrick Thaddeus Jackson, Karin Fierke, Lene Hansen, David Campbell, and James der Derian.

as groups of signs ... but as practices that systematically form the objects of which they speak" (Foucault 1972: 49). In Chapters 6 and 7 we outlined ethnography and studying social meanings. This chapter and the next examine discourses of terrorism and counterterrorism in order to note meanings and identities produced therein.

The key point here is, of course, that discourses are *social practices* that constitute objects, including objects of analysis. As Foucault puts it, "we must show that they [pre-existing forms of continuity in discourses] do not come about of themselves, but are always the result of a construction, the rules of which must be known, and the justifications of which must be scrutinized" (1972: 25). It is these "rules" – as evidenced in the language and practices used to describe events – that a study of terrorism as discourse will lead to. In IR, definitions of discourse itself are drawn from a variety of fields, including linguistics, sociology, and social psychology. As such, "discourse" has been used to refer to a diverse range of methods, methodologies and ways of knowing the world around us (Potter and Wetherell 1987: 6–7). One clear definition of discourse from outside IR is provided by Jonathan Potter. Potter writes that a focus on discourse means "the concern is with *talk and texts as parts of social practices*" (1996: 105; emphasis in original). In IR, Jutta Weldes writes, "Discourses – like that of neoliberal globalization – are sets of rules for ordering and relating discursive elements (subjects, objects, their characteristics, tropes, narratives, and so on) in such a way that some meanings rather than others are constituted" (2006: 179).

While definitions of discourse range from "discourse" as sets of statements to "discourse" as language and practices to "discourse" as emerging from specific ideological standpoints, in all these definitions, "discourse" draws attention to *how* things have been "put together," i.e. how meanings become known as commonsensical and how particular identities are produced. Thus, a study of terrorism as discourse means illustrating the processes by which our commonsensical understandings of the world are formulated. It also means being aware of the links between issues and social actors that are labeled "dangerous" and those countering the dangers. For example, the traditional narrative of counterterrorism as having terrorists who perform their violent acts first and then the response by the counterterrorist state itself becomes open to question. But because of the many definitions of discourse in IR, it is incumbent upon the researcher to specify which discursive tradition her research draws upon prior to starting research.

The study of terrorism as discourse takes the view that language and practices are foundational to analysis and construct what count as terrorism and counterterrorism in the first place. Terrorism is therefore a socially constructed phenomenon, its meanings emerging from social interaction and analyzable through studying language use and visual media. As Hodges, discussing the "war on terror," writes, "Discourse infuses events with meaning, establishes widespread social understandings, and constitutes social reality" (2011: 5). Meanings in official counterterrorist discourses draw upon popular meanings elsewhere. Discourse analysts call this intertextuality. Simply, "intertextuality" is how meanings in different discourses refer to each other. While "discourse" is more all-encompassing than "language," it is the study of language-in-use that allows us to delineate various identities (or "subject positioning") within different discourses. The analysis of discourse can be done by analyzing language as it is used ("language-use"), with "language" broadly defined as written, spoken, visual, and body languages.

Thus, language and how it is used are key in understanding identities and interests constituted within discourses. Foucault writes that the task of analyzing discourses is not reducible to language (1972: 49) but, we would argue, studying practices includes studying "language-in-use" or, language as it is *used* during particular social interactions. Wetherell et al. (1984) clarify this link between language use and identity formation as they point out how discourse analysis takes as foundational that language is both constructed (by social practices and how it is used) and constructive (of meanings and identities). They draw attention to the implications of particular language (words, phrases, and labels) being used during specific social interactions.

It is important to be aware that "language" here encompasses written, spoken, and visual data as well as performances, and this is the data for a discourse-analytical project.

Discourse analysis is about the public use of language since, as Potter and Wetherell explain, "to look at how the self is constructed, the social scientist should research the grammatical matrix and everyday language usage" (1987: 107). For example, to study the counterterrorist state, it is important to examine the state's language about itself and about its "others," and about security and threats. This will be further discussed in Chapter 9. Analyzing language use is also tied in with questions of power, as Potter and Wetherell explain:

> people become fixed in position through the range of linguistic practices available to them to make sense. The use of a particular discourse which contains a parti-cular organization of the self not only allows one to warrant and justify one's actions ..., it also maintains power relations and patterns of domination and sub-ordination. In constructing the self in one way, other constructions are excluded, hence ... the creation of one kind of self or subjectivity in discourse also creates a particular kind of subjection.
>
> (1987: 109)

Traditions of Discourse: Critical and Poststructural/Foucauldian

In IR, there are two main traditions of discourse, Critical Discourse Analysis and Poststructural or Foucauldian Discourse Analysis.

Critical Discourse Analysis

This is the "big C" Critical tradition linked with Max Horkheimer, Theodor Adorno, and Jürgen Habermas (amongst others) who have inspired discourse theorists such as Theo van Dijk, Ruth Wodak, Paul Chilton, and Norman Fairclough. The majority of terrorism scholars who use discourse analysis have followed this tradition, under the umbrella of "Critical Terrorism Studies."

There is a normative commitment to emancipation in Critical (big "C") terrorism scholarship and Critical Discourse Analysis (CDA). As Richard Jackson writes, "a central aim of critical discourse analysis lies in revealing the means by which language is deployed to maintain power; what makes critical discourse analysis 'critical' is its normative commitment to positive social change" (2005: 25). For many Critical ter-rorism scholars, emancipation is a process of "freeing up space for dialogue and delib-eration" (McDonald 2007: 252). Responding to potential criticisms by scholars who may argue emancipation is a subjective process, McDonald writes, "a reflexive com-mitment to emancipation as the removal of unnecessary structural constraints through a process of freeing up space for dialogue provides a basis for both analytically impor-tant and normatively progressive research on 'terrorism' in international politics" (2009: 111).

There are two avenues for critical research here:

1. research on social meanings of "emancipation" by noting how people use "emancipation" in their daily lives;
2. asking what research utilizing a different standpoint on emancipation would lead to.

The CDA view on emancipation is drawn from the Western European philosophical background of the Frankfurt School of scholars. This second track of research could ask what a different philosophical understanding and standpoint on emancipation lead to.

Hence, further research could ask questions such as "Whose emancipation?," "How does this emancipation occur?" and "What *is* emancipation?" Such questions are best answered using an interpretive methodology which explains *how* social actors in different contexts make sense of emancipation. Research could then empirically delineate how different societies understand and experience emancipation and how its meanings differ. From a discourse-analytical perspective, "emancipation" and its deployment – when, where, by whom and with what effects? – become a central concern for critical research on terrorism.

Poststructural or Foucauldian Discourse Analysis

The second tradition of discourse in IR is inspired by Michel Foucault. This is a poststructuralist understanding of discourse which has been adopted by critical security scholars such as Jutta Weldes, David Campbell, and the Copenhagen School. Language use is central here, but physical enactments and also buildings and structures can be "interpreted" for analysis. Studying language use in the poststructural tradition is not to reveal the ideological underpinnings or to call for emancipation but to illustrate how self–other identities are produced and legitimated within particular discourses. This poststructural understanding of discourse and language is best exemplified by Lene Hansen in critical security scholarship. For Hansen, language use is social, political, and inherently unstable (Hansen 2006: 18–20).

In order to do research using poststructural discourse analysis, the process of fixing the meaning of language within particular contexts is an empirical exercise that (a) determines how language constitutes identities and interests; and (b) makes us continuously aware that the "fixing" or the "stability" of the language examined is temporary and often an analytical convenience. Hansen writes how self–other identity formation is usually self–other*s* as the other is situated in a web of identities and not just in binary opposition to the self as is often theorized (Hansen 2006: 40). A discursive analysis of foreign policy, for Hansen, reframes research questions and has a different meaning of "foreign" than that using traditional methods.

In the 1990s, poststructural discourse analysis was the methodological choice of many critical security scholars, especially those who prioritized "speech acts" in the study of security. The best-known example here is the Copenhagen School – a loosely connected group of scholars – who sought to denaturalize pre-given identities of threats while emphasizing security can be studied as a "speech act." This meant that, instead of looking at language as incidental or supplementary to the main issue of security, these scholars posited language use and social interactions as foundational to analysis and as constitutive of issues and identities. This move from defining what threats are to how they are represented, with language being the means through which this representation is done, was key to questioning traditional ways of studying security and to conducting research on what (and who) was being securitized.

The Copenhagen School's theory of securitization centralizes language use in the analysis of security. Describing securitization, Waever writes, "with the help of language, we can regard security as a *speech act.* In this usage, security is not of interest as a sign that refers to something more real; the utterance *itself* is the act. By saying it, something is done (as in betting, giving a promise, naming a ship)" (Buzan et al. 1998: 26). Successful securitization has three steps:

1.   the identification of existential threats;
2.   the proposal of emergency action;
3.   the breaking free of regular rules of security.

For these scholars, security is understood as "the move that takes politics beyond the established rules of the game and frames the issue either as a special kind of politics or as above politics" (Buzan et al. 1998: 23). This approach to security does not seek to define security (and, relatedly, insecurity) but details what the use of the language of security *does* in terms of forming boundaries between self and others, security and threats. While there have been critiques of the Copenhagen School, these criticisms do not mitigate that the School focused on studying *how* threats were defined (by states and others). Copenhangen scholars linked the tasks of defining threats and responding to them, tasks which were often studied separately. A similar study could be conducted for terrorism in which the "terroristization" of a particular issue or a group of people is the focus of the research. Similar to the Copenhagen School, the Paris School of CSS also draws attention to the socially constructed nature of security and terrorism. Paris School scholars have studied the field of meanings from which insecurity, including fear of terrorism, is produced and on defining (and understanding) practices of exclusion (Bigo and Tsoukala 2008: 2–3).

The Paris School's interest has been on how "liberal" states with their pregiven "liberal" identities deal with insecurity. These are grounds for further research. Another option is to be aware that the discourse of the liberal democratic state is one of many possible discourses available for meaning-making purposes and state officials continually interpret acts and actions as "dangerous." For example, under Bigo et al.'s framework, Britain's relations with the IRA could be investigated as "a liberal democratic state's" response to terrorism or how British security officials (or related personnel) constructed insecurity. What repressive security practices *do* to the state's liberal democratic identity would be the focus. On a related but slightly different note, a more poststructuralist approach to terrorism would not take the liberal democratic nature of states for granted but would examine "democracy" as one of a series of rhetorical tropes that states use when describing threats and constructing their own identity, often in contrast to terrorism.

For poststructural discourse analysis as a whole, danger and those responding to danger are co-constituted in the process of making sense of events and actions. Looking at identities and interests as socially constructed and centralizing interpretation means researchers can focus on how particular identities and outcomes were made possible and, importantly, how they were legitimated. For example, the link made between local Maoist rebels in Nepal and global terrorists in the 2001–2006 period legitimated the

Nepalese state's actions as against terrorism and allowed for continued military assistance including (but not limited to) from the USA. However, at the same time, many other possible identities and choices for actions were also present with different identities for the Maoists and the Nepali state but these were marginalized within the terrorism discourse.

Discourse Analysis in Terrorism Studies

Terrorism scholarship that utilizes discourse analysis has been expanding. For example, since the events of September 11, 2001, there has been an increasing amount of terrorism research from a critical perspective. Some scholars have drawn attention to other examples of "September 11" (e.g., Elden 2009; Hodges 2011) or to other contexts where terrorism was not used despite there being acts of violence (e.g., Blakeley 2009). The term "September 11" or, more commonly, "9/11," has become a rhetorical commonplace that is re-deployed in other contexts. This could be noted after the 2008 Mumbai bombings, when media reports in India claimed this was "India's 9/11." In IR, Richard Jackson's research on US counterterrorism discourse is one of the best-known examples of the study of terrorism as discourse. In his 2005 book *Writing the War on Terrorism: Language, Politics and Counter-terrorism,* Jackson uses CDA to analyze the US's counterterrorism policy after September 11, 2001. After specifying that "discourses form the foundation for [counterterrorism] practice" (Jackson 2005: 21), he analyzes official documents and speeches by US government officials to note how the identity of the USA, its allies, and its enemies were socially constructed.

Discussing the meaning-making of September 11, 2001, in official accounts, R. Jackson points out there were four key features:

1. The attacks were "discursively constructed" as exceptional tragedy.
2. The language used portrayed the attacks as an "act of war" rather than a criminal act or mass murder.
3. The attacks were linked with other "meta-narratives" such as threats against the USA (e.g., Pearl Harbor) and the opposition of civilization and barbarism.
4. Finally, the way the event was represented closed off avenues for other possible meanings.

(R. Jackson 2005: 31)

Here, R. Jackson is outlining what a discourse-analytical approach to US counter-terrorism strategies can help us understand. Instead of seeing the meaning of September 11, 2001, as natural and self-evident, its socially constructed nature and the mechanics (repeated use of specific terms by US officials) of that construction become centralized. Furthermore, Jackson examines how the identity of the "terrorist enemy" as evil, alien, and inhuman is produced through and in representations (R. Jackson 2005: 62–63). On a related note, the identity of Americans is produced as "good," as freedom-loving, compassionate, heroic, innocent, and united against this evil terrorist threat (R. Jackson 2005: 76–88). One goal of the discourse analysis here is to note the production of self (US state) and others (terrorists, allies of the US, "enemies" of the US) identities.

R. Jackson's is the clearest use of discourse analysis – CDA – in the study of terrorism. However, there have been other scholars who have studied discourse. One of these scholars is Joseba Zulaika. His concern is partly to reduce the mystique of terrorism and make people aware of the loaded connotations of the use of the term itself. In his 2005 book *Terrorism: A Self-Fulfilling Prophecy*, he writes, terrorism discourse "must be disenchanted if it is to lose its efficacy for all concerned" (Zulaika 2005: 1). Zulaika writes that "Terrorism creates its own reality" but then says "My arguments here go beyond discourse analysis. Terrorism is premised on the *will* of insurgents, rebels, fighters, terrorists" (2005: 2). This gives a "reality" to terrorism that is extra-discursive, which fits in with the CDA method. As such, Zulaika assumes there is something more than discourse that discourse obscures, an understanding that fits in better with CDA and one that R. Jackson's book (and subsequent work) also presume. In another example of the use of discourse analysis to study terrorism, Graham, Keenan and Dowd examine George W. Bush's "war on terror" discourse and compare it with other "call to arms" in the past. Their work outlines how the war on terrorism was legitimated using what they call a "discourse-historical approach." In this, they compare Bush's declaration of a "war on terror" with past declarations, including Queen Elizabeth I in the sixteenth century and Adolf Hitler in the early twentieth century (Graham et al. 2004).

In addition to focusing on how identities are formed and policies legitimated, studying discourses of terrorism also interrogates and makes transparent the processes of categorization. For example, R. Jackson selected a series of texts to analyze how the phrase "Islamic terrorism" has been used and the effects of such labeling (R. Jackson 2007b). Jackson examines "over 300 political and academic texts." He writes that the categorization process draws upon previous "Orientalist" scholarship as well as negative media reports about Arabs and Muslims. He concludes that the label of "Islamic terrorism" posits Islam as inherently violent, even terrorist and has the long-term effect of increasing fissures in society. This "making of commonsense" is a key feature of discourse-analytical research:

> America's "response" to those [September 11, 2001] attacks was not obvious, not "natural," nor based on some objective standard of "common sense." Policy had to be built on a narrative that could be shared amongst those who felt threatened; and that had to be America's government and, importantly, American society as a whole.
>
> (Croft 2006: 1)

Croft's discourse-analytical analysis examines how the American government and society were represented as under threat. While R. Jackson concentrated on official speeches and documents, Croft examines popular culture as well, thus studying the intertextuality of meanings in official and popular terrorism discourses.

Other scholars have examined media texts to note how terrorism is constructed therein. Zulaika and Douglass write that the media did not generally label political violence as terrorism until the early 1970s (Zulaika and Douglass 1996: 45). They add that, since 1972, events which were previously not called terrorism were then labeled as such, especially when describing actions in Northern Ireland (Zulaika and Douglass 1996: 46). Hulsse and Spencer (2008) analyzed the German media's representations of al-Qaeda after September 11, 2001, and the Madrid and London bombings of 2004 and 2005 respectively. They write how the representations of terrorism shifted from war to crime over this period. Similarly, Yufang Qian examines China's *People's Daily* newspaper and the United Kingdom's *The Sun,* the two most-read newspapers in each country, to see how these two sources used "terrorism" and the identities and policies produced.

Qian argues how there is not just one main "terrorism discourse" but different ways in which terrorism is understood even within the same context (Qian 2010). These scholars focus on who is labeled terrorist and how "terrorism" is used in the respective newspapers and also provide examples of the type of research a discourse-analytical project could lead to.

In terms of "how to" do discourse analysis, while many researchers conduct interviews and analyze visual or textual data, there has been a rise in qualitative data analysis software. For example, Qian's analysis uses software (Wordsmith tools), a practice that may be more common when doing discourse analysis in the future. Some of Qian's findings on terrorism in *The Sun* included a shift from organization-based language (dissident, loyalist, Republican) to individual (Osama bin Laden); lack of words referring to religion to an increase in religion-based words ("Islamic," "fanatic," "extremist" were more common in the post-9/11 period); a move from discourse of crime (police, crime, imprisonment) to discourse of war (fighters, suicide bombers); and from local threat of terrorism (IRA, Irish, Republican, loyalist) to worldwide terrorist threat (network, suspected, raising, and funds). As such, before September 11, 2001, terrorism in the UK was constructed as an Irish-based locally originating threat that was part of a criminal problem. After September 11, 2001, this changed to terrorism meaning globally oriented war led by extremist religious individuals (Qian 2010).

Yet other scholars have studied how social actors reconceptualize US or global discourses on terrorism in different contexts. Erjavec and Volcic study Serbian intellectuals' discourses to note how violence against Muslims in Bosnia and Kosovo was legitimated as against terrorism (Erjavec and Volcic 2007). While using a "foreign" discourse – US language about the global "war on terror" – local actors in Serbia used analogies to then link Muslims with terrorist threats. "They equate the attacks on the WTC and the Pentagon with the former Yugoslav wars and they position and represent former Yugoslav Muslims as terrorists" (Erjavec and Volcic 2007: 123). Terrorism or terrorist violence is linked with all Muslims, hence constituting Muslims from the former Yugoslavia as terrorist. Erjavec and Volcic utilize qualitative methods, gathering their data from methods with thirty-two Serbian intellectuals, aged between twenty-three and forty. Intellectuals included journalists, writers, teaching/research assistants, and politicians.

Research Design: Questions, Discourses, Discursive Formations, and Identities

To study terrorism as discourse, the main two traditions of discourse analysis – Critical and poststructural/Foucauldian – are appropriate. As Richard Jackson's *Writing the War on Terror* (2005) is exemplary of a CDA approach, the rest of this section will broadly sketch out what a poststructural discourse analysis of terrorism could study.

The research question should focus on identity-related issues. This means questions such as "What causes terrorism?," "What are the socioeconomic factors that lead to terrorism?" are inappropriate for a discourse-based research project since such questions assume the objective "reality" of terrorism, an assumption that poststructural discourse analysts do not share. Instead, the link between insecurity and identity and the shift in particular identities should be focused upon. For example, Roxanne Doty (1993) asked how US–Filipino relations were described such that it seemed commonsensical for the USA to militarily intervene in another sovereign state. Hansen asks how the meaning of Bosnia became understood as a site (and people) where Western military intervention was permissible. Graham et al. (2004) studied how the US move to war was legitimated. Qian (2010) and Hülsee and Spencer (2008) study media discourses in different countries and how they construct the terrorist identity differently, thus questioning the "natural" response of counterterrorism as well as indicating other meanings of events and actors labeled as terrorism. R. Jackson (2007a) performs a similar task with reference to academic discourses and the concept of "Islamic terrorism." Hence, discourse-analytical questions about terrorism may range from asking how particular policies were legitimated to how the terrorist subject is produced within specific discourses to how alternative discourses were sidelined in the process of establishing a particular terrorist or "counterterrorist" identity.

Once the question and the time period for analysis have been selected, the next step is to decide upon which level(s) of discourse should be studied. Much of the discourse-analytical work done in security studies has focused on official discourse analysis (R. Jackson, Weldes, Campbell, among others) or the media and popular culture texts (Spencer and Hülsse, Qian, Dowd et al.). However, there is also the possibility of analyzing popular discourses via interviews, studying other forms of discourse (security officials, counterterrorism personnel, local people, and so on). The main level of analysis should be clearly specified. It is also important to consider if the researcher is pursuing a genealogical or historical analysis in which one main discourse is analyzed over a period of time (Figure 8.2) or one time period is focused on and the formation of terrorism or terrorist identity within a range of discourses is to be studied (Figure 8.1). These are two different types of research projects and the researcher would benefit from clarifying which research study she is conducting (see Figures 8.2 and 8.3).

Following Hansen, one of the goals of discourse analysis, after identifying the level of analysis and time period(s) for study, could be to go from a series of texts to identifying what she calls basic discourses (2006: 51). To identify basic discourses, the researcher should conduct a thorough reading of data available. "Basic discourses" are ideal-typical analytical tools for the researcher. They are usually not the most commonly argued and nor are they the ones that are proposed by governments (Hansen 2006: 51). Basic discourses "provide a lens" from which different positions and policies within particular debates can be noted.

Hansen's research design fits in better with a research project that seeks to understand how different discourses construct the issue in question (as a problem, as a site that needs intervention, and so on; see Figure 8.2). For Hansen, basic discourses should outline the "main structural positions within a debate" and indicate how different others and selves are articulated. A related point here is that "one would expect that basic discourses articulate rather different foreign policies" (Hansen 2006: 54). A comprehensive analysis of a series of sources during the specified time period is necessary because "one basic discourse will be argued relatively quickly as an issue manifests itself on the foreign policy agenda, while the other basic discourse(s) will be argued in response to and in criticism of this position" (Hansen 2006: 54). So, basic discourses are identified from the researcher's analytical design and study of diverse range of sources. These sources are usually texts but can be audio or visual sources as well.

Overall, the goal then is to identify the number of selves outlined in these basic discourses at the period(s) of time specified in the study. By utilizing both texts from the time of study (official documents, media, academic sources as well as travelogues and novels) as well as "historical material" (civilizational discourse, novels), Hansen builds up a series of connected texts to identify basic (and competing) discourses and identities. This is similar to the research design outlined in Figure 8.2, wherein an issue (the

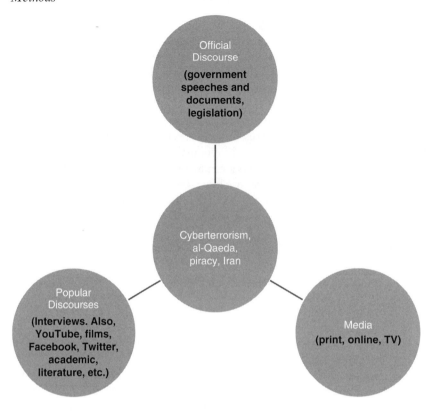

Figure 8.1 A general outline of data for a discourse analysis project

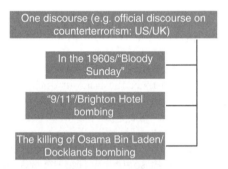

Figure 8.2 Analyzing one discourse, two to three events/time periods

war in Bosnia and the intervention by "the West") and a time period (period before intervention) are clearly specified and a wide array of sources presents the data for analysis of foreign-policy-making.

Some other ways of doing discourse analysis include Potter's emphasis on strategies by which identities are constructed and legitimated and, in IR, Jutta Weldes' (1999) analysis using articulation and interpellation as well as Roxanne Doty's "discursive practices" approach (1993). P. Jackson (2006a) utilizes "rhetorical commonplaces." Rhetorical commonplaces retain a history of their use but also gain new meanings as they are used in different times and places. They can be empirically delineated by examining sources during various events where self–others identities are constituted. In all these examples, the analysis of discourse is to study how identities are constructed and legitimated. The instability of meanings is illustrated by outlining other possibilities for meaning-making that were present at the time. This also serves to challenge the "commonsensical" meanings and identities.

Conclusion: Analyzing Language in Use, Questioning Common Sense

To sum up, discourse analysis focuses on identifying how particular identities – self and others – are produced within particular discourses (see Figure 9.1 on p. 130). Hence, labels are important, and noting how, when, by whom, and with what effects labeling is conducted is key to discourse analysis of both the CDA and poststructural types. The researcher's goal is to describe how this "social object" (its identity) is produced within these texts and visual data and what is left out when certain meanings are normalized.

One of the main outcomes of a discourse-analytical project is to indicate how identities and interests are not "natural." Instead, what we usually consider common sense is itself socially constructed and communicated. As such, the focus on legitimation – whether of counterterrorism policies or of identifying a particular group as terrorists – leads to the researcher showing how such identities and policies are always one of many possible options. Discourse analysis points out the connections between knowledge and power. For example, Stuart Croft writes,

> If the recognition of the new "reality" in the "post 9/11" world is to be understood fully, it must be achieved by identifying and deconstructing the meaning of the "war on terror" as discourse. Not only that, but the "common sense" that is produced in that discourse must be problematized in order to understand that which counts as knowledge and that which does not; that which constitutes identity with a particular group, and that which constitutes identity against a particular group.
>
> (2006: 27)

As such, an overall goal of discourse analysis is to note how "that which counts as knowledge and that which does not" is produced, communicated, legitimated and resisted.

Questions to consider

- What are two main types of discourse analysis? What are some key differences among them?
- Identify some basic discourses in discussion about a particular security issue. Some ideas are: militias, "homegrown extremism," insurgencies, female suicide bombers, etc.
- What are some key rhetorical commonplaces in the "global war on terror"? What does this indicate about mainstream discourse about the "global war on terror"? What does this leave out?
- Are discourses real?
- Outline how an issue has been securitized in the post-9/11 period. How was this issue represented prior to 9/11?
- What are some similarities and differences between discourse analysis and ethnography?

Further Reading

Ahluwalia, P. (2010), *Out of Africa: Post-Structuralism's Colonial Roots*, London and New York: Routledge.

Der derian, J. and Shapiro, M. (Eds.) (1989), *International/Intertextual Relations: Postmodern Readings of World Politics*, New York: Lexington Books.

Fairclough, N. (2003), *Analysing Discourse: Textual Analysis for Social Research*, London and New York: Routledge.

Foucault, M. (1995), *Discipline and Punish: The Birth of the Prison*, trans. A. Sheridan, New York: Vintage.

Gavey, N. (2011), "Feminist Poststructuralism and Discourse Analysis Revisited," *Psychology of Women Quarterly*, 35 (March): 183–188.

Hansen, L. (2006), *Security As Practice: Discourse Analysis and the Bosnian War*, London and New York: Routledge.

Milliken, J. (1999), "The Study of Discourse in International Relations: A Critique of Research and Methods," *European Journal of International Relations*, 5 (2): 225–254.

Potter, J. (1996), *Representing Reality: Discourse, Rhetoric and Social Construction*, London: Sage.

Redfield, R. (2009), *The Rhetoric of the War on Terror*, New York: Fordham University Press.

Slembrouck, S. (2001), "Explanation, Interpretation and Critique in the Analysis of Discourse," *Critique of Anthropology*, 21 (1): 33–57.

Van Dijk, T. A. (2008), *Discourse and Power*, Houndsmills: Palgrave.

Wodak, R. (2007), "What Is Critical Discourse Analysis?: Ruth Wodak in Conversation with Gavin Kendall," *Qualitative Research*, 8 (2). Available online at: http://www.qualitative-research.net/index.php/fqs/article/view/255/561.

Weblinks

Forum: Qualitative Social Research has a special issue enitled "From Michel Foucault's Theory of Discourse to Empirical Discourse Research" (vol. 8, no. 2, 2007), available at http://www.qualitative-research.net/index.php/fqs/issue/view/7. (Some of the articles are in German and some in Spanish.)

See the Google scholar page for Jonathan Potter at http://scholar.google.co.uk/citations?user=kRrsam UAAAAJ& hl = en.

D. Howarth and A. Norval outline a course on "Postcolonialism, Feminism and Radical Democracy: Poststructuralist Perspectives" at http://www.victoria.ac.nz/criticaltheories/week3. aspx (2008). The website gives reading lists, including one on "A Poststructuralist Perspective," which will be useful for scholars adopting a poststructural discourse analysis approach to research.

A pioneer of visual and textual analysis outlines his perspective in Theory Talks #36, "Interview with Michael Shapiro": www.theory-talks.org/2010/02/theory-talk-36.html.

Jutta Weldes also outlines three ways of studying discourse and identity in IR in her speech at an Ohio State University Conference. See https://kb.osu.edu/dspace/bitstream/handle/1811/31957/Weldes%20Comments.pdf?sequence=30.

9 Discourse Analysis of the Counterterrorist State

Introduction

In Chapter 8, we outlined two types of discourse analysis and how a discourse-analytical research project could proceed. To summarize, discourse analysis is useful for explaining how particular identities and policies are deemed commonsensical. It draws attention to how such normalization ignores and sidelines other ways of making sense. The analytical focus is therefore on studying what has been done, said, written, or made visible ("language use") to note how particular meanings emerged and were normalized. This chapter will follow on from that but focus specifically on state and terrorist identity formations, analyzing discourses of counterterrorism. The first part of the chapter situates the role of the state in TS in general and discusses different ways the state and terrorist identities can be studied using discourse analysis. The second part outlines the method of genealogy and provides some examples. The final part discusses some further concerns for researchers interested in discourse analysis.

The Role of the State in Terrorism Studies

There are three main ways in which the state–terrorism relationship can be studied in terrorism scholarship:

1. states that "produce" terrorists by funding them;
2. states that counter terrorists;
3. state terrorism.

Let us discuss each in more depth.

States That Fund and Train Terrorists

In conventional TS, state terrorism usually refers to the state that "sponsors" or "supports" terrorism by training or funding terrorists. An example is Walter Laqueur's *The New Terrorism,* which has a chapter on state terrorism in which Laqueur writes that the former Soviet Union was a main sponsor of terrorism and that it and other Communist countries were heavily involved in international terrorism (2000: 158). The longevity of state sponsorship of terrorism is pointed out by Laqueur who writes, "state-sponsored terrorism, warfare by proxy, is as old as the history of military conflict" (2000: 156). The terms "state sponsors of terror" or "state-sponsored terrorism" are almost always used to refer to states that are separated from liberal, democratic (often Northern) states by space and time. Indeed, the USA is the state that categorizes and communicates other states as "state sponsors of terrorism." In 2011, Cuba, Iran, Sudan, and Syria were all on record as being state sponsors of terrorism, according to the US State Department.

There are two implications for future research here:

1. to note other understandings of state terrorism in addition to the normalized one of the US State Department classification (discourse analysis could be used to interrogate this normalized understanding);
2. a focus also on the liberal democratic state and its use of violence.

Conventional terrorism scholarship has classified terrorism as a form of violence that *others* (not the liberal democratic state) are involved in. This, as some scholars (e.g., Blakeley 2007, 2009) have pointed out, is a weakness in the scholarship on state terrorism.

A discourse-analytical project could interrogate these silences about the role of the state. One way of doing this is by studying processes of labeling: Who does the labeling of acts and actors as terrorism? What practices are justified? Who is left out from the categorization of "state sponsors of terrorism"? On the subject of labeling, in an article written after the killing of Osama bin Laden, Noam Chomsky calls it "a political assassination." He criticizes the naming of the operation – Geronimo – as arising from an "imperial mentality" which is glorifying bin Laden by linking him with "courageous resistance against genocidal invaders" (2011). Thus, a discourse-analytical research project would question the representational practices of all states, not just those categorized as "state sponsors of terrorism" (a categorization that itself emerges from a particular sociopolitical standpoint).

States That Counter Terrorists

Implicitly or explicitly, this is the most common form of the state found in much of TS. A discourse-analytical project questions this normalized counterterrorist identity. For example, a discourse-analytical project can study the *spaces* where this counterterrorist state operates, and the sites where the counterterrorist identity is reproduced. An example here is R. Jackson's research on terrorism "experts." Jackson claims the embedded nature of terrorism "experts" is a problem for research on terrorism. This is because such "experts" are usually allied to institutions which are part of or are funded by governments (R. Jackson 2007b). Thus, the counterterrorist state is not just present in official statements but also produced and reproduced in talks and actions of these "experts."

Another possible research track is to question the state's use of violence. Traditional TS links terrorism with a unique kind of violence and avoids discussing the state's use of violence as terrorist. Cindy Combs writes, "It is only the act that can accurately be labeled as terrorist, not the individual or the group, and certainly not the cause for which the tactic is employed" (2003: 17). However, "terrorism" is then *only* applied to the acts of non-state actors even though a consistent use of her definition would logically mean state actions could also be considered terrorist. Arce and Sandler begin by defining terrorism as "the premeditated use of threat of violence by individuals or subnational groups" (2005: 183). In the definition itself, terrorism is limited to the use of violence by non-state actors, thus making states' use of violence *not* terrorism. In a recent book on "the political economy of terrorism," Enders and Sandler outline their book as, "unlike other books, this book identifies rational explanations for observed behavior – for example, why terrorist groups cooperate and form networks with one another, while targeted governments are slow to cooperate" (2005: xi–xii). States (in this formulation) can only be *targeted* by terrorists; they cannot be terrorist themselves. This, of course, reconstructs and reifies the *(good) states counter (evil) terrorists* narrative found in the majority of conventional scholarship on terrorism.

All these examples – Combs, Arce and Sandler, and Enders and Sandler – safeguard the state's counterterrorist identity by leaving out the state itself from the category of terrorist. R. Jackson analyzed over 100 texts on terrorism to conclude that state terrorism is mostly absent from the literature on terrorism (R. Jackson 2008). He writes, "In the vast majority of the more than 100 texts I examined, the terms 'state terrorism' or 'state terror' did not even appear" (R. Jackson 2008: 7). Jackson asks why "such obvious cases of terrorism" of states (including Western democratic states) using terrorism are "so rarely studied by terrorism scholars" (R. Jackson 2008).

State Terrorism

To respond to this "silence" on state terrorism, these are two ways discourse analysts can study this subject:

1   studying the state's use of (terrorist) violence;
2   studying "the state" and terrorism as co-constituted (state/terrorism).

Adding the State and Its Use of (Terrorist) Violence as a Research Topic Within TS

Recently, scholars have repeatedly called for the state to be "brought back" to TS.[1] For example, Ruth Blakeley examines violence used by Northern states in the Global South. She writes, "State terrorism along with other forms of repression, has been an ongoing feature of the foreign policies of democratic great powers from the North and the United States (US) in particular" (2007: 228). Within this approach, the state is now added as another user of terrorist violence. In addition to Blakeley, Jeffrey Sluka, Noam Chomsky, and essays in *Contemporary State Terrorism* have all begun to study the terrorist use of violence by the state (Blakeley 2007; Chomsky 2003; Sluka 2000; R. Jackson et al. 2009a). For critical terrorism scholars, this adding of the state to examine its terrorist actions is one avenue of research.

Studying "the State" and Terrorism as Co-constituted: State/Terrorism

The second way to study the state in terrorism scholarship is to take labeling and language-use seriously and study labeling practices as co-constituting terrorist threats as well as the counterterrorist state. Here, the state is not just a user of violence or a participant in violent acts but it is socially constructed as a particular type of state (counterterrorist) within various discourses. This means, instead of arguing whether certain violent acts are terrorist or not, the focus is on when and how the term terrorist is used and, relatedly, when it is *not* used and the implications of this usage for the state's and others' identity formations. The variable usage of the term terrorism and the implications of such usage are centralized in analysis. It goes without saying that the terrorism label can and often is used by other social actors as well (see Chapters 6 and 7, as well as examples provided in Chapter 8).

State/terrorism draws attention to the mutual co-constitution of terrorist and state identities. In this view, the counterterrorist state emerges from processes of representing actions and actors as terrorist. Here, the silences which are pervasive in research regarding states and terrorism, as identified above, are made visible such that the focus is on studying how the traditional narrative of (good) states counter (evil) terrorists emerged and became normalized. The research focus is then on the processes of labeling that produces counterterrorist states and dangerous terrorists. At the same time, other spaces wherein the state operates and where terrorist meanings become normalized can also be studied. State/terrorism concentrates attention not just on the politics of representation but on the practices of represent*ing*.

Much of the current discourse-analytical research on counterterrorism has studied the USA in the post-9/11 era. For example, by comparing how terrorists are described in the post-9/11 era with a US action from the past, John Collins draws attention to the inconsistent usage of "terrorism" and to the different ways in which violence is interpreted (2002: 156). He quotes a paragraph that decries terrorist actions and then reveals it is from an Edward Said article written after the US bombing of Libya in 1986, rather than from the post-9/11 period. He clarifies,

> What we think we "know" about terrorism is not an objective reality; on the contrary, the very idea of terrorism is the product of specific efforts by specific people to define certain examples of political violence (typically violence committed by those who are opposed to U.S. policies in the world) as illegitimate.
>
> (2002: 157–158)

Collins's data is a series of speeches and texts as he concludes that a lack of definition of terrorism is part of how the USA (and its allies) avoid being labeled terrorist while applying the label to others (2002: 166–169). Collins thus questions the commonsensical understanding of (counter)terrorism by examining other times and spaces where the term was (or was not) used. Collins utilized a genealogical method to study counterterrorism. The next section will briefly outline the usefulness of a genealogical research project and provide some examples.

Box 9.1 Foucauldian concepts and their use in studying terrorism

The following section refers to some common Foucauldian concepts and illustrates ways in which researchers using Foucauldian discourse analysis may be able to use them in their own work. This is not an exhaustive list of concepts and the examples provided are brief but they will hopefully serve as a starting point for further research.

For a list of "key concepts," please see http://www.michel-foucault.com/concepts/index.html. A useful book is: Taylor, D. (ed.) (2011), *Michel Foucault: Key Concepts*, Durham: Acumen.

Concepts

Archaeology: An archaeology of terrorism (knowledge) would examine systems of thought (and modes of being) in which particular "terrorist" identities (e.g. "radical Islam" or "Irish" or "Palestinian") emerged. What counts as (terrorism) knowledge is thus based on a system of rules and norms – which can be outlined through analyzing texts, visuals, talks, etc.

Biopolitics: This refers to Foucault's understanding of power which circulates through institutions (broadly defined) and produces a certain body (or life). In other words, biopolitics refers to the operations and techniques of biopower and, in Foucault's works, is often used to refer to various techniques and modes by which states relate to their populations. Foucault focused on how "processes of life" were modified, managed and reproduced within particular forms of power. For terrorism scholarship, a focus on biopolitics could draw attention to how life and ways of understanding it become the referent points for terrorism studies (as a discipline) and for counterterrorism strategies (as something to be controlled and managed).

In security studies, there have been numerous theorizations and applications of biopolitics, some of which are listed below:

Resources on biopolitics and security

Campbell, D. (2005), "The biopolitics of security: oil, empire, and the sports utility vehicle," *American Quarterly*, 57(3) (September): 943–972.

Debrix, F. and Barder, A. (2011), *Beyond Biopolitics: Theory, Violence and Horror in World Politics*, Routledge.

Dillon, M. and Lobo-Guerrero, L. (2008), "Biopolitics of security in the 21st century," http://www.biopolitica.cl/docs/Lobo_Biopolitics_of_Security_21stCentury.pdf.

Dillon, M. and Reid, J. (2001), "Global liberal governance: biopolitics, security and war," *Millennium*, 30(1) (January): 41–66.

Rai, A. S, (2005), "The promise of monsters: terrorism, monstrosity, and biopolitics," *International Studies in Philosophy*, 37(2): 81–92.

Reid, J. (2009), *The Biopolitics of the War on Terror: Life Struggles, Liberal Modernity and the Defence of Logistical Societies*, Manchester University Press.

Biopower: A new form of power conceptualized by Foucault, biopower refers to how a network of power relations (e.g. a system of state surveillance and monitoring), helps produce particular type of bodies ("docile bodies"). It refers to how power operates in and through networks rather than in a top-down fashion. Biopower operates to both discipline and produce specific bodies (subjects).

For more on biopower and terrorism

Dauphinee, E. and Master, C. (Eds.) (2006), *The Logics of Biopower and the War on Terror: Living, Dying, Surviving*, Basingstoke: Palgrave Macmillan.

Duffield, M. (2004), "Carry on killing: global governance, humanitarianism and terror," Danish Institute for International Studies. Working Paper (December), http://www.diis.dk/sw8141.asp.

Rai, A. (with Puar, J.) (2002), "Terrorist, monster, fag: the war on terrorism and the production of docile patriots," *Social Text*, 22(3) (Fall): 117–148.

Rai, A. (2004), "Of monsters: biopower, terrorism and excess in genealogies of monstrosity," *Cultural Studies*, 18(4): 538–570.

See also the list on biopolitics.

Body: This can refer to an individual body or a social body (population, group, the state, global organization) and refers mostly to the influence of biopower upon the body. In terrorism studies, research can be conducted on the body of the condemned (e.g. detainees in Guantánamo, people arrested under counter-terrorism legislation in different states, etc) as well as on the production of "docile bodies" (e.g. people who do not question policies and practices of the state and other counterterrorism entities; people who report and are suspicious of "Islamists," etc.). Related research could be on militarized bodies, examining how post-9/11 states around the world have become increasingly militarized and how such militarization is becoming normalized as a way of dealing with terrorists. A focus on the body in research also draws attention to how surveillance and monitoring techniques, often but not always of the state and its institutions, proliferate and manage populations.

Discipline: This is related to bodies and spatial divisions/categorizations. In Foucault's own words: "Discipline is an art of rank, a technique for the transformation of arrangements. It individualizes bodies by a location that does not give them a fixed position, but distributes them and circulates them in a network of relations"(1995: 146) … "Discipline is no longer simply an art of distributing bodies, of extracting time from them and accumulating it, but of composing forces in order to obtain an efficient machine." (1995: 164). Discipline, as an analytical tool, draws attention to how bodies are surveilled, managed, controlled and produced as specific (e.g. "terrorist" or "counterterrorist") bodies.

Discursive formation and discursive practice: While discursive formation is "roughly similar to a scientific discipline" (www.michel-foucault.com), discursive practice draws attention to the norms and rules wherein some meanings make sense while others seem nonsensical. As such, these concepts are closely interrelated. For example, "Terrorism studies" could be considered a discursive formation. On a related note, the discourse of "Islamist groups" draws attention to how Islam is now divided into normal or "moderate" Islam and abnormal or "radical" "Islamist" bodies. Thus, talking about moderate Islamists does not make sense.

Charles Antaki provides another example which focuses on texts (described below). A similar example can be drawn out for visual or audio data.

Antaki's example:

> Discourse analysts (of whatever kind) look for how things are constituted by what they call "discursive practices." If you set out on an investigation into a certain social phenomenon, you will find an identifiable set of things that go together. …
>
> e.g. particular words, phrases, terms of reference, metaphors, rhetorical styles, systematizations of knowledge (e.g. rule books, catechisms, manuals, style guides) … which, together, construct that pheonomenon as a certain kind of social object (e.g. "homosexuality," "Science" "Muslims" etcetera).
>
> In each of those cases, the social object is being constructed by the discourse's *choice of description,* and the *associations* it implicitly makes.
>
> e.g. the choice between:
>
> Muslim vs Islamic
>
> fundamentalist vs devout

and the association between "Muslim" and ... terrorism vs insurgency vs freedom vs. ... ?

Whichever choice you make, and whatever associations you imply, you will help to construct (or "constitute') a certain social object. For DA (in common with many theories of language in general) the choice of one description over another, and the association of one description with another, are significant. The categories of the world are not ready-made, nor is any use of them neutral. (Antaki 2007)

An overview of "discursive practices" and its use in anthropology is provided here: http://www.anthropology.hawaii.edu/programs/Specializations/Discursive%20Practice/index.html.

Dispositif: For a short definition and reference to Foucault's own use of the term, see: http://foucaultblog.wordpress.com/2007/04/01/what-is-the-dispositif/

Dispositif, as an analytical concept, could be applied to study the myriad forms and institutions which proliferate in the labeling, categorization and control of "terrorists" and, relatedly, non-terrorists. First, discourses (e.g. official, popular), institutions (government departments, "fusion centers" in the USA, think tanks, private security organizations), architectures (spaces which are under higher surveillance as well as spaces which are now militarized, e.g. public transport stations, restrooms, roadways), laws (PATRIOT Act but also less obvious examples such as Greyhound USA asking for ID and AMTRAK employing sniffer dogs), etc. all form part of the data that can be analyzed in order to depict the "elements of the dispositif (apparatus)."

Second, by outlining the "elements of the dispositif," the researcher can note connections amongst these seemingly diverse factors and draw attention to how a particular discourse (e.g. official terrorism discourse) emanates from certain institutions (e.g. the Department of Defense in the US) but also forms justification for other practices (e.g. the "if you see something, say something" posters visible at some Metro stations in Washington, DC, in November 2011). Discourses are thus embedded and circulated within seemingly non-security spatial areas (e.g. metro stations in Washington, DC). Finally, "dispositif has a dominant strategic function" in this example, which is that of counterterrorism. This, of course, relates to who (or what) is considered "terrorist" and the subsequent surveillance, monitoring and control of specific groups of people as well as ways of establishing and maintaining these practices.

Event: This is an analytical concept that delineates and limits the period of research. For example, the choice to study the Moro Islamic Liberation Front (MILF) from 1980 to 2011 or examine the 10-year memorialization of "9/11" is one that the researcher herself makes. For Foucault, "every human experience, activity, idea and central form can be analyzed as an event or as a series of events." Events-based analysis thus questions "metaphysical essences in history." (www.michel-foucault.com).

Gaze: Draws attention to the actor doing the gazing and thus links the gazed (the object that is being "known") and the gazer. For example, feminist analysis discusses how the world is ordered according to the (often heterosexual) male gaze (see Chapter 5). A researcher could study how terrorism scholarship generally presents women as needing to be rescued (if they are present at all) or outline how the male gaze operates to make invisible and silence women, children, LGBT people's views during discussions on terrorism. Here, media discourses would be a good source for analysis.

Genealogy: See Box 9.2 and Box 9.3.

Governmentality: Foucault's early work discussed governmentality in the context of Europe and the rise of the sovereign state as a political order (www. michel-foucault.com). Later, he expanded his definition so that governmentality described how individuals and populations were governed by particular techniques at all levels. For terrorism, Bigo and Tsoulakis' edited volume examines some of the ways in which governmentality can be used as a concept to study the formation of the terrorist threat and its related effect on the social body of the liberal state.

Resources on governmentality

Burchell, G., Gordon, C., Miller, P. (Eds.) (1991), *The Foucault Effect: Studies in Governmentality*, Chicago: University of Chicago Press.

On governmentality and the war on terror: http://www.cas.sc.edu/socy/faculty/ deflem/zgovernterror.html.

Listserv on governmentality (which includes more sources on the topic): http:// edtheory.ning.com/group/governmentality.

Heterotopia: This concept draws attention to the spatial aspects of Foucault's thought and refers to areas that are sites which are "something like counter-sites" which exist alongside and within "real sites." These are heterotopia. Analyzing practices of domination and resistance within prisons (e.g. Abu Ghraib) or studying surveillance methods in a sports stadium (e.g. during the Olympics or the soccer World Cup) are potential research agendas utilizing heterotopia.

Foucault's own views are outlined in "Of other spaces (1967), Heterotopias" http://foucault.info/documents/heteroTopia/foucault.heteroTopia.en.html.

History of the present: A genealogy is a "history of the present." See Genealogy.

Ideology: Foucault is not in favor of ideology. He sees it as masking what is supposed to be "the truth," with the assumption then that researchers can unmask the truth by removing or being aware of ideology. Foucault critiques this notion of the truth, especially one that is universally understood through history and across cultures. Thus, Foucault did not find ideology a particular useful analytical tool especially as his own work collapsed the idealism/materialism duality and did not accept there was a universal truth.

Interpretation: Much if not all of Foucault's work was based on interpreting historical social practices.

Panopticon: For one definition of the panopticon, see: http://foucaultblog. wordpress.com/2007/04/08/what-is-the-panopticon/.

For Foucault, the Panopticon served as a way to describe how power operates in society. For terrorism, research on the state, prisons, government buildings/ departments, and even villages and towns can utilize the concept of the panopticon to note how biopower operates and "docile bodies" are produced.

Power/knowledge: A concept that draws attention to how power and knowledge co-constitute each other and notes this is a self-perpetuating relation. One cannot have knowledge without relations of power which include rules and norms for what counts as "knowledge" in the first place. For example, the definition of particular groups as "terrorist" means the related production of a (counterterrorist) state.

Foucault explained the relationship as follows:

> Each society has its regime of truth, its "general politics" of truth; that is, the types of discourse which it accepts and makes function as true; the mechanisms and instances which enable one to distinguish true and false statements, the means by which each is sanctioned; the techniques and procedures accorded value in the acquisition of truth; the status of those who charged with saying what counts as true.   (1980: 131)

Investigating this "regime of truth" regarding terrorism in different times and cultures could be a feature of research.

The state: The state is an institution and is the terminal form of power relations, for Foucault. He adds that the state is a practice not a thing. As such, a Foucauldian discourse analytical project can seek to explicate this "practice" of the state in different sites.

For more on Foucault's views on the state, see: *History of Sexuality, Volume 1* and *Security, Territory, Population.*

Subject and subject positioning: For Foucault, there are no universal subjects which move linearly through history. Instead, subjects are produced within particular discourses. The subject is produced within particular discourses (e.g. the Islamist terrorist subject within the discourse of global Jihadi terrorism; the "teen mom" within US popular television discourse, etc.). Instead of talking about "the subject," it would make more sense to talk about "subject positioning." Subject positioning implies that individuals/states/other collectives have choices within which they act. These choices are constrained by particular discursive practices but they are also a source of power (and resistance). As such, "subject positioning" refers back to Foucault's notion of power as relational and his suspicion of the use of "ideology" as an analytical tool.

One view distinguishing subject positions and subjectivities is Epstein, C. (2008), *The Power of Words in International Relations: Birth of an Anti-Whaling Discourse*, Cambridge, MA: MIT Press.

Davies, B. and Harré, R. (1990) "Positioning: the discursive production of selves," http://www.massey.ac.nz/~alock/position/position.htm discuss "selves" and "positioning" from a Foucauldian standpoint.

A Genealogy of the Counterterrorist State

Defining a Genealogical Project

A genealogy is a historical analysis whose goal, in Foucault's words, is not to show us the essential beginning, the undisputed origin of things but the chaos and "disparity" of practices from which particular identities are produced (1980: 79). Therefore, a genealogy or "the search for descent" is "not the erecting of foundations: on the contrary, it disturbs what was previously considered immobile; it fragments what was thought unified; it shows the heterogeneity of what was imagined consistent with itself" (Foucault 1980: 82). In this sense, studying discourses of counterterrorism help understand strategies that work to produce authoritative and commonsensical public accounts of states' actions in relation to terrorist groups. It also points out how there have been alternative, dissenting voices *within* and *alongside* official discourses. Foucault writes, "the purpose of history, guided by genealogy, is not to discover the roots of our identity, but to commit itself to its dissipation" (1980: 95). It is this challenge that a genealogical analysis of counterterrorism could undertake – not to examine history to try to discover "best practices" for states against terrorists, but to see how such practices, whether attacking terrorists or talking to them, were made possible.

What is considered common sense or normal? How did it become that way? These are some of the questions a genealogical method draws attention to (see Box 9.2). As an example, discussing the "war on terror," Dauphinee and Masters write:

> The war on terror animates particular forms of political violence, while simultaneously obscuring the historical contexts in which these violences have emerged. Ascribing the violence of our current political situation to the events of September 11 and their aftermath erases the fact that many of these practices are not new ... The war on terror levels an obvious gaze at the places we expect to find it: in the narrow field of vision associated with "what counts" as "international relations" – in states and the administration of states and in the battlefields of war (physical, cyber, informational). But the war on terror also produces violences in spaces where our gaze *is not* – where our disciplinary vision is murkier. To recognize this is to tell different stories and to tell stories differently.
>
> (2006: vii)

Box 9.2 A history of the present: British counterterrorism and the 1984 Brighton bombing

The British state's counterterrorism discourses and the shift in relations between the state and citizens ("terrorists" and non-"terrorists") indicate how practices that are commonsensical in the post-9/11 era were not seen as normal in the past, even after a violent "terrorist" act. An analysis of British counterterrorism discourses during and after the Brighton bombing would be useful as part of a genealogy of counterterrorism. The Brighton bombing refers to the IRA bombing of the hotel where the annual Conservative Party Conference was being held. In terms of the number of people who died during the Northern Ireland conflict, there were other incidents which were deadlier. In terms of the publicity received by the event and it being the first (and only) time the entire British ruling party had been targeted, Brighton is a suitable site to study "state" and "terrorist" relations in Britain. On the one hand, official accounts represented the Brighton bombing as an exceptional act of violence against the British state and its citizens. This meant there was a *reinscribing* of the democratic, freedom-defending anti-terrorist identity of the British state, an identity which had been questioned during the IRA hunger strikes and by other incidents including ongoing protests by miners over pit closures. This counterterrorist identity became reproduced in media and subsequent government accounts and was followed by more stringent anti-terrorist legislation.

However, these were not the only responses after the Brighton bombing. Instead, there were also concerns over increased anti-terrorist measures and there was a spirited debate about the meaning of security in official discussions about the event. The need for politicians to be publicly accessible to the public was something official accounts repeatedly mentioned. This concern was expressed, among others, by the Deputy Prime Minister Viscount Whitelaw, "I have already made known my own view that total, impregnable security is not compatible with the free society we enjoy. We must continue to search for improvements in security arrangements but without calling into question the entire basis upon which public life in this country is conducted" (1984).

In view of the counterterrorism measures we experience today in 2011, this call for the public to have easy access to politicians seems unusual and even unthinkable. It is also important to keep in mind that the Grand Hotel, where the conference was being held, had easy public access during the conference. A report in *The Times* mentioned, "Journalists and delegates said that from late evening onwards they were able to come and go through the doors of the Grand Hotel ... without showing their passes. Photographers' bags were not being checked" (Staff Reporters 1984: 1–2).

A genealogical research design is thus useful in noting how counterterrorism strategies were not the only option and how they were not even the most common option at different times. It is useful in reminding us how often possibilities which were deemed unthinkable later were commonplace during specific historical periods. This brief analysis of the Brighton bombing indicates some of the benefits of doing a genealogy: first, it provides indication that alternative meanings – for example, that "total security" is never possible in a free society – were present in addition to the outcomes that became normalized (increased anti-terrorist measures by the British state). Second, it points out that practices we take for granted today (heavy security during governmental meetings) were not the case in the past, as the relatively open access to the Grand Hotel indicated.

This task – "to tell different stories and to tell stories differently" – is a genealogical undertaking. What is emphasized when legitimating counterterrorism? What counts as "important"? Analyzing the usage of terrorism also leads to noting connections made between seemingly disparate contexts, as Dixit's work on Nepal and Northern Ireland indicates. In Nepal, the state drew upon a globally available language of "war on terror" and "terrorism" in the post-9/11 context. However, the language of counterterrorism in Nepal also drew upon historical practices, such as the British experience in Northern Ireland, as well as localized meanings of Nepal as a "Zone of Peace" and the birthplace of the (peaceful) Buddha. In this formulation, Maoist "terrorist" violence could be presented as abhorrent and abnormal to the social body. As such, there were connections made across space and time as the term "terrorist" was used to label people within the state's political boundaries, thus creating spaces of exclusion within the state. At the same time, these groups' actions were linked with a global terrorist threat (in the case of Nepal) and long-term grievances against a democratic state (in the case of the UK).

On the whole, a genealogical project examines struggles or encounters from which particular identities and policies are produced. This means it combines a broader sweep of how identities shift through time with particular emphasis on specific encounters. The researcher can study state and terrorist encounters at specific sites or events (see Figure 9.1). For example, in *Terror, Culture, Politics: Rethinking 9/11*, Sherman and

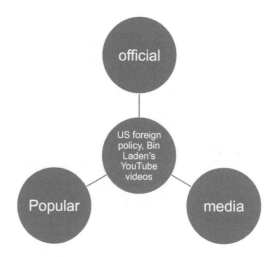

Figure 9.1 Different discourses, one issue

Nardin have collected essays that study different social constructions of 9/11 and different spaces in which the memorialization of it occurs. It is not just official discourses which are analyzed. How September 11, 2001, has been "imagined" in popular culture – whether in photographs, sculpture, comic books, maps, and architecture – form the basis of the chapters here. Authors share "a common spirit of critique" (Sherman and Nardin 2006: 2) as they examine spaces and forms which are normally invisible in the dominant representations and memorializations of 9/11.

In another example, analyzing a source that is often "invisible" in IR – comic books – Henry Jenkins notes "themes of jingoism, xenophobia and warmongering" in mainstream comics published after 9/11. However, Jenkins also analyzes alternative-press comics where "both characters and plot lines challenge readers to think carefully about reflexive violence and the inclination to blame foreigners for insecurity" (2006: 8). Here, a general overview of US national identity is combined with a specific examination of post-9/11 meanings on dangers and threats to indicate parallels with official representations about "9/11" but also to indicate sites and practices of resistance.

Genealogy and Meanings

Genealogy points toward alternative meanings. Genealogical analysis thus draws attention to *silences* in how terrorism is commonly understood. For example, normalizing counter-terrorism as a state's goal means that states' actions cannot be considered terrorism. At the same time, assuming a state is normally (and automatically) against terrorism ignores that actions and actors need to be interpreted as terrorist prior to formulating and legitimating "anti-terrorism" policies. Kyle Grayson reminds us of this as he indicates the lack of discussion of US casualties in the "war on terror," the caution against showing body bags and the lack of discussion of civilian deaths are not just strategies that "deflect responsibility for the consequences of the U.S. administration's actions" but also a means by which to focus memory on the desire for vengeance for 9/11 (2006: 101–102). Representations create and communicate meanings.

Alternative meanings can be noted through a strategy of *decentering*. This focuses attention on processes of displacement as that which is considered central – e.g., conventional

TS, the state in terrorism scholarship, masculinized ways of looking at the world – are shifted from their central position. One way of *decentering* is through studying sites where terrorism is not usually found as well as drawing out the *intertextual* meanings between official and other discourses. Intertextuality refers to how similar meanings emerge and draw from different discourses. In Martin and Steuter's *Pop Culture Goes to War* (2006), links between popular culture in the form of films and television shows and the legitimation of counterterrorism are explored. The authors argue the "militarism" of US foreign policy is linked to popular culture, which serves to legitimate US militarism. At the same time, however, they indicate how an alternative discourse – that of resistance to militarism – can also be noted in some pop cultural sites (e.g., *The Daily Show*). Here, as in Jenkins' study, the counterterrorist state is both reproduced and resisted in the sites of various popular cultural artifacts. Hunt and Rygiel's edited volume *(En)gendering the War on Terror* (2006) provides another standpoint – that of gender – from which to study counterterrorism. Stuart Elden's *Terror and Territory* (2009) begins with an excerpt of a speech on terrorism by a US president. The quote, which sounds very similar to post-9/11 speeches, is actually from US President Clinton after the US Embassy bombings in Kenya and Tanzania in 1998.[2] Part of Elden's goal here, similar to Collins' described earlier, is to decenter commonsensical understandings of terrorism and terrorist and of the "war on terror." Utilizing a spatial perspective, Elden proceeds to investigate connections between territory, the state, and terror(ism) and draws the reader's notice to previous US practices in relation to those labeled terrorist. This serves to remind his reader that "counterterrorism practices" are not commonsensical and nor are they unchanging over time.

In a similar vein, Jeffory Clymer in *America's Culture of Terrorism,* examines literature from the late nineteenth and early twentieth centuries and points out, "if during the last decade the imagined figure of the terrorist in America was always, correctly or incorrectly, a religious zealot of Middle Eastern descent, in the 1880s the terrorist was, equally inevitably, identified as an anarchist from Germany, Russia, or Bohemia" (2003: 11). This draws upon a genealogical understanding that there is no unitary, universal subject moving through history but that norms and practices of who or what is terrorist have changed over time. Clymer's data is popular discourses, and his analysis examines the terrorist subject produced therein.

But, why else do a genealogy? The simplest answer is that a genealogical project draws attention to power relations that produce particular subjects, objects, and the practices that link them. For example, "the British state" which negotiated with Sinn Féin, the political wing of the terrorist IRA, was produced within official security discourses that helped legitimate the shift in identity of the British state. This shift was from a state which had previously claimed it would never negotiate with terrorists to a state which entered into negotiation with Sinn Féin, despite continued use of violence by the IRA. An analysis of statements made by British officials after the 1996 Docklands bombings – which occurred in the middle of the British–IRA peace talks – indicates how the conventional taboo against talking to terrorists was broken. Table 9.3 outlines self (British state) and others (IRA/the people) identities during the Docklands bombing.[3]

Genealogical Data

The data for a genealogy is the same as that for discourse analysis in general: language as it is used in the form of talks, texts, songs, and visuals. As we wrote in Chapter 8, it is the use of language (broadly defined as talks, texts, and visuals) that is central to analysis. Hodges explains this as: "Only through language are such events [like those of September 11, 2001] turned into a full account of that experience. Through language, we name protagonists, ascribe motivations, and provide explanations" (2011: 3–4). As we have outlined, official discourses of counterterrorism can form the topic of research; popular discourses as seen in media and film can be analyzed to note how the state's identity is socially constructed in different sites. Interviews can be conducted for understanding popular meaning-making. For example, if conducting a genealogy of TS, a researcher could study texts that list terrorist incidents from the past (e.g., Hoffman, Combs, Laqueur). Returning to Hoffman, a genealogist would argue Hoffman's list of a series of suicide bombings or of twentieth-century terrorist events are not useful to show us terrorist trends or even counterterrorism practices. It is also a contradiction to claim, as Hoffman does, that terrorism has drastically changed in the recent past while, at the same time, drawing terrorist motivations from earlier terrorist incidents (Hoffman 2006: ix). Instead, for a genealogical analysis, these lists of terrorist incidents and actors are interesting to note what links them together (terrorists are non-state actors; usually liberal, democratic states are counterterrorist while other states are producers and sponsors of terror, etc.) and what that says about how we, as researchers, define and understand terrorism and counterterrorism.

In another example, utilizing textual data, Aditi Bhatia studied official US counterterrorism discourse from 2001 to 2004. She discusses what she calls the discursive strategy of "evilification" wherein groups and individuals are categorized as "evil" terrorists and linked with tropes which signify danger and inhumanity (2009: 282). Further strategies are the *criminalization* of particular social actors and linking them with tyranny and barbarism. As such, it is similar to R. Jackson's research on US counterterrorism. The link between representations of terrorism and the construction of the state's counterterrorist identity is also the focus of Lauderdale and Oliverio whose work "stresses the relevance of examining the role of the state in the construction of terrorism and terrorists" (2005: 2). As is clarified by the term "construction" here, Lauderdale and Oliverio are not talking about the state's use of a particular type of violence (however defined) but about the effects of its labeling practices in defining certain actors and actions as "terrorist". Within this framework, their book contains essays on the link between representations and what counts as "moral" (Ben-Yehuda), processes of remembering and forgetting (Tota), and on the inconsistent labeling of acts of violence as terrorism (Lauderdale and Oliverio). The common thread in all the essays is how terrorism is represented and its "symbiotic relationship" (2007: 8) to the state.

Two of the tasks of a genealogical project: how the label "terrorism" is used to draw boundaries between self and others and how a diverse range of practices are linked as "anti-terrorist" are exemplified in the essays in Stephens and Vaughan-Williams' *Terrorism and the Politics of Response* (2009). Studying the London train bombings of July 2005, Bulley examines "one way in which the events were discursively constructed: the way the terrorism was made 'foreign'" (2009: 81) even though the perpetrators of the act were British. Molloy conducts a similar analysis but looks at the arrest of the "Toronto 17" in Canada. She argues that representations of these men – all Canadian – worked to constitute them as "foreign" and "a challenge" to Canada's multiculturalism (2009: 112–113). Vaughan-Williams examines an event that occurred some time after the bombings – the shooting of Jean Charles de Menezes by British anti-terrorist officials. He questions the conventional discourse of it being a "mistake" and seeks to "examine how the dominant discourse of the 'mistake' has legitimized and/or obscured particular political practices in the aftermath of the shooting of Menezes" (2009: 97). Statements by public officials and media reports are the data for these analyses.

Some Research Concerns for Analyzing (Counter)Terrorism Discourses

Theorizing Resistance

Discussions of resistance within a discourse-analytical project can take two forms: First, in outlining the self–others identities constructed within various discourses, the researcher is drawing attention to the possibility of alternative meanings and identities that are present. This also focuses on subjugated knowledges and sites which are often deemed outside of "normal" (conventional) TS. For example, claiming that a counter-terrorist state is not self-evident in its meaning is itself a form of resistance. Second, and this is something that critical-discourse analysts assume: Resistance can take the form of identifying particular ideologies that underlie discourses or calling for eman-cipation. These two notions of resistance operate under different understandings of "discourse" (as outlined in Chapter 8) and from different ontological standpoints.

A poststructuralist discourse-analytical project about the state could outline mechanisms of governmentality and examine the manifestations of biopower as exhibited by the state's counterterrorist practices (Bonditti 2004; Neal 2006; Reid 2006). Resistance, here, does not arise from unearthing ideology or calling for emanci-pation but noting the mechanisms of power which proliferate in different sites as well as "cracks" in the dominant discourse itself. Jutta Weldes et al. clarified this mode of resistance as, "any representation can potentially be contested and so must actively be reproduced ... In addition, discourses are themselves not perfectly coherent but always entail internal contradictions and lacunae." (1999: 16).

The Role of the Researcher

It is important to constantly remind oneself that discourses are not natural objects waiting to be discovered but are analytical constructs that the researcher herself iden-tifies through empirical research. As Helle Malmvig writes in *State Sovereignty and Intervention:*

> It is not the objects of observation in themselves, which tell us how they are [wish] to be studied, but the analyst who makes the objects appear, who constructs the objects of investigation. Therefore, discourses *do not exist* prior to our investiga-tions of them, as it sometimes unfortunately seems to be implied. It is the analyst who constructs them through the analytical choices and definitions made in order to identify them in the first place.

> (2006: 24)

Terrorism scholars such as Schmid and Jongman have cautioned that "the [terrorism] researcher should not confuse his roles. His role is not to 'fight' the terrorist fire; rather than a 'firefighter,' he should be a student of combustion" (2006: 179).

Motivations and Mental States

Discourse analysis notes how the language of interests and motivations plays into legitimating and delegitimating particular identities and policies. In this view, language use does not reflect mental states but constitutes them. Potter and Wetherell spell this out:

> Discourse analysis takes a rather different position when faced with this problem of the relationship between utterances and mental states. We argue that the researcher should bracket off the whole issue of the quality of accounts as accurate or inaccurate descriptions of mental states. The problem is being constructed at entirely the wrong level. Our focus is exclusively on discourse itself: *how it is constructed, its functions, and the consequences which arise from different discursive organization.*
>
> (1987: 178)

Taking this seriously, descriptions of mental states – the irrational terrorist; the calm and rational soldier who only fires "aimed shots" at protesters – then become discursive social practices open to investigation instead of reflective of these actors' mental states or motivations. Discourse analysis moves away from asking what terrorism really is to asking what the *use* of the language of terrorism does. In doing so, it links language and practices, discourse and identity formation.

Moving Research Beyond the Idealist/Materialist Divide

This way of understanding social life as beyond the idealism/materialism divide was clearly laid out by Ernesto Laclau and Chantal Mouffe:

> Our analysis rejects the distinction between discursive and non-discursive practices. It affirms a) that every object is constituted as an object of discourse, insofar as no object is given outside every discursive condition of emergence; and b) that any distinction between what are usually called the linguistic and behavioural aspects of a social practice, is either an incorrect distinction or ought to find its place as a differentiation within the social production of meaning.
>
> (2001: 107)

Analyzing terrorism as discourse is, therefore, not to deny that terrorism exists but to make a different claim – that the "materiality" of terrorists and terrorism does not make sense until they are represented and communicated as such in and through language and practices. This means that the question of whether, ontologically, terrorism exists is less important than *how* terrorism and terrorists are represented and the practices which are authorized on behalf of and against terrorism. Hansen (2006) explains why the idealism–materialism divide does not make sense in poststructural/Foucauldian discourse analysis.

Conclusion

A genealogy of the counterterrorist state could thus examine different types of state and terrorist relations in TS, as we have briefly outlined here. As R. Jackson writes, "it is crucial to our understanding of the 'war on terrorism' to examine and explain how the discourse of counter-terrorism constructs the practice of counter-terrorism" (2005: 24). In this way, language and practices of terrorism are implicated in the formation of what is considered terrorism and the practices put in place to counter such terrorism.

Genealogy is one way of doing discourse analysis. It draws attention to the fact that how things are was not always the case. It also points towards different spaces where the counterterrorist state identity is reproduced and legitimated. Additionally, a genealogical approach emphasizes there are usually more than one discourse and multiple possible identities for the state present during particular time periods (see Box 9.3). As R. Jackson, Hodges, and others have shown in their research, counterterrorism was not the only option available to the USA after September 11, 2001. Table 9.2 outlines some identities and responsibilities for the state within different discourses. Indeed, it is the strategies of construction – how a counterterrorist state is produced and legitimated within particular discursive frameworks – that a genealogy foregrounds. As such, analyses of counterterrorist discourses can be conducted at different levels – official, popular, academic and media.

Box 9.3 Genealogy

The best way to begin grasping what Foucault's conceptualization of a genealogy is and its relation to historical analysis is by reading his (fairly short) essay "Nietzsche, Genealogy, History" (Foucault 1980). Genealogical analysis assumes there is no one origin to things (and ideas) but a series of accidents and small changes eventually lead to particular meanings and practices being seen as commonplace. For example, a brief survey of some of the definitions of terrorism in the world today indicate that the term is used to refer mainly to non-state actors (see Bruce Hoffman's (2006) definition of terrorism in *Inside Terrorism,* a definition which explicitly excludes states and their actions). But this commonsensical understanding of terrorists as non-state actors cannot be traced to one "origin" since there is no particular time in history when this meaning emerged. Instead, a series of practices including colonial counterinsurgency and suppression of anti-colonial groups, the consolidation of the use of violence by newly-formed states in Europe and elsewhere, the delegitimation of protest movements in the mid-twentieth century as anti-state and communist, etc. all combined to justify states' use of military force while making illegal those who acted against the state. This then had the related effect of linking various other forms of anti-state protests as "terrorist," a practice that then continued.

In order to do a genealogy, the data is similar to historical analysis: texts, visual data and oral data. The majority of genealogies involve texts (archives) as data.

Defining "genealogy"

Foucault (1980: 83) defines genealogy as follows: "Let us give the term *genealogy* to the union of erudite knowledge and local memories which allows us to establish a historical knowledge of struggles and to make use of this knowledge tactically today."

A genealogy of counterterrorism could examine "erudite knowledge," or official discourses about terrorism. At the same time, other data, such as local ways of making sense of violence (e.g. popular understandings of violence as depicted in films, cartoons, comics) could form part of "local memories."

Example of genealogical anlaysis

A genealogy draws attention to the workings of power, so, when doing a genealogy, Foucault's questions are relevant: "What are these various contrivances of power, whose operations extend to such differing levels and sectors of society and are possessed of such manifold ramifications? What are their mechanisms, their effects and their relations?" (Foucault 1980: 88).

Taking up this challenge, a brief example could be to examine the Filipino state's actions regarding terrorism. Examining the shift in the Filipino state's relation to its Muslim citizens would indicate "contrivances of power." For example, Filipino Muslims were traditionally deemed outside the political order of the colonizing Spanish authority. The effects of these practices of exclusion, combined with the distance of the Muslim-majority areas from the center (which made it difficult for the Spanish and, later, other Filipinos from traveling to the South) served to further distance the Muslims from the "imaginary community" of the Filipino state.

Here, the historical practices of the Spanish colonizers and their local allies combined with spatial distancing of the Muslims from the center (Manila) created and maintained relations in which "Muslims" were seen as "other" to the emerging Filipino national identity. This "othering" was further assisted by policies such as mass internal migration in the post-WWII period, religious nationalism (in which Catholicism was linked with the nation-state), and conflict over land as new migrants in the South claimed land which traditionally belonged to Muslims. Thus, the "contrivances of power" are not just present in overt spaces of government policies (which are, mostly, egalitarian and applicable to Muslim and non-Muslim Filipinos) but in different spaces, institutions and levels – historical relations, geography, notions of nationalism linked with Catholicism, etc.

To review Foucault's own work utilizing genealogy, *Discipline and Punish* is the best example. Foucault describes how regimes of punishment in Western societies have changed from a focus on the individual body to a focus on the social body, with a related shift in modes of observation and categorization. Instead of an abnormal individual body that can be excised from the social body (by hanging, for example), we now have categorizations which depict what is "normal" in terms of a social body and classify any changes from this as "abnormal." Continued surveillance and monitoring are necessary to ensure the social body remains "normal." With the example of the panopticon, Foucault proposes that individuals eventually begin to monitor each other and to police their (and others) behaviors. This is summed up in Foucault's words: "Power has its principle not so much in a person as in a certain concerted distribution of bodies, surfaces, lights, gazes; in an arrangement whose internal mechanisms produce the relation in which individuals are caught up" (1995: 202).

A genealogical understanding takes as foundational that there is no universal subject (e.g. that of "the terrorist"). Instead, a series of norms and techniques produce particular identities during different periods.

A genealogy as a history of the present connects how rules, institutions, norms, and subjects developed over time; and outlines how inclusion/exclusion into the social body occurred.

Foucault writes, "I would like to write the history of this prison, with all the political investments of the body that it gathers together in its closed architecture. Why? Simply because I am interested in the past? No, if one means by that writing a history of the past in terms of the present. Yes, if one means writing a history of the present" (1995: 30–31).

There are different ways this "history of the present" can be done in practice. Following on with our Filipino example, an avenue for research could be to examine how the Filipino Muslims have reclaimed and re-used the term "Moro," as in the Moro Islamic Liberation Front (MILF). A related example is the concept of "bangsamoro," where "bangsa" is a Malay word meaning "nation" or "people" and this could be an alternative conceptualization of nationalism and a reworking of "moro." Tickell's (2010) genealogy of "Thuggee" (described in Chapter 5) is an example of a "history of the present."

Table 9.1 Identities for the state within different discourses

Discourse	Responsibility of the state
Human rights	Protect citizens, especially vulnerable groups
Socioeconomic	Promote economic and social growth
Terrorism	Counter "terrorists"

In this chapter, we have used the term state/terrorism to refer to a poststructural discourse-analytical (genealogical) analysis of the state's relationship with terrorism. We also outlined other ways of using discourse analysis to study this relationship. In the next chapter, the use of SNA to study terrorism will be described.

Research Design

Box 9.2 outlines a genealogical project. Table 9.2 indicates how other scholars have analyzed terrorism and counterterrorism discourses at different levels of analysis. Table 9.3 outlines one way of doing discourse analysis wherein common terms used to refer to "self" (the British state in this example) and "others" (the IRA/Sinn Féin) are presented and the identities produced outlined.

In short, these are some of the characteristics of a discourse analysis of the counterterrorist state:

- *Research question*: How did the terrorist identity of X group emerge?
- *Data*: Documents (textual, visual, oral) about the terrorist and other identities of X.
- *Analysis*: Outline the sociopolitical implications of labeling X as terrorist. What other possible identities were present and sidelined? Who did the labeling? How

were the labelers themselves representing their own actions? What were the identities and policies ultimately legitimated? Were there challenges to the dominant meanings and identities? By whom? How?

Table 9.2 Examples of some discourse analytical research on terrorism and counterterrorism

Author	Research question	Source/data	Level(s) of analysis
R. Jackson (2005)	How has the language of terrorism been used to justify the "war on terror"?	Speeches, government documents, legislation	Official
Hodges (2011)	How was the "war on terror" (re)contextualized?	Presidential speeches, media reports and focus group interviews with 26 "politically active college students" (p. 11)	Official (supplemented by media and popular)
Debrix (2008)	How did representations of the "war on terror" construct reality?	Advertisements, personal narratives of military officials, academic studies, tabloid media	Popular (tabloid); also "intellectuals"
R. Jackson (2007a)	How does the language of "Islamic terrorism" affect state–society relations?	"> 300 written and spoken English-language Western texts" from 2001–2006, official speeches, think tank texts, academic books (p. 396)	Elite (official, think tanks, academic)
Martin and Steuter (2010)	How do popular culture texts legitimate US militarism?	Films, TV shows, songs, and also scholarly books	Popular (academic as supplementary)
Clymer (2003)	How is "terrorism" made sense of in the US? Goal: "to uncover a genealogy of modern terrorism" (p. 5)	Literary and cultural texts from 1890s–1910s	Popular (media as supplementary)
Erjavec and Volcic (2007)	How did Serbian intellectuals justify violent actions against Muslims?	Data from qualitative interviews with Serbian intellectuals, aged 23–40	Popular
Hunt and Rygiel (2006)	How is war, specifically the "war on terror" engendered?	"Official war stories" from US/Western governments, policy documents, speeches, mainstream media coverage	Official (media as supplementary)
Qian (2010)	How has the "war on terror" been represented?	*The Sun* (UK) and the *People's Daily* (China)	Popular (media)
Blain (2007)	How does the discourse on terrorism legitimate the politics of a liberal-democratic state?	240 speeches by US President Bush (2001–2005) (p. 49)	Official

Table 9.3 Self/others representations in British security discourses immediately following the 1996 Docklands bombing

The state	IRA and Sinn Fein
Will move peace process forward	– no doubt "the evil act" was the work of the IRA
– protection of the public is our first priority	– IRA callously sacrificed innocent lives
– government sought to make "appropriate and proportionate" response	– "No shred of an excuse" for this return to violence by the IRA
– reduced security measures during ceasefire	– IRA never said it was a permanent ceasefire
– moved the peace process forward	– "the IRA peace was not a true peace"
– "no one took more risks for peace than the government"	– IRA continued to train and plan for terrorist attacks
– SF should decommission to create confidence	– IRA remained ready to resume full-scale terrorism
– remained cautious about the IRA's motives	– IRA continued punishment beatings and killings
– remained strongly committed to a political settlement in NI	– SF must decide if it's democratic or a front for the IRA
– will work for peace with "all the democratic political parties and with the Irish government"	– SF called for all-party talks (but IRA continue to plan for terrorist attacks)
– cannot meet with SF without an end to the violence	– SF misrepresented the Mitchell Report and decommissioning proposal
– in line with Irish government's views	– SF has to return to the ceasefire if it is to participate in future talks
– support popular will, which is for peace	
– peace process has received a setback from "the men of violence"	
– ceasefire led to benefits	
– will not be deterred by terrorism	
– will leave "no stone unturned" in search for peace, both now and in the future	
– people of GB and NI deserve peace	

Notes: Analysis based on official statements, parliamentary discussions and media reports for a period of two weeks after the event. One of the interesting narratives here was the separation of Sinn Féin and the IRA, a separation that was not as evident in previous official British narratives on counterterrorism. GB = Great Britain; NI = Northern Ireland; SF = Sinn Féin.

Questions to consider

- What are some features of a genealogical project? How did Michel Foucault define a genealogy? What are some key features and goals?
- Choose a series of government documents or media sources and outline some of the ways in which the state and others (terrorist) have been socially constructed within these. Take Figure 9.1 and Table 9.3 as guidelines. What identities and meanings of the state and terrorism are produced? What are some meanings that have been sidelined?
- What are three ways in which the state–terrorist relationship has been conceptualized in TS? What does a discourse analysis of these modes of relating tell us about the development of TS?
- Can a state be terrorist? Why or why not?
- What are some research concerns when conducting discourse analysis? How will your research address these?

Notes

1 See R. Jackson (2008: fn 14) for a detailed list of scholars who have done research on state terrorism.
2 Part of the speech is, "our battle against terrorism did not begin with the bombing ... nor will it end with today's strike ... we will not yield to this threat. We will meet it, no matter how long it may take" (Elden 2009: xi).
3 Hodges (2011: 23) outlines self (US state) identities under different discourses – terrorism and criminal.

Further Reading

Engle, K. (2009), *Seeing Ghosts: 9/11 and the Visual Imagination*, Kingston, Ontario: McGill-Queen's University Press.
Foucault, M. (1980), *Power/Knowledge: Selected Interviews and Other Writings 1972–1977*, ed. C. Gordon, trans. C. Gordon, L. Marshall, J. Mepham, and K. Soper, New York: Pantheon Books.
Foucault, M. (1984), "Nietzsche, Genealogy, History," in P. Rabinow (Ed.), *The Foucault Reader*, New York, Random House, pp. 76–100.
Foucault, M. (2007), *Security, Territory, Population*, trans. G. Burchell, Basingstoke: Palgrave Macmillan.
Hodges, A. (2011), *The "War on Terror" Narrative: Discourse and Intertextuality in the Construction and Contestation of Sociopolitical Reality*, New York: Oxford University Press.
Vucetic, S. (2011) "Genealogy as a Research Tool in International Relations," *Review of International Studies*, 37 (July): 1295–1312.

Weblinks

For more on Foucault and genealogy, see http://www.english.ugent.be/da/socialtheory#mfoucault.
For a list of philosophical concepts related to Foucault and genealogy, see http://www.philosopher. org.uk/index.htm.
For Foucault and social theory, see http://www.english.ugent.be/da/socialtheory#mfoucault.
For a list of sources on biopolitics/biopower, see http://www.keele.ac.uk/bos/resources/war.htm.
For the biopolitics of Baghdad, see http://web.mac.com/derekgregory/iWeb/Site/The%20biopolitics%20of%20Baghdad.html.
Recently, some scholars have claimed there is a difference between "biopower" and "biopolitics." For more, see http://www.generation-online.org/c/cbiopolitics.htm.

10 Terrorism and Social Network Analysis

Introduction

This chapter contributes to the development of a critical study of terrorism that draws from SNA. In particular, we discuss some of the basic concepts of SNA, the methodology, theoretical tools, and methods of analysis and data-gathering that have been used or could be used to study terrorism from a critical perspective.

Basic Social Network Concepts

SNA offers a distinctive approach to the critical study of terrorism. This section works to draw out that distinctiveness. At the same time, while not aiming to be terminologically exhaustive, we highlight some important concepts used in SNA.

Perhaps the most useful way to illustrate the distinctive methodological underpinnings of SNA is to compare it with other approaches to terrorism. Most studies of terrorism approach the topic from an individualistic, atomistic or dispositional angle. Charles Tilly has offered some relevant criticisms in this regard. He argues that individualistic modes of explanation start by positing the existence of "coherent entities" or terrorists (Tilly 2005b: 19). The focus is then on explaining these individual terrorists' behaviors by referring to internal causal factors, such as motives, emotions, decision logics or ideologies (Tilly 2005b: 19). Jessica Stern (2003) takes precisely this individualist approach. She explains terrorist behavior by focusing on individual emotional, psychological, and motivational causes of action that derive from long-standing and contemporary grievances and traumas (Stern 2003; Tilly 2005b). Martha Crenshaw also takes an individualistic approach. For her, explaining individual terrorists' behaviors is a psychological matter; it could be an emotional drive for vengeance, a particular personality type, or perhaps an attitude that causes certain behaviors (Crenshaw 2011: 43–48). In either case, the terrorist is posited to exist and their behavior is claimed to be caused by factors internal to the individual.

A thoroughly relational CTS, as we show, operates from a distinct methodological perspective that is non-individualist and can offer systematic, empirically rich constitutive and causal explanations.

Relations to Social Sites

In contrast to individualistic approaches, SNA places *relationships* at the center of analysis. Relations, in general terms, are composed of observable informational and material content. The specific kind of relationship can vary widely: from physical and symbolic media, to communications, to instrumental connections, to relations of political and/or religious authority, to kinship, friendship, competition, meaning, and identity (Knoke and Kuklinski 1982: 15–16; Boissevain 1974; White 2008).

The standard individualist view, which we mentioned above, assumes that individuals come first and then they establish relations with other persons or organizations. A relational perspective, however, inverts that claim. It asserts that relations come first and through those exchanges social sites emerge and are defined in context (Jackson and Nexon 1999; Emirbayer 1997; Abbott 1995, 2007). Or, to phrase it a bit differently, relational approaches assume "that actions, not actors, are the primitives of the social process" (Abbott 2007: 7). Through ongoing actions in specific circumstances, actors, sites, or nodes become defined in relation to other social sites. A social site is a "loci in which organized human action occurs" and can include individual people, aspects of individual people, organizations, places (Tilly 2003: xi), concepts, categories, and narrative clauses (Mutzel 2009: 874).

What does this mean for a CTS that draws from a relational SNA? Charles Tilly suggests one possible answer: terrorism can be studied as a relational strategy and process performed by a wide variety of governmental and non-governmental social sites interwoven into a more or less dynamic network of violence, intimidation, and coercion (Tilly 2005b). Another possible answer is that terrorism can be studied as a category of practice (Stump and Dixit 2012; Dixit and Stump 2011; Stump 2009, 2011).

> Terrorism as a practice entails that researchers withhold making claims about what counts as "real" descriptions and characteristics of terrorism and, instead, closely and systematically examine the empirically available practices through which some community of people concretely build up and sustain the danger of terrorism and the various identities and security policies associated with that construction of danger.
>
> (Stump 2011)

A third possible answer to a CTS that draws from SNA would be to study narrative networks. Peter S. Bearman and Katherine Stovel studied the identity narratives generated by actors who became Nazis and maintained that particular sense of self after the demise of the Nazi regime (2000). Along similar lines, it would be possible to study the narrative networks that multiple social sites generated around the process of becoming a terrorist or militant. The aim would be to transform the various elements (e.g., people, places, things, events, ideas, etc.) into nodes connected together by narrative clauses, which can reveal structural similarities among different sites and unique configurations of identity.

In either case, from the perspective of SNA, researchers should not posit the existence of an actor, terrorist or otherwise, prior to analysis. Rather, by making interactions primitive, it becomes possible to account for the relational construction of the social actor in question. That is to say, SNA can account for how some actor becomes a Nazi (Bearman and Stovel 2000), a state and/or person (Jackson and Nexon 1999; Jackson 2006b), an enemy or ally (Jackson 2006a), and, how that particular self in question persists across changing contexts. Indeed, from a relational perspective, explaining change is trivial; the primary goal is to offer a systematic explanation of the formation and stability of some set of sites in a network (Abbott 2007: 8). So, for a CTS that draws from SNA, the goal is to account for the process through which some site becomes and sustains their self as a terrorist actor. This process could include the way, for instance, a state terror network was formed and sustained over time through various political, economic, communicative, and symbolic connections between the USA, Chile, and Argentina (McSherry 2002). Or, it could include an analysis of the processes through which an individual actor comes to meaningfully define themselves, through a variety of observable linguistic and nonlinguistic exchanges, as a terrorist or member of some militant group and how that redefinition of self made new courses of action possible. By interviewing formerly successful traffickers of illegal goods and services who were serving prison sentences, Michael Kenney was able to measure and map out criminal networks operating in Columbia (2009). However, Kenny does not investigate how, through a series of connections, these imprisoned traffickers *became* the kind of actor who traffic in illegal goods and services. The gap in the literature is apparent in the study of criminal networks and networks of terrorism, which creates an excellent avenue for possible research.

Networks

Ongoing relations form specific social sites. The set of "socially relevant nodes connected by one or more relations" is a basic network (Marin and Wellman 2011: 11). Networks should not be seen as static arrangements. Granted, some relations are more durable than other sets of relations. Tilly, for instance, has argued that relations of inequality can often be durable, spanning whole careers, lifetimes, and even organizational histories (1999). However, Tilly makes clear that these ties are not an essential and unchanging feature of some group or individual but ongoing constructions of inequality that take work and can be explained by recurring mechanisms. The point is that social networks are dynamic arrangements that depend on participation and that "participation depends on circumstance" (Fine and Kleinman 1983: 99). In changing circumstances, relational participation may decline, completely evaporate, or persist – how that process occurs in regards to the topic of terrorism is the key point of explanation for a CTS that draws from SNA.

The sites and relations that compose any particular network can range widely in scale: from the "bundle of identities" (White 2008: 3) that compose the individual self, to an individual actor's networks of dyads, triads, and small group clusters that make up personal communities (Chua et al. 2011), to larger regional and global systems of relations among states and other institutions (Kick et al. 2011; Chase-Dunn and Grimes 1995), and global criminal and clandestine networks (Kenney 2009; Kahler 2009). The critical study of terrorism could focus on any of these network scales and would entail the appropriate data gathering methods, which we discuss in more detail later in this chapter. The focused study of the individual terrorist self, for instance,

---

Box 10.1 Components of networks

Relations – informational, material, or symbolic links between sites.

Sites – wide variety of loci in which organized human action occurs.

Network – set of sites connected by ongoing relations.

would probably entail observational and interview data. Studying global and/or regional systems of state terror, for instance, might entail archival research, like McSherry (2002) conducted when she described the development and implementation of Operation Condor throughout the Americas. The point is that a critical study of terrorism that draws from SNA has a wide range of possible networks to research. Figure 10.1 depicts the conceptual components of social networks.

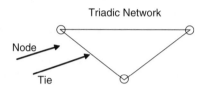

Figure 10.1 Ties and nodes in a network

Measuring Networks and Ties Between Sites

There is a continuing divide among network analysts: structural approaches focus on measuring networks and interactional approaches focus on networks as culturally meaningful arrangements (Mutzel 2009; Fuhse 2009). For a CTS that draws from SNA, both measurement and meaning can be important components of the study. Thus, we suggest a CTS that combines more formal structural analysis of patterns of relations with interpretive analysis of the practices enacted by actors. This enables the researcher to concretely ground their analysis of broader patterns of relations.

Social network analysts measure a number of observable relations between sites. This is not an exhaustive list of possible measurements, but a useful start.

Structural measures

SIZE

The size of a network is, most simply, the number of sites within a network or data set. According to Boissevain, size is one of the most important measures of a network because all of the other structural measures are calculated as a proportion of the actual and possible nodes in a network (1974: 35). So, the size of a network includes the actual nodes used by an actor and the latent nodes not explicitly used by an actor. This means that measuring the size of a network can become immensely complex. To manage the complexity, number of sites, and to more clearly mark out the boundaries of a particular terrorist network, for instance, Koschade limited the size measurement to "actors within the terrorist cell or those involved with terrorist activities in association with the cell [in question]" (2006: 568).

DENSITY

The density of a network is a measure of the connections that do actually exist between sites. Or, put differently, the degree that members of a particular actor's network are "in touch with each other independently" of that actor is density (Boissevain 1974: 37). A denser network of ties is generally seen as more efficient at, for instance, dispersing information (Wasserman and Faust 1994: 101), but it is more vulnerable to disruption, or the removal of one site is more likely to compromise the overall network (Koschade 2006: 568). A less dense network, like the cell of terrorists who carried out the September 11, 2001, attacks in the USA, however, is less efficient and less vulnerable to disruption because sites are less dependent on each other (Krebs 2002). The following equation is a measure of density

$$LD = -g(g - 1)/2$$

where D is density; L is the total number of ties present in the network; and g is the total number of sites in the network (Koschade 2006: 568).

DEGREE

The degree of connection is a measure of the average number of ties that each site has with other sites in the same network. Measuring degree can help qualify the density measure and allow more comparisons between different networks (Koschade 2006: 568). The equation for measuring degree is

$$2Ld = -g$$

where d is degree; L is the total number of ties present in the network; and g is the total number of sites in the network.

CENTRALITY

The measure of centrality is the degree to which a particular site in a network is accessible to other sites in the network. A more central site in a network is, generally speaking, a leader or site of critical importance (Koschade 2006: 568) in the network and has a greater possibility of manipulating other sites, information, or material flowing through the network (Boissevain 1974: 41). The centrality measure is calculated like this:

$$\frac{\text{Sum of shortest distances from every member to every other member}}{\text{Sum of shortest distances from site in question to every other member.}} = -C$$

Transactional measures

CONTENT

What is observably exchanged among actors is an important relational measure. The specific content can range from spoken and written words, to body language, to concrete objects. The specific content is an important measurement to consider because what is exchanged between sites is indicative of the kind and value of connections being generated.

DIRECTIONAL FLOWS

Generally speaking, flows of content between actors will be equal, complementary, or unequal (Boissevain 1974: 33). Symmetrical and complementary transactions of content are indicative of more egalitarian positions among actors, while asymmetrical transactions are indicative of unequal positions among actors (Boissevain 1974: 33). Directional flows are important measurements because they help account for actors' positions in the network.

FREQUENCY AND DURATION

The frequency of interactions among actors "often leads to and is a result of the quality of the relationship" or its strength, but not always (Boissevain 1974: 34). Daily interactions between a militant and store attendant, for instance, are usually indicative of less valuable ties than compared to less frequent (once weekly) interactions among family members or religious connections. Duration of interaction is perhaps a better indicator of the quality of the tie. The shop owner is frequently interacted with for short periods of time; family members and religious connections, however, are seen less frequently but for extended durations of time. Frequency and duration are important indicators of the strength and quality of some tie or set of ties.

We have already indicated that these structural measures have been adopted by conventional TS, especially after the events on September 11, 2011. How do these measurement techniques relate to CTS? A more formal approach to CTS could map out the structure of state terror in the Americas. Building on and formalizing McSherry's (2002) analysis of Operation Condor in the Americas, for instance, the size of the state terror network, how densely the sites were interconnected, the centrality of various sites, what kinds of content were transacted, their direction, and the strength of particular ties could all be measured and mapped out. Similarly, given that there are often observably close relations between agents of state terror and non-state terror (Tilly 2005b), one could explore and measure the network of sites that gave rise to the Mujahideen. Going beyond Sageman's (2008) analysis of friendship and kinship ties between individual militants, a researcher may examine the density and centrality of connections between the Central Intelligence Agency, Israel, Egypt, Pakistan, and various militant groups and individuals, as well as the kinds of content transacted and the strength of those ties over time. One final example of a possible avenue of research in which a more formal network approach could be harnessed for the critical study of terrorism. Policy networks have long been studied by analysts of social networks (Knoke 2011). A researcher, for instance, could study how networks (policy-makers, their various institutions, and media channels) issue and circulate warnings of terrorism that garner sociopolitical benefit.[1] A researcher could longitudinally map out and measure the expanding size and density of the warnings of terrorism network, which sites are most central to this process of issuing warnings, and the frequency of such warnings. A study of this sort could help researchers better understand and describe the flows and distribution of warnings of terrorism and how some sites, especially policy-making networks within and between states, garner measurable sociopolitical benefit from such warnings.

Interpreting Relational Meaning and Identity

At the same time, as we discussed above, since the 1980s and especially the 1990s, meaning and identity have become important components of network analysis. Meaning and identity go well beyond the measurement of specific network structures and transactions. To be clear, not all network studies will use more formal measurement techniques. Some will focus exclusively on how actors draw on particular ties in the process of making sense of changing situations.

Meaning, or the process of sense making, is neither a psychological matter nor an objective matter. Rather, meaning is an intersubjective construction, where ongoing circumstances are comprehended by actors explicitly through words and bodily movements that function "as a springboard to action" (Taylor and Van Every 2000: 40; quoted in Weick et al. 2005: 409). As Herbert Blumer notes, meaning arises through the process of interaction; it is a social product created, sustained, and challenged "through the defining activities of people as they interact" in different contexts (1998: 5). To put it a bit differently, meanings arise when an actor indicates (through linguistic and non-linguistic interactions) in different contexts "what is significant to them," "who we are," "who we are opposed to," "what kind of situation we're in," and "how we should act in this situation." In this way, the "very terms or units involved in a transaction derive their meaning, significance, and identity from the [changing] functional roles they play within that transaction" (Emirbayer 1997: 287). We therefore come to describe a "chair" as a "chair," for instance, through the indications of others (Blumer 1998: 11). Or, more relevant, we come to describe some event as terrorism or some actor as terrorist through the combination of mass-mediated connections (e.g., TV, Internet, Twitter, print news, etc.) with which we continually interact.

Closely related to the study of meanings generated by actors is the concept of identity. Identity consists of

> clusters of relations linked by their associated histories and projects. These include relations based on organizational affiliations (e.g., membership in political parties or religious organizations), institutional positions (student, agronomist, citizen), and broad cultural associations (e.g., race, gender, or nationality). Such performances involve representations of alignments and boundaries (distinguishing who you are from who you are not) as well as orientation toward possible future actions. Identities are multiple and shifting, as individuals move between social setting and as those settings themselves are transformed over time.
>
> (Mische 2008: 47)

At this interactional level, what should be the focus of examination for a CTS? Until now, this way of studying terrorism has largely been overlooked. As we mentioned above, most SNA of terrorism has centered on the formal, mathematically sophisticated tradition of study, which avoids questions of meaning and identity. Even Marc Sageman's books (2004, 2008), which focus on explaining the process of joining a terrorist organization and the global rise of terrorist networks, fail to consider the practices of sense-making, identity formation, and how they relate to conduct.

From this relational SNA approach, a researcher may examine how members of terrorist organizations make sense of their networks. In particular, we suggest that a researcher could focus on the ways that the actors in question mediate contingencies by selecting some ties and not others, articulating some identities and not others. For instance, as ethnographers have shown, terrorist identity is not an essential component of their being; rather, it is constructed and contingent (Toros 2008). So, a CTS that draws from SNA might focus on explaining how, as actors move between contexts (clandestine meetings between militants to a day-time job as shop worker), they connect with

> **Box 10.2 Additional components of relational Social Network Analysis**
>
> **Sense-making** – ongoing process of constructing meaningful action out of changing circumstances.
>
> **Identity** – ongoing and circumstantial process of defining who "I" and "we" are in relation to some other site or set of sites.

different actors, make sense of those connections in varying ways, articulate varying identities, and engage in varying modes of conduct.

Or, consider policy-makers participating in state terror. In terms of state terror networks, a researcher might explain how policy-makers construct public or front stage identities compared to backstage committee identities. In a more public context, policy-makers might draw on particular ties to present a particular self, and, in a more exclusive context, they may draw on another set of ties that enables a very different construction of self. The focus of a CTS that draws from SNA, in this instance, would be on explaining how identities are sustained or varied as actors switch between contexts.

Another avenue of research would be to investigate how some connections open up opportunities for certain lines of sense-making, identity, and action, while other ties close down those possibilities. Along the lines of Sageman's book (2004), some connections make it possible to join a terrorist network. But going beyond his analysis, one might study how those connections enable the actor in question to make sense of the world differently, to define their self in new and varying terms, and to justify actions that would previously have been outside the realm of possibility.

Finally, one might investigate the emergence and diffusion of stories and categories through a network of connections. In terms of US state terror networks in Latin America, one might explain how certain stories and categories about "Communism," "free trade," and "democracy," for instance, emerged and circulated through key policy-making sites in and between the US context so that certain policies directed at Latin America became justifiable.

Understanding and Explaining

The difference between understanding and explaining some phenomena is basically between "explanations that answer different kinds of questions" (Wendt 1998: 104). Some research questions entail descriptive explanations and some research questions entail causal explanations; both are useful in the context of studying terrorism (Dixit and Stump 2011: 507). In SNA, formal structural analyses and measurements offer descriptive accounts; they allow the researcher to discern and describe ongoing patterns of activity out of immense complexity. For instance, Krebs' (2002) excellent research on the terrorist cell that carried out the events on September 11, 2001, in the USA offers no causal claims; rather, it depicts or maps out the network of ties that composed the cell's organization. In general, then, these structural studies of terrorism say very little in terms of causation. Indeed, insofar as the most recent literature on political networks is concerned, there is very little agreement in regards to conceptualizing causation or making generalizable causal claims (see Fowler et al. 2011).

In the context of a CTS that draws from SNA, we are talking about situated, or singular, causation that draws on a process- and mechanisms-based explanatory framework (Jackson 2006a: 276; McAdam et al. 2001). This mode of causal analysis is "more speculative," offering arguments that claim neither necessity nor sufficiency, but plausibility. "In other words," as Jackson puts it, "scholars know that some configuration of factors is causally adequate if they cannot plausibly conceive of that configuration *not* producing the outcome in question" (2006a: 276).

Causal mechanisms are analytically defined, recurring processes and patterns of social actions that come together to generate outcomes (Jackson 2006a: 276; Tilly 1995). The specific processes and mechanisms that come together in any particular context are historically unique. At the same time, generalization and comparison occur not across cases but at the level of mechanisms and their concatenation (Jackson 2006a: 276). For example, Tilly often refers to the mechanism of brokerage, which is the recurring action of bringing two previously unconnected sites together. In specific contexts, brokerage will combine with historically unique factors and other mechanisms to produce some specific outcome; however, the mechanism of brokerage occurs across a number of different contexts, which entails that one can make generalizable claims about brokerage and how its combination with other factors and mechanisms in different contexts generates variable outcomes. Tilly has used the mechanism of brokerage to explain a wide variety of relational phenomena, including the activity of ethnic leaders, rural landlords, Stalin's effort in forming his political machine, the work of a small manufacturing entrepreneur, householders in urban neighborhoods, and immigrants who sell craft goods and food (Tilly 2005a: 86–87).

How does this relate to CTS? Both descriptive and explanatory approaches are relevant and warranted for a CTS that draws from SNA. As we have suggested above, descriptive approaches could map out the sociopolitical landscape of state terror networks, the dispersion across media networks and policy-making sites of politically beneficial terrorist warnings, and so on. At the same time, in terms of causal explanations, studies could seek to analytically identify and define new and important mechanisms, compare how similar mechanisms concatenate in contextually dependent ways, and explain situated outcomes. For instance, one could study and compare how brokers connect different militant and clandestine groups together into a larger network and how brokers connect militant and clandestine groups with governmental agencies. Or, focusing more on the cultural construction of identity and meaning through intersubjective networks, one might use rhetorical mechanisms to explain how actors circumstantially specify the meaning of terrorism and counterterrorism and how they legitimate a course of action by joining particular ties together and breaking other connections.[2] The general point is that a CTS that draws from SNA should continue to break ground by describing and explaining the phenomena of terrorism in ways outside the conventional paradigm.

Accessing Data

Data Limitations

While the study of meaning and identity often entails more intimate data gathering strategies, such as observation and interviewing, the data used in many formal network studies of terrorism are publicly available documents. For various reasons, for example, officials may not release some information for strategic and tactical reasons and may in fact be releasing misinformation, the data should be seen as incomplete and possibly inaccurate. In dealing with this concern, Valdis E. Krebs turned to studies of other "covert, secret, or illegal networks" (2002: 44). He indicates four points worth considering when gathering network relevant data on terrorism:

1. *Incompleteness.* It is practically inevitable that the researcher will miss important sites and linkages in the network (Krebs 2002: 44; Sparrow 1991), so this limitation should be explicitly factored into the study and discussed.
2. *Limits of the network.* It is difficult to determine the limits of the terror network regarding who is to be included and who is to be excluded from a study (Krebs 2002: 44; Sparrow 1991). Generally, there are two legitimate ways to consider these limitations. The more inductive approach would be to adopt the experiential limits by "all or most actors that are members of the entity" (Knoke and Kuklinski 1982: 22). Alternatively, the researcher could impose closure on the network for analytical purposes based on certain definitions of relations, such as social class where all workers have a "common relation to a mode of production" (Knoke and Kuklinski 1982: 22).
3. *Dynamism.* Networks are not static, as we mentioned before. So, instead of determining the presence or absence of a particular tie, the data should be longitudinal and focused on the "waxing and waning strength of a tie" (Krebs 2002: 44; Sparrow 1991) and how meaningful identities change or are sustained over time and across contexts.
4. *Archives.* Given the difficulty of obtaining interviews and directly observing people involved in terror networks or state terror networks, archival documents often provide more useful sources of data (Krebs 2002: 44; Baker and Faulkner 1993).

Data-Gathering Strategies

Given these limitations to gathering data about the topic of terrorism, it is often difficult, impossible, or unwarranted to conduct random samples when studying terrorism from the social network angle. Network studies of voting patterns or other overt political activities may rely on random samples (see Fowler et al. 2011; Christakis and Fowler 2008; Knoke and Kuklinski 1982) or a combination of random sample and snowball methods of data gathering (Knoke and Kuklinski 1982: 23). Indeed, nonrandom snowball sampling, which is when the initial contact is invited to provide additional names of people in their network, is the most widely used strategy in network analysis because it "is a better way of finding a hidden population" (Newman 2010: 58–59). Studies of genocide or other violent political activity may entail purposeful sampling strategies, such as the "'funnel' method," which covered a range of actors and actions but sampled increasingly small subgroups more thoroughly (Fujii 2008: 574). Similarly, historical studies may use purposeful strategies of data-gathering. A study of becoming a Nazi, for instance, would lead a researcher to purposefully select the appropriate data and to avoid random sampling strategies (Bearman and Stovel 2000). In general, then, random sampling is not required for network analyses and may actually hinder an SNA study. The goal should be to gather a rich data set that allows one to plausibly answer their research questions.

Sources of Data

With all of these limitations and the range of possible sampling strategies, in order to study a sociopolitical problem from a network perspective you must gather data. Generally, as we have indicated in other chapters, there are three general sources of data and the methods of gathering associated with those sources:

1. interviews;
2. documents;
3. participant observations.

Interviews

One of the most common ways to gather network relevant data is through interviews. In Chapter 6, we discussed surveys, semi-structured interviews, and unstructured interviews. For ethnographers, we said that most employed semi-structured and unstructured interview techniques. Neopositivist hypothesis testers usually use surveys. Depending on the research design of the study, network analysts can use surveys, semi-structured interviews, and unstructured approaches to interviewing.

Surveys are uniformly organized and applied. So, the researcher will ask the same questions to all of the people involved in the study and there is often some limit to the possible answer choices. If a researcher is interested in describing networks, then a survey should seek to generate names of sites. For instance, a classic study of friendship networks asked students to give friends' names. The wording went like this:

- My best friend at _____ Junior High School is:
- My second-best friend at _____ Junior High School is:
- My third-best friend at _____ Junior High School is:
                    (Rapoport and Horvath 1961; quoted in Newman 2010: 40)

The blank "_____" was filled in with the school's name. The list stopped at the eighth-best friend, a limit dependent on workload and resources available to the researcher. The important point is that a survey of this sort is *asymmetrical* insofar as person A names person B as their friend and there is no guarantee that person B will name person A as their friend. An asymmetrical survey process such as this is thus best illustrated as a *directed* network: linkages between sites run in particular directions. If two persons name each other as best friends, then the illustration will show this with two directed linkages running in both directions (Newman 2010: 41). These two scenarios are shown in Figure 10.2.

Not all surveys that are illustrated with networks are directed. Some are *nondirected*. This is often seen with research focused on sexually transmitted disease (see Klovdahl et al. 1994; Liljeros et al. 2001). In these surveys, respondents are asked simple yes or no questions about their sexual contacts. "Did you have sex with person B?" A linkage in such a network is nondirected, which illustrates that person A and B did have sex; no linkage illustrates that person A and B did not have sex. These two scenarios are illustrated in Figure 10.3.

Beyond generating names of other sites in a network, interviewing can help researchers get at the particular content of the linkages between sites and the frequency and duration of those linkages (Newman 2010: 42–43). Researchers can employ semi-structured techniques to gather information on specific content. An interviewer may

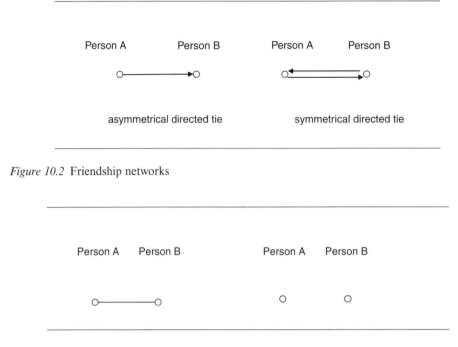

Figure 10.2 Friendship networks

Figure 10.3 Sexual contact networks

ask an interviewee to describe their relationships with other people or things. For instance, a researcher may ask:

- When you need help fixing a _____ problem, who do you turn to for advice?
- The last time that you were emotionally distraught, who did you turn to for support?
- When you want authoritative information about _____ , which television/radio/ internet program do you view?

These semi-structured interview questions help researchers flesh out the content of certain ties. Similarly, the strength of a tie can be measured through interviews. Interview questions aimed at measuring the strength of some tie may ask about frequency of connections to a person or object:

- How often do you see _____ ?
- How often do you talk with _____ ?
- How frequently do you use the _____ ?

To measure the duration of some connections to a person or object, then a researcher might ask questions along these lines:

- When you speak with _____ , how long does your conversation usually last?
- When you see _____ , how long do you usually look?
- When you use the _____ , how many minutes/hours/days/weeks/months does this happen?

So, interviews can help researchers gather data regarding the establishment of network connections, their content, duration, and frequency. Beyond measures of content and strength, as we have argued in Chapters 6–9, interviews can also serve as data to study sense-making processes.

For example, Lee Ann Fujii studied the Rwandan genocide and the role of local ties, especially family and friendship ties, in creating and resisting the violence. Her data consisted of 231 intensive interviews conducted with eighty-two people in two separate communities in two different regions of the country (Fujii 2008: 572). In contrast to surveys, her questions were semi-structured, which allowed respondents to articulate open-ended answers. Examining the micro-interactions of mass violence entails the analysis of sense-making processes, or "how people made sense of the violence and how people made sense through violence" (Fujii 2008: 572). As Fujii puts it, her "goal was not to test hypotheses about specific variables but to uncover the subjective and intersubjective meanings that people used to explain what they had lived through, survived, participated in, or witnessed" (2008: 578). While Fujii does not provide examples of the questions she asked, semi-structured questions might be similar to this:

- Can you describe why the violence started?
- When you engaged in violence, can you describe why a particular target was selected?
- Why didn't you join the violence?
- Is there "x" where you live now?
- Is "x" good or bad?
- What do you think "x" means?
- To you, what is "x"?

In general, then, it is important to keep in mind that a researcher's goal when conducting semi-structured and unstructured interviews is to access the meanings generated by those speaking. The goal is not to correct, judge or instruct the speaker. At the same time, for surveys the goal is to map out connections, to understand the content flowing between sites, and to measure the frequency and duration of particular ties.

Documents

As we mentioned above, archived documents may be the easiest source of data to gather, especially when studying terrorism. Archived documents are another important source of data for network analyses. Compared to interviews, archived documents are less labor-intensive to gather and are more voluminous. As we indicated in Chapters 6 and 7, possible types of archived documents range widely. Some historical studies have looked at private, family archives of trade relations, marriage ties, and other connections for ruling European families (Newman 2010: 48). Studies of contemporary networks have looked at contemporary email logs and address books, telephone-call graphs, Facebook and LinkedIn networks, dating websites, online message boards, and scholarly citation indexes (Newman 2010: 47–50).

A more relevant example to political science and IR in general is David Kinsella's analysis of the global small-arms network (2006). The raw data was drawn from the Black Market File Archives located at the Norwegian Initiative on Small Arms Transfers. The archive is composed of information gathered from news reports of illegal arms shipments that cross interstate borders. In particular, Kinsella observed the "transfer *event* – that is, a shipment of weapons from an originator to a recipient, possibly intercepted along the way" (2006: 106). Each event was then coded according to established and standardized rules that indicated:

- the source of the arms;
- those people involved in the transaction;
- the characteristics of the arms transferred;
- the journey that the shipment took after leaving the source;
- and the destination of the shipment (Kinsella 2006: 106).

While noting the limitations of data regarding illegal activities, Kinsella shows how South Africa and Angola are especially central to the global small-arms network, as are Romania, Bulgaria, and the Ukraine.

Even more relevant to network-based studies of terrorism are publicly available news documents. These documents are generally archived by the publisher and are also available online through various search engines, like Lexis Nexis. For instance, in the journal *Connections,* Valdis E. Krebs published the first systematic network analysis of the terrorist cell that carried out the attacks on September 11, 2001 (2002). His data consisted of information released by major newspapers such as the *New York Times,* the *Wall Street Journal,* the *Washington Post,* and the *Los Angeles Times.* Along similar lines, David Martin Jones, Michael L. R. Smith, and Mark Weeding used a combination of publicly available sources in their effort to piece together the origins, growth, and direction of al-Qaeda in Southeast Asia (2003). In particular, they collected news documents from sources such as the *Manila Times, The Guardian,* the *Sydney Morning Herald,* the *Washington Times,* and official sources such as the Philippines Directorate for Intelligence and police reports. Similarly, Herman used news documents to study the global network of national security state terror (1983).

Beyond the news, other archived documents are used to study networks of terror. From a variety of countries researchers have gathered court proceedings, corroborated statements from those with direct access to information, uncorroborated statements from those with direct access to information, secondhand statements from people who had heard the information (Qin et al. 2005: 292), sworn testimonies, captured documents found in computer hard drives, and intercepted conversations of terrorists unaware that they were being recorded (Sageman 2004; 2008: 26–27). Other researchers have built semi-automated data collection, filtering, analysis, and visualization systems that focus on monitoring "39 Arabic terrorist Web sites" (Chen et al. 2008: 1348). Looking at state terror networks, such as those associated with Operation Condor that tied the USA, Argentina, Chile, Uruguay, Paraguay, Bolivia, and Brazil together, researchers have also examined unclassified government documents (McSherry 2002; Petras 1987).

Similar to interviewing, these documents are used by researchers to sketch out the network of connections, their content, and strength. For instance, Stuart Koschade's network analysis of Jemaah Islamiyah coded the documentary data according to two criteria: "Transactional Content" and "Frequency and Duration of Interaction" (2006: 564). The content is the basic "substance" of the interaction; it could be information exchanges that concerned the tactical operation, for instance. The frequency and duration of the interaction measure the strength of the tie in question. Koschade used a scale of 1 to 5; 1 indicates a weak tie such as a single text message exchange or a financial transaction and 5 indicates a strong tie such as individuals who live together or who communicate regularly during the period under study (2006: 564 and 567). Another example is Justin Magouirk, Scott Atran, and Marc Sageman's analysis of the Global Transnational Terrorism Project data set (2008). In terms of content, they examined friendship, kinship, religious, and instrumental ties. Using a method that the authors developed to "discern differences in the strength of ties over time and in the reliability of the ties based on the available open-source information," they rank ordered the connections from 1 to 3. Weaker ties consisted of in-laws and acquaintances with whom little time was spent and the strongest ties included the nuclear family, where actors would spend the most time and see that cluster of people most frequently (Magouirk et al. 2008: 4).

Documents can also be used to study the construction of identity and meaning through cultural networks. For instance, Peter Bearman and Katherine Stovel used network analysis to study the written, autobiographical accounts of becoming and being a Nazi. Narratives, or stories, are seen from this perspective as "one mechanism for organizing and generating social meanings," especially identities (Bearman and Stovel 2000: 70). Narrative processes of identity construction, Bearman and Stovel argue, can usefully be studied through a network lens by treating specified elements of stories as nodes connected by causal linkages. By using these techniques, they are "able to identify some core elements of the process by which individuals became Nazis" and to analyze the "structure associated with *being* a Nazi" (Bearman and Stovel 2000: 71). Similarly, Charles Tilly has studied documented identity stories that indicate "Who are you?" "Who are we?" and "Who are they?" More specifically, he has focused on how these transactions constitute the boundaries and contentious politics between different sites in religious networks, revolutionary networks, democratizing networks, and terrorist networks (Tilly 2003, 2004, 2005a, 2005b).

Participant Observations

A final source of data available to network researchers is direct observation. Researchers attempt to directly observe transactions between people and people and things. In Chapters 6 and 7, we discussed participant observation in relation to terrorism in more depth. Here, we bring participant observation and network analysis together and discuss how they might work together in the study of terrorism.

Earlier in this chapter we mentioned that network analysts have often regarded themselves as structuralist and drawn heavily from mathematics. At the same time, as a way of grounding more abstract mathematically derived networks in concrete interaction, social network analysts have also used participant observation as a central method for gathering data. Educational psychologists directly observed children's play and interactional networks in the 1920s. Anthropologists have also studied kinship networks through fieldwork. Fieldwork, as we noted earlier in the book, entails meeting informants, gaining entrance into their community by making contacts with certain members, and building up a rapport. For this reason, Alvin W. Wolfe says that ethnographic methods and anthropology in general offer an "excellent grounding for a network orientation" (1978: 57).

Similar to interviews and documents, direct observation enables the researcher to measure the content and strength of relationships. By participating and observing interactions, the specific content of networks, whether ties are based on kinship or friendship or utility or authority or religion, can be described in more or less systematic terms. When trying to discern the content of some set of relationships, it is useful to take field notes that focus on detailing:

1. *Actors.* Both the focal subject and the others with whom he or she transacts. Does the focal subject interact with religious figures, police or other figures of governmental authority, with brothers and cousins, with friends, or with business associates?
2. *Actions.* The focal behaviors under study, including specific acts or ongoing flows of actions, the content of speech, and the observable consequences of their actions. How are actors acting and interacting in specific instances or over the course of a specified duration of time? How do actors move from one setting to another? What do actors say in specific locals (e.g., at home compared to in church), over the course of time (before, during, and after church), and in the movement between locals (between home and church)?
3. *Settings.* The locale where actions occur, including details of the physical space where actors act and interact, and the props used by actors in the course of acting and interacting. Where are actors acting? What are they touching, talking about, manipulating, pointing at, etc. (Johnson and Sackett 2000: 309)?

At the same time, direct observation and participation enable researchers to measure the strength of relationships. As we mentioned earlier in discussing interview and archival data-gathering methods, researchers often construct rank order scales that focus on measuring:

1. *Frequency*: the number of occurrences of an act or interaction during a given period of time. Over the course of a month, how many times does the focal subject speak with his or her business associates compared to religious figures compared to brothers compared to friends? The higher the frequency of occurrences, then we are warranted in saying that the tie is stronger.
2. *Duration*: the length of time that some action or interaction occurs during a period of time. Over the course of a month, with whom did the focal subject interact with the longest period of time? The longer the duration, then we are warranted in saying that the tie is stronger.
3. *Intensity*: the pace at which the action or interaction is performed during a period of time. Over the course of a month, was the pace of religious training compared to military training compared to working at a job more leisurely or vigorous? The more intense the action or interaction, then we are warranted in claiming that the tie is stronger (Montoye et al. 1996; quoted in Johnson and Sackett 2000: 310).

Beyond the observable measurement of the content and strength of ties is the analysis of interpretive interaction and the search for meaningful action or, as Clifford Geertz put it: "Cultural analysis is (or should be) guessing at meanings, assessing those guesses, and drawing explanatory conclusions from better guesses" (1973: 20). There are a number of accepted ways to do this type of analytical work. Yanow and Schwartz-Shea, for instance, have compiled a useful list of interpretive methods (2006: xx) that students of CTS could learn and employ. Some of the interpretive methods Yanow and Schwartz-Shea note include:

- ethnography;
- ethnomethodology;

- symbolic interaction;
- metaphor analysis;
- dramaturgical analysis;
- oral history;
- grounded theory;
- frame analysis;
- discourse analysis.

P. Jackson has outlined specific analytical techniques (2006c: 144–145), as has Stacie E. Goddard (2006); both explicitly relate their mechanism-centered approaches to SNA. Other researchers who have combined formal and relational-interactional SNA have developed their own interpretive analytical techniques. Mische, for instance, along with her structural analysis, conducted fieldwork of Brazilian political activists. To study relational practices enacted by activists, Mische developed a relational approach to SNA that was grounded in the theoretical developments of Georg Simmel, George Herbert Mead, John Dewey, Alfred Schutz, Erving Goffman, and Harrison White. The point, to bring our discussion back home, is that there is no one single way to do interpretive analysis well. Though not always, it often entails fieldwork; that means selecting a research site or set of sites, establishing connections with locals, gaining entrance into the groups under study, and taking copious fieldnotes – all of which was discussed in greater detail in Chapters 6 and 7.

Research Design

How, then, can one design their research project? In general, research design can be schematically broken down into a series of practical steps:

1. Identify a topic of interest. For our purposes, terrorism is the topic.
2. Identify an event, outcome, or course of action to be explained. Perhaps one wants to explain how terrorism is constructed in major print media in the USA.
3. Pose an answerable research question that would set the stage for an empirical, systematic investigation of the event, outcome, or course of action one is trying to explain. For our selected event, the research question may go something like this: How has terrorism been represented in US print media between 1900 and 2010?
4. Identify what types of data (interviews, observations, documents) would enable one to study that event, outcome, or course of action and where that data can be accessed. In this case, the primary type of data would be documents and they are generally available through online archives such as Lexis Nexis.
5. Collect the relevant data into a rich corpus that can more easily be analyzed.
6. Systematically go through the data and map out the rhetoric of terrorism.

Depending on the mode of analysis one was using, the focus could be on the predication of terrorism or the metaphor of terrorism or any other way of studying the interpretive meaning of terrorism. Studying the predication of terrorism, for instance, might entail

- mapping out the clusters of predicates connected to terrorism between 1900 and 2010;
- showing that the clusters of predicates linked to terrorism have changed over time;

- showing that some clusters of predicates linked to terrorism are more central, more frequent, and endure for longer periods of time compared to other clusters;
- and showing how changing clusters of predicates linked to terrorism entailed different meanings and were occurring in the context of changing counterterrorist policies.

Our study might show that from 1900 through the 1960s, the most central, frequent, and enduring predication of terrorism was "East European," "Soviet," "Bolshevik," and "communistic'; by the 1970s through 2010, the most central, frequent, and enduring predication of terrorism are with "Middle East," "Muslim," and "Islam"; and that these changing structures of meaning were associated with changing US counterterrorist policies.

Software for Network Analysis

This chapter is not the best venue to write extensively about the computer software available to SNA. Already there are more in-depth and comprehensive overviews of the various software packages available for SNA. More recently, for instance, Mark Huisman and Marijtje A. J. van Duijn, wrote "A Reader's Guide to SNA Software," which is an excellent primer for new students of SNA (2011: 578–596). For our purposes, it should suffice to say that there is software available for both formal and interactional approaches to SNA and both kinds of software can be used in the critical study of terrorism.

Questions to consider

- What is a network and what are its basic components?
- What are the two basic approaches to the study of social networks? How are they different and similar?
- What are some structural and transactional measures that SNA scholars often employ?
- How does the interpretation of meaning and identity construction compare to the measurement of network characteristics?
- What types of data do network analysts gather?
- What are the limitations to gathering data on terrorism and counterterrorism networks?

Notes

1 Robert E. Goodin offers an excellent discussion on how warnings of terrorism could be terroristic too, particularly if policy-makers are politically profiting from their public speech (2006: 78–155).
2 Jackson has used the rhetorical mechanisms of specification, breaking, and joining to explain how post-WWII Germany was defined as part of "Western civilization" and the Marshall Plan was legitimated as a course of action.

Further Reading

Emirbayer, M. (1997), "Manifesto for a Relational Sociology," *American Journal of Sociology*, 103 (2): 281–317.

Knox, H., Savage, M. and Harvey, P. (2006), "Social Networks and the Study of Relations: Networks as Method, Metaphor, and Form," *Economy and Society*, 35 (1): 113–140.

Koschade, S. (2006), "A Social Network Analysis of Jemaah Islamiyah: The Applications to Counterterrorism and Intelligence," *Studies in Conflict and Terrorism*, 29 (6): 559–575.

Krebs, V. E. (2002), "Mapping Networks of Terrorist Cells," *Connections*, 24 (3): 43–52.

McSherry, P. J. (2002), "Tracking the Origins of a State Terror Network," *Latin American Perspectives*, 29 (1): 38–60.

Mische, A. (2008), *Partisan Publics: Communication and Contention Across Brazilian Youth Activist Networks*, Princeton, NJ: Princeton University Press.

Tilly, C. (2005), "Terror as Strategy and Relational Process," *International Journal of Comparative Sociology*, 46 (1–2): 11–32.

Wasserman, S. and Galaskiewicz, J. (1994), *Advances in Social Network Analysis: Research in the Social and Behavioral Sciences*, Thousand Oaks, CA: Sage.

Websites

The *International Network of Social Network Analysis* provides a number of professional services and discussion among practicing researchers. They also provide a comprehensive list of software available to SNA. See http://www.insna.org.

Wikipedia also provides a very useful and regularly updated list of software packages available to SNA. See http://en.wikipedia.org/wiki/Social_network_analysis_software.

The NetLab is a site developed and run by Berry Wellman, a sociologist at the University of Toronto who specializes in SNA. See http://homes.chass.utoronto.ca/~wellman/netlab/index.html.

Harvard University also has a Program on Networked Governance. See http://www.hks.harvard.edu/netgov/html/index.htm.

11 Conclusion

Critical Research on Terrorism

Others have outlined possible futures for a CTS research agenda elsewhere (Jackson et al. 2009a, 2012). We detail some possible concerns and pathways regarding the "how to" of doing critical research on terrorism. TS occupies a marginal role in IR and even more so in security studies. Of that, critical scholarship on terrorism is further marginalized and often ignored in mainstream texts on terrorism. In our previous chapters, we have sketched out some critical research approaches which can be used to study and understand terrorism. Some common themes that have emerged are as follows.

Truth, Ontology, and Epistemology

All research approaches presume certain ontological and epistemological commitments on the part of the researcher regarding terrorism. Traditional TS approaches often seek (big T) Truths regarding terrorism. For instance, TS scholars often want to identify or debate about how best to identify the root motivational or environmental causes of terrorism (Bjorgo 2005; Pedahzur 2006). Many critical approaches interrogate research that seeks the (big T) Truth of terrorism and argue such understandings are flawed because they fail to take into account the standpoint of those doing research. Big "T" truthseekers might also fail to recognize the different meanings of terrorism in different sociopolitical contexts. Instead, critical researchers are either wary of the Truth (ethnographers, poststructural discourse analysts) or theorize possibilities of reaching consensus via dialogue (Frankfurt School-influenced scholars, [some] feminists and postcolonial theorists) and the opening up of space for such dialogues to occur.

The majority of critically oriented research calls for a clarification of the ontological and epistemological presuppositions of any research design prior to conducting research. This assists in transdisciplinary dialogue as researchers across disciplines can understand, collaborate, and critique each other's work. Critical theorists are (often) critical realists though, as we have argued, this need not be the case. Ethnographers take social constructionism as their ontological presupposition, while feminists might adopt a more dialogue-leads-to-truth stance in their calls for emancipation, and so on. However, it is important to remember that not all research approaches have only one ontological presupposition; for example, feminists may be critical realists or poststructuralists. Among discourse analysts, CDA presumes a world "out there" and is realist in orientation while poststructural/Foucauldian Discourse Analysis adopts a social-constructionist approach to meaning-making. The lack of one specific ontology tied in with a particular research approach makes the need to specify and communicate one's ontological and epistemological standpoint even more relevant to producing accessible research.

Ethics

Another common feature when conducting critically oriented research on terrorism (or any research on terrorism in general) is a concern with and for ethics. Here, "ethics" is not just the conventional academic institutional approval that needs to be received prior to conducting research but a more all-encompassing use of the term, one which includes responsibility to oneself (the researcher), one's research participants as well as the final research outcome itself. Thus, questions of access to the field and to one's research participants are tied in with issues of selecting texts and choosing interviewees, being aware of whose voice(s) are heard and who get(s) silenced in the process of researching and writing, and being sensitive to the possible dangers faced by research participants who choose to talk to the researcher about what is bound to be a sensitive and controversial topic. As Potter and Wetherell wrote in 1987, "terrorism" is an evaluative term and already has judgment as part of its articulation (Potter and Wetherell 1987). This means research on such a topic requires thoughtfulness and self-awareness on the part of the researcher. At the same time, however, the researcher's safety also becomes a central concern more so than when conducting research on less "sensitive" subjects. Breen Smyth (2009) outlines some of the major ethical issues when dealing with terrorism, including a lack of primary data, excessive focus on secondary data, and the links between researchers and government organizations and counterterrorism especially with regards to the funding of research on terrorism. Her statement: "it is important to ask who research on terrorism is for" (2009: 214) is something that all critical researchers should consider.

On a personal level for the researcher, in addition to being aware of safety considerations both for oneself and for one's research subjects, there are other related considerations. Earlier chapters have discussed issues of standpoint analysis, wherein the researcher's standpoint is key in the knowledge that is produced and communicated. We have also discussed reflexivity and the practices of reflexivity in both self (the researcher) and the work itself. A key aspect to conducting research on terrorism is transparency – keeping fieldnotes and diaries when doing ethnographic fieldwork, being clear about the criteria for choosing visual and textual data for discourse analysis, laying out guidelines and procedures for interviewing and participant observation and outlining one's role in the production and communication of knowledge about terrorism.

Causality

Another possible research pathway is to conduct further analysis of non-linear *causality*. Currently, the "critical" view appears to be that critical research is primarily *not* about causation. Instead, the terms often used are "co-constitution" or "combinability." But there is no reason to discount causality when doing critical research on terrorism. It should be made clear, however, that there is more than one way of understanding causality. The conventional way of equating causality with a linear understanding is just one of several possible options. Thus, critical research provides opportunities to reconceptualize causality itself to something where, for example, social practices allow for a range of identities and policies to be produced and understood. In this sense, then, co-constitution *is* causal. Examining non-linear causality from a discourse-perspective: Jackson claims that "rhetorical commonplaces and the legitimation processes involving them can certainly be understood as causal, to the extent that the overall 'shape' of the discursive environment contributes to the formulation of policy initiatives" (P. Jackson 2005: 41). Outlining this "shape" in CTS would be a research project that is still causal, even if the understanding of causality is different to that from conventional IR. More research in this direction is warranted.

Applied and Basic Research

An important distinction among TS and CTS that has been alluded to but not directly discussed is that between applied and basic research. Applied research, in general terms, is policy-relevant research that aims to solve, improve, or manage a practical problem. Much of the TS literature has been applied research aimed at improving a state or government's ability to counter the threat of terrorism, which has been a point of criticism leveled by CTS scholars. Conversely, basic research does not necessarily have an applicatory aim but is rather focused on systematically answering research questions, solving empirical and theoretical puzzles, and generally producing knowledge for the sake of knowledge. Much of the CTS literature has been basic research, and this also has been a point of criticism leveled by TS scholars.

In practice, the distinction between applied and basic research is not so sharp when it comes to the study of terrorism. Gunning has pointed out that CTS approaches with an emancipatory political aim should be producing policy-relevant research (2007b: 239–240). The policy-making communities, however, are not limited to the government but can also include NGOs and everyday citizens. Similarly, as the US Army's controversial Human Terrain System has shown, ethnographically informed research can have on-the-ground policy relevance for soldiers operating in foreign contexts. On the flip side, orthodox TS is not all noncritical applied research. Weinberg and Eubank (2008) and Horgan and Boyle (2008) both argue that orthodox approaches have been self-critical.

What is important for the future of CTS? It seems to us that while there is an increasingly strong and justified push to make CTS policy relevant, it is equally important to leave open space for basic research that aims to systematically answer research questions and to sharpen the methodological positions and methods used to answer those questions. Hence, our emphasis in this book on the transdisciplinarity of CTS with fields such as philosophy, literature, and rhetoric and cultural studies. These disciplines have studied the phenomena of terrorism and counterterrorism but have had little connection to CTS. By emphasizing more cross-fertilization between disciplines that have little application to seemingly practical problems and by also encouraging applied research especially as it relates to emancipatory politics, CTS can successfully be situated in the gray zone between applied and basic research. Both are important, in other words, because, as Nobel Laureate George Smoot noted: "People cannot foresee the future well enough to predict what's going to develop from basic research. If we only did applied research, we would still be making better spears" (quoted in Haurwitz 2011).

The Way(s) Forward

A more inclusive definition of "critical," with a clear specification of methodological standpoint prior to doing research is likely to benefit CTS as it could lead to discussions and dialogue across disciplines. As we have outlined throughout this book, the use of critical research approaches have been fairly limited in TS in general as compared to their usage in IR. For example, while feminist IR has grown rapidly since its emergence in the 1990s, feminist TS remains scarce. As such, it is essential to outline clear research techniques and draw upon examples of critical studies of terrorism from beyond IR so that future researchers have illustrations and instances to learn and critique. The development of a vibrant CTS requires thoughtful attention toward *how* researchers have conducted research; not just *what* should be studied.

For example, as indicated in Chapter 4 and the discussion therein regarding the use of CT, future CTS research could clarify analytical concepts that are drawn from specific research traditions.

As Chapter 2 indicates, there remains limited circulation of terrorism research done by scholars from the Global South or from non-Western areas in general. Greater attention to such scholarship is likely to broaden the definitions and understanding of terrorism as well as outline how terrorism is studied and made sense of in contexts outside of the academic and sociocultural contexts of the Global North. For example, Dixit became aware of the lack of interest in and disinclination to talk about terrorism and conflict amongst locals during her experiences in Nepal in 2002. Instead, concerns were more about daily life: the rising cost of food, the lack of jobs and educational opportunities. This was at a time when the Nepali government had established extensive anti-terrorism legislation and was receiving outside assistance (both military and financial) to counter Maoist terrorists. Greater attention to how people outside Western areas of the world make sense of their lives in relation to terrorism and counterterrorism would be one way to demystify our phenomena of study.

Following on from this, an attention to "subaltern" knowledges and their production would broaden CTS and bring in feminists and postcolonial scholars (among others) to the study of terrorism. Here, the goal would be "[an] insurrection of subjugated knowledges" (Foucault 1980: 82). According to Foucault, "subjugated knowledges" mean "historical contents that have been buried or disguised in functionalist coherence or formal systemization" (1980: 81–82). Such knowledge also means, "something which in a sense is altogether different, namely a whole set of knowledges that have been disqualified as inadequate to their task or insufficiently elaborated" (1980: 82). By utilizing some of the critical research approaches outlined in this text (e.g., ethnography, discourse analysis, postcolonialism and feminism) and by paying attention to methodological and geographical plurality, CTS can move towards elaborating such knowledges.

Expanding the range of data available for research is another key goal. CTS scholars have already pointed out the lack of primary data available on terrorism (R. Jackson et al. 2009a). By examining how terrorism and counterterrorism are socially constructed in different settings, visual data (comic books, art, advertising, films, TV shows, etc.) as well as oral narratives and even buildings and architecture (physical changes to space due to counterterrorism measures such as roadblocks and immigration stations; buildings memorializing deaths due to terrorism, such as the "Ground Zero," etc.) are sources of studying how different cultures make sense of terrorism as well as how counterterrorism policies are enacted.

Pursuing network-based analysis of terrorism is also important, especially by drawing from relational and interactionist approaches. Employing these methods can enable connections (or lack thereof) among various terrorist and counterterrorist actors to be traced and systematically studied. For example, connections may exist among think tanks, academics, government institutions and funding agencies in the USA and network analysis would be a useful tool to visualize and explain the impact and meanings of these connections.

When research on terrorism is presented, communicated and legitimated, the epistemological question ("How do we know?") should be foregrounded. This leads to an interrogation of current modes of research on terrorism and challenges all researchers to justify how their research was conducted and warranted.

Transdisciplinarity is crucial. The future of CTS research could build on feminist and postcolonial understandings of *transversal politics,* not just in terms of disciplines but also in terms of forming coalitions of researchers and research across geographical spaces. The term "transdisciplinarity" is more suited than interdisciplinarity since it draws attention to the need for change.

Transversal politics is a term borrowed by Nira Yuval-Davis from Italian women activists:

> Transversal politics recognizes the differential power positions among participants in the dialogue, but it nevertheless encompasses these differences with equal respect and recognition of each participant. Moreover, transversal politics resists autocratic decision-making mechanisms in which certain individuals take upon themselves to "represent" their communities.
>
> (Yuval-Davis 1999: 98)

Here, the focus is on various critically oriented researchers remaining open to dialogue while being aware of the differences in methodological approaches amongst them. Transversal politics and the action of building transversal coalitions can help address the question of how to relate to differences in a wide range of settings – while researching violence that may be outside of the usual experience of the researcher or, more mundanely, while discussing one's research with another researcher with a different methodological approach.

Bibliography

Abbott, A. (1995), "Things of Boundaries," *Social Research*, 62 (1): 857–882.

——(2007), "Mechanisms and Relations," *Sociologica*, 2 (2): 1–22.

Abufarha, N. (2009), *The Making of a Human Bomb: An Ethnography of Palestinian Resistance*, Durham, NC: Duke University Press.

Ackerly, B. A, Stern, M., and True, J. (Eds.) (2006), *Feminist Methodologies for International Relations*, Cambridge: Cambridge University Press.

Ackerly, B. and True, J. (2008), "Reflexivity in Practice: Power and Ethics in Feminist Research on International Relations," *International Studies Review*, 10 (4): 693–707.

Agamben, G. (1998), *Homo Sacer: Sovereign Power and Bare Life*, trans. Daniel Heller-Roazen, Palo Alto, CA: Stanford University Press.

——(2005), *State of Exception*, trans. Kevin Attell, Chicago: University of Chicago Press.

Agger, B. (1991), "Critical Theory, Poststructuralism, Postmodernism: Their Sociological Relevance," *Annual Review of Sociology*, 17 (17): 105–131.

Ahmad, E. (2001), *Terrorism: Theirs and Ours*, New York: Seven Stories Press.

Alexander, Y. and Craft, M. (Eds.) (2008), *Evolution of US Counterterrorism Policy*, 3 vols., Westport, CT: Praeger Security International.

Altheide, D. (1987), "Ethnographic Content Analysis," *Qualitative Sociology*, 10: 65–77.

——(1994), "An Ecology of Communication: Toward a Mapping of the Effective Environment," *Sociological Quarterly*, 35 (4): 665–683.

——(2000), "Identity and the Definition of the Situation in a Mass Mediated Context," *Symbolic Interaction*, 23 (1): 1–27.

——(2004), "Consuming Terrorism," *Symbolic Interaction*, 27 (3): 289–308.

——(2006), *Terrorism and the Politics of Fear*, Lanham, MD: Altamira Press.

Alway, J. (1995), *Critical Theory and Political Possibilities: Conceptions of Emancipatory Politics in the Works of Horkheimer, Adorno, Marcuse, and Habermas*, Westport, CT: Greenwood Press.

Antaki, C. (2007), "Lecture/Seminar 10: The Basic Ideas of Discourse Analysis," and "Lecture/Seminar 11: Varieties of Discourse Analysis II," in *Analysing Talk and Text: Lectures for Barcelona Students*, Universitat Autònoma de Barcelona. Available online at http://www.staff.lboro.ac.uk/~sscal1/ttlecture10da1.htm (accessed October 19, 2012).

Arce, D. G. and Sandler, T. (2005), "Counterterrorism: A Game-Theoretic Analysis," *The Journal of Conflict Resolution*, 49 (2): 183–200.

Aretxaga, B. (1997), *Shattering Silence*, Princeton, NJ: Princeton University Press.

——(2001), "Terror as Thrill: First Thoughts on the 'War on Terrorism'," *Anthropological Quarterly*, 75 (1): 139–150.

——(2005), *States of Terror: Begona Aretzaga's Essays*, Reno, NE: University of Nevada.

Argenti-Pillen, A. (2003), *How Women Contain Violence in Southern Sri Lanka*, Philadelphia, PA: University of Pennsylvania Press.

Armstrong, A. and Prashad, V. (2006), "Bandung Women: Vietnam, Afghanistan, Iraq, and the Necessary Risks of Solidarity," in R. Riley and N. Inayatullah (eds), *Interogating Imperialism: Conversations on Gender, Race, and War*, Basingstoke: Palgrave Macmillan.

Arquilla, J. (2007), "The End of War as We Knew It? Insurgency, Counterinsurgency and Lessons from the Forgotten History of Early Terror Networks," *Third World Quarterly*, 28 (2): 369–386.

Ashcroft, B., Griffiths, G., and Tiffin, H. (1998) *Key Conceptes in Post-Colonial Studies*, London and New York: Routledge.

Ashcroft, B., Griffiths, G., and Tiffin, H. (Eds.) (2005), *The Post-Colonial Studies Reader*, London and New York: Routledge.

Atran, S. and Sageman, M. (2006), "Connecting the Dots," *Bulletin of the Atomic Scientists*, July/August, p. 68.

Auge, M. (1998), *A Sense for the Other: The Timeliness and Relevance of Anthropology*, Palo Alto, CA: Stanford University Press.

Axel, B. (2001), *The Nation's Tortured Body: Violence, Representation, and the Formation of a Sikh Diaspora*, Chapel Hill, NC: Duke University Press.

Baker, W. and Faulkner, R. (1993), "The Social Organization of Conspiracy: Illegal Networks in the Heavy Electrical Equipment Industry," *American Sociological Review*, 58 (6): 837–860.

Barkawi, T. and Laffey, M. (2002), "Retrieving the Imperial: Empire and International Relations," *Millennium*, 31 (1): 109–127.

——(2006), "The Postcolonial Moment in Security Studies," *Review of International Studies*, 32 (2): 329–352.

Barnes, J. (1954), "Class and Committees in a Norwegian Island Parish," *Human Relations*, 7 (1): 37–58.

Basu, S. (2011), "Security as Emancipation: A Feminist Perspective," in J. A. Tickner and L. Sjoberg (Eds.) *Twenty Years of Feminist International Relations: A Conversation About the Past, Present and Future*, London and New York: Routledge.

Bauer, K. (2009), "Adorno's Intellectual Praxis," in A. J. Drake (Ed.), *New Essays on the Frankfurt School's Critical Theory*, Cambridge: Cambridge Scholars Publishing.

Bearman, P. S. and Stovel, K. (2000), "Becoming a Nazi: A Model for Narrative Networks," *Poetics*, 27 (2–3): 69–70.

Beer, J. (1986), *A Passage to India: Essays in Interpretation*, New York: Barnes and Noble Books.

Berenson, A. (2010), *The Silent Man*, New York: G. P. Putnam's Sons.

Berger, M. T. and Guidroz, K. (2009a), "Conversation with Founding Scholars of Intersectionality: Michelle Fine, Kimberle Grenshaw, Nira Yuval-Davis," in M. T. Berger and K. Guidroz (Eds.), *The Intersectional Approach: Transforming the Academy through Race, Class and Gender*, Durham, NC: University of North Carolina Press, pp. 61–80.

Berger, M. T. and Guidroz, K. (Eds.) (2009b), *The Intersectional Approach: Transforming the Academy through Race, Class and Gender*, Durham, NC: University of North Carolina Press.

Berkowitz, S. D. (1982), *An Introduction to Structural Analysis: The Network Approach to Social Research*, Toronto: Butterworth-Heinemann.

Bevir, M. (2006), "How Narratives Explain," in D. Yanow and P. Schwartz-Shea (Eds.), *Interpretation and Method: Empirical Research Methods and the Interpretive Turn*, New York: M. E. Sharpe.

Bhatia, A. (2009), "The Discourses of Terrorism," *Journal of Pragmatics*, 41 (2): 279–289.

Bigo, D. and Tsoukala, A. (2008), "Understanding Insecurity," in D. Bigo and A. Tsoukala (Eds.), *Terror, Insecurity and Liberty: Illiberal Practices of Liberal Regimes After 9/11*, London and New York: Routledge.

Bilgin, P. (2011), "The Politics of Studying Securitization? The Copenhagen School in Turkey," *Security Dialogue*, 42 (4–5): 399–412.

Bird, K. R. and Brandt, E. B. (2002), "Academic Freedom and 9/11: How the War on Terrorism Threatens Free Speech Off Campus," *Communication, Law and Policy*, 7 (4): 431–459.

Bjorgo, T. (2005), *Root Causes of Terrorism: Myths, Reality and Ways Forward*, London and New York: Routledge.

Blain, M. (2007), "On the Genealogy of Terrorism," in D. Staines (Ed.), *Interrogating the War on Terror: Interdisciplinary Perspectives*, Newcastle: Cambridge Scholars Publishing.

Blakeley, R. (2007), "Bringing the State Back into Terrorism Studies," *European Political Science*, 6 (3): 228–235.

——(2009), *State Terrorism and Neoliberalism: The North in the South*, London and New York: Routledge.

Blanchard, E. M. (2003), "Gender, International Relations, and the Development of Feminist Security Theory," *Signs: Journals of Women in Culture and Society*, 28 (4): 1289–1312.

Blumer, H. (1998), *Symbolic Interactionism*, Berkeley, CA: University of California Press.

Boehmer, E. and Morton, S. (Eds.) (2010), *Terror and the Postcolonial*, Oxford: Wiley-Blackwell.

Boissevain, J. (1974), *Friends of Friends: Networks, Manipulators and Coalitions*, New York: Blackwell.

Bonditti, P. (2004), "From Territorial Space to Networks: A Foucauldian Approach to the Implementation of Biometry," *Alternatives*, 29 (4): 465–482.

Booth, K. (1991), "Security and Emancipation," *Review of International Studies*, 17 (4): 313–328.

——(Ed.) (2005), *Critical Security Studies and World Politics*, Boulder, CO: Lynne Reiner.

Borradori, G. (Ed.) (2003), *Philosophy in a Time of Terror: Dialogues with Jürgen Habermas and Jacques Derrida*, Chicago: University of Chicago Press.

Bott, H. (1957), *Family and Social Network*, New York: The Free Press.

Bourgois, P. (1996), *In Search of Respect: Selling Crack in El Barrio*, Cambridge, Cambridge University Press.

Boyce Davies, C. (1994), *Black Women, Writing and Identity: Migrations of the Subject*, London and New York: Routledge.

Britan, G. M. (1979), "Some Problems of Fieldwork in the Federal Bureaucracy," *Anthropological Quarterly*, 52: 211–220.

Bronner, S. E. (2011), *Critical Theory: A Very Short Introduction*, Oxford: Oxford University Press.

Bruff, I. (2010), "European Varities of Capitalism and the International," *European Journal of International Relations*, 16 (4): 615–638.

Bulley, D. (2009), "'Foreign' Terror? Resisting/Responding to the London Bombings," in A. Closs Stephens and N. Vaughan-Williams (Eds.), *Terrorism and the Politics of Response*, London and New York: Routledge, pp. 81–95.

Burawoy, M. (2003), "Revisits: An Outline of a Theory of Reflexive Ethnography," *American Sociological Review*, 68 (5): 645–679. Available online at http://burawoy.berkeley.edu/methodology/revisits.asr.pdf (accessed February 24, 2012).

Burchell, G., Gordon, C., and Miller, P. (Eds.) (1991), *The Foucault Effect: Studies in Governmentality*, Chicago: University of Chicago Press.

Burnett, J. and Whyte, D. (2005), "Embedded Academics and Counter-Insurgency in Bullying and Lateral Violence." Available online at http://www.creativespirits.info/aboriginalculture/people/bullying-and-lateral-violence.html (accessed August 16, 2012).

Butler, J. (2009), *Frames of War: When Is Life Grievable?*, New York: Verso.

Buzan, B., Waever, O., and De Wilde, J. (1998), *Security: A New Framework for Analysis*, Boulder, CO: Lynne Reiner.

Campbell, D. (1998a), *Writing Security: United States Foreign Policy and the Politics of Identity*, Minneapolis, MN: University of Minnesota Press.

——(1998b), *National Deconstruction: Violence, Identity and Justice in Bosnia*, Minneapolis, MN: University of Minnesota Press.

Caprioli, M. (2004), "Feminist IR Theory and Quantitative Methodology: A Critical Analysis," *International Studies Review*, 6 (2): 253–269.

Césaire, A. (2000), *Discourse on Colonialism*, trans. R. D. G. Kelly, New York: Monthly Review Press.

Chakrabarty, D. (2000), *Provincializing Europe: Postcolonial Thought and Historical Difference*, Princeton, NJ: Princeton University Press.

Chaliand, G. and Blin, A. (2007), *The History of Terrorism: From Antiquity to Al Qaeda*, Berkeley, Calif.: University of California Press.

Chase-Dunn, C. and Grimes, P. (1995), "World-Systems Analysis," *Annual Review of Sociology*, 21: 387–417.

Chen, H., Chung, W., Qin, J., Reid, E., Sageman, M., and Weimann, G. (2008), "Uncovering the Dark Web: A Case Study of Jihad on the Web," *Journal of the American Society for Information Science and Technology*, 59 (8): 1347–1359.

Chilton, P. (1996), *Security Metaphors: Cold War Discourse from Containment to Common House*, New York: Peter Lang.

Chomsky, N. (2003), *Power and Terror: Post-9/11 Talks and Interviews*, ed. J. Junkerman and T. Masakazu, New York: Seven Stories Press.

——(2011), "Noam Chomsky: My Reaction to Osama Bin Laden's Death," *Guernica*, May 6, available online at http://www.guernicamag.com/blog/2652/noam_chomsky_my_reaction_to_os (accessed June 20, 2012).

Chowdhry, G. (2007), "Edward Said and Contrapuntal Reading: Implications for Critical Interventions in International Relations," *Millennium: Journal of International Studies*, 36 (1): 101–116.

Chowdhry, G. and Ling, L. H. M. (2010), "Race(ing) International Relations: A Critical Overview of Postcolonial Feminism in International Relations," in R. A. Denemark (Ed.), *The International Studies Encyclopedia*, Oxford: Blackwell Publishing.

Chowdhry, G. and Nair, S. (2002), "Introduction: Power in a Postcolonial World – Race, Gender and Class in International Relations," in G. Chowdhry and S. Nair (Eds.), *Power, Postcolonialism and International Relations: Reading Race, Gender and Class*, London and New York: Routledge, pp. 1–32.

Christakis, N. A. and Fowler, J. H. (2008), "The Collective Dynamics of Smoking in a Large Social Network," *The New England Journal of Medicine*, 358 (21): 2249–2258.

Chua, V., Madej, J., and Wellman, B. (2011), "Personal Communities: The World According to Me," in John Scott and Peter J. Carrington (Eds.), *The Sage Handbook of Social Network Analysis*, Thousand Oaks, CA: Sage.

Cloud, D. L. (2004), "'To Veil the Threat of Terror': Afghan Women and the 'Clash of Civilizations' in the Imagery of the US War on Terrorism," *Quarterly Journal of Speech*, 90 (3): 285–306.

Clymer, J. A. (2003), *America's Culture of Terrorism: Violence, Capitalism, and the Written Word*, Chapel Hill, NC: University of North Carolina Press.

Collins, J. (2002), "Terrorism," in J. Collins and R. Glover (Eds.), *Collateral Language: A User's Guide to America's New War*, New York: New York University Press, pp. 155–174.

Comaroff, J. (2007), "Terror and Territory: Guantánamo and the Space of Contradiction," *Public Culture*, 19 (2): 381–405.

Combs, C. (2003), *Terrorism in the Twenty-First Century*, 3rd edn, Upper Saddle River, NJ: Prentice Hall.

Cook, T. E. (1986), "The Electoral Connection in the 99th Congress," *PS Political Science*, 19 (1): 16–22.

Cox, M. (2005), "Empire by Denial," *International Affairs*, 81 (1): 15–30.

Cox, R. (1981), "Social Forces, States, and World Orders: Beyond International Relations Theory," in R. O. Keohane (Ed.), *Neorealism and Its Critics*, New York: Columbia University Press.

——(1987), *Production, Power and World Order: Social Forces in the Making of History*, New York: Columbia University Press.

Crenshaw, M. (2011), *Explaining Terrorism: Causes, Processes and Consequences*, London and New York: Routledge.

Croft, S. (2006), *Culture, Crisis and the War on Terror*, Cambridge: Cambridge University Press.

Darby, P. (Ed.) (2006), *Postcolonizing the International: Working to Change the Way We Are*, Hawaii: University of Hawaii Press.

Darby, P. (2009), "Recasting Western Knowledges About (Postcolonial) Security," in D. Grenfell (Ed.), *Rethinking Insecurity, War and Violence: Beyond Savage Globalization?* London and New York: Routledge, pp. 71–85.

Darby, P. and Paolini, A. (1994), "Bridging International Relations and Postcolonialism," *Alternatives*, 19 (3): 371–397.

Dauphinee, E. and Masters, C. (Eds.) (2006), *The Logics of Biopower and the War on Terror: Living, Dying, Surviving*, Basingstoke: Palgrave Macmillan.

Davies, B. and Harré, R. (1990), "Positioning: The Discursive Production of Selves," *Journal for the Theory of Social Behavior*, 20 (1): 43–69. Available online at http://www.massey.ac.nz/~alock/position/position.htm (accessed May 20, 2012).

Davies, C. B. (1994), *Black Women, Writing and Identity: Migrations of the Subject*, London and New York: Routledge.

Davies, M. W., Nandy, A., and Sardar, Z. (1993), *Barbaric Others: A Manifesto on Western Racism*, Boulder, CO: Pluto Press.

Debrix, F. (2008), *Tabloid Terror: War, Culture and Geopolitics*, London and New York: Routledge.

Debrix, F. and Barder, A. (2011), *Beyond Biopolitics: Theory, Violence, and Horror in World Politics*, London and New York: Routledge.

De Kock, L. (1992), "Interview with Gayatri Chakravorty Spivak: New Nation Writers Conference in South Africa," *A Review of International English Literature*, 23(3): 29–47.

DeLillo, D. (2007), *Falling Man: A Novel*, New York: Scribner.

Der Derian, J. and Shapiro, M. (1989), *International/Intertextual Relations: Postmodern Readings of World Politics*, Lexington, MA: Lexington Books.

Deutsch, K. W. (1957), *Nationalism and Social Communication: An Inquiry into the Foundations of Nationalism*, Cambridge, MA: MIT Press.

——(1963), *The Nerves of Government: Models of Political Communication and Control*, New York: The Free Press.

Dillon, M. and Lobo-Guerrero, L. (2008), "Biopolitics of Security in the 21st Century," *Review of International Studies*, 34: 265–292. Available online at http://www.biopolitica.cl/docs/lobo_biopolitics_of_security_21stcentury.pdf (accessed May 20 2012).

Dillon, M. and Neal, A. (Eds.) (2008), *Foucault on Politics, Security and War*, Basingstoke: Palgrave Macmillan.

Dillon, M. and Reid, J. (2001), "Global Liberal Governance: Biopolitics, Security and War," *Millennium*, 30 (1): 41–66.

Dixit, P. (2010), "State/Terrorism: The Social Construction of 'States' and 'Terrorists' in Northern Ireland and Nepal," Ph.D. dissertation, American University, Washington DC.

Dixit, P. and Stump, J. L. (2011), "A Response to Jones and Smith: It's Not as Bad as It Seems; or, Five Ways to Move Critical Terrorism Studies Forward," *Studies in Conflict and Terrorism*, 34 (6): 501–511.

Domhoff, G. W. (1967), *Who Rules America?* Englewood Cliffs, NJ: Prentice Hall.

Donohue, L. (2008), *The Cost of Counterterrorism: Power, Politics and Liberty*, Cambridge: Cambridge University Press.

Doty, R. (1993), "Foreign Policy as Social Construction: A Post-Positivist Analysis of US Counterinsurgency Policy in the Philippines," *International Studies Quarterly*, 37 (3): 297–320.

——(1996), *Imperial Encounters: The Politics of Representation in North-South Relations*, Minneapolis, MN: University of Minnesota Press.

Duffield, M. (2004), "Carry on Killing: Global Governance, Humanitarianism and Terror," Danish Institute for International Studies Working Paper (December), available online at http://www.diis.dk/sw8141.asp (accessed May 20, 2012).

Eagleton-Pierce, M. (2011), "Advancing a Reflexive International Relations," *Millennium Journal of International Studies*, 39 (3): 805–823.

Earp, J. and Jhally, S. (2006), (Dirs.), *Reel Bad Arabs: How Hollywood Vilifies a People*, DVD, Media Education Foundation (Documentary). Available online at http://video.google.com/videoplay?docid=-223210418534585840# = (accessed May 20, 2012).

Elden, S. (2009), *Terror and Territory: The Spatial Extent of Sovereignty*, Minneapolis, MN: University of Minnesota Press.

Emerson, R. M., Fretz, R. I., and Shaw, L. L. (1995), *Writing Ethnographic Fieldnotes*, Chicago: University of Chicago Press.

Emirbayer, M. (1997), "Manifesto for a Relational Sociology," *American Journal of Sociology*, 103 (2): 281–317.

Enders, W. and Jindapon, P. (2010), "Network Externalities and the Structure of Terror Networks," *Journal of Conflict Resolution*, 54 (2): 262–280.

Enders, W. and Sandler, T. (2005), *The Political Economy of Terrorism*, Cambridge: Cambridge University Press.

Enloe, C. (2007), *Globalization and Militarism: Feminists Make the Link*, Lanham, MD: Rowman & Littlefield.

——(2010), *Nimo's War, Emma's War: Making Feminist Sense of the Iraq War*, Berkeley, CA: University of California Press.

Epstein, A. L. (1961), "The Network and Urban Social Organization," *Rhodes-Livingston Institute Journal*, 29: 29–62.

Epstein, C. (2008), *The Power of Words in International Relations: Birth of an Anti-Whaling Discourse*, Cambridge, MA: MIT Press.

Erickson, B. H. (1981), "Secret Societies and Social Structure," *Social Forces*, 60 (1): 188–210.

Erickson, C. W. (2007), "Counterterror Culture: Ambiguity, Subversion, and Legitimization?" *Security Dialogue*. Special Issue on Securitization, Militarization and Visual Culture in the Worlds of Post-9/11, 38 (2): 197–214.

——(2008), "Thematics of Counterterrorism: Comparing *24* and *MI-5/Spooks*," *Critical Studies on Terrorism*, 1 (3): 343–358.

Erjavec, K. and Volcic, Z. (2007), "'War on Terrorism' as a Discursive Battleground: Serbian Recontextualization of G. W. Bush's Discourse," *Discourse and Society*, 18 (2): 123–137.

Etzioni, A. (2005), *How Patriotic Is the Patriot Act? Freedom Versus Security in the Age of Terror*, London and New York: Routledge.

Fairclough, N. (1995), *Critical Discourse Analysis*, London: Longman.

Falkenrath, R. A. (2001), "Problems of Preparedness: US Readiness for a Domestic Terrorist Attack," *International Security*, 25 (4): 147–186.

Faludi, S. (2007), *The Terror Dream: Fear and Fantasy in Post 9/11 America*, New York: Metropolitan Books.

Fanon, F. (2004), *The Wretched of the Earth*, trans. R. Philcox, New York: Grove Press.

Feldman, A. (1991), *Formations of Violence: The Narrative of the Body and Political Terror in Northern Ireland*, Chicago: University of Chicago Press.

Fenno, R. (1978), *Home Style*, Boston: Little, Brown.

Fierke, K. (1998), *Changing Games, Changing Strategies: Critical Investigations in Security*, Manchester: Manchester University Press.

——(2005), "The 'War on Terrorism': A Critical Perspective," *Irish Studies in International Affairs*, 16 (16): 51–64.

——(2007), *Critical Approaches to International Security*, Malden, MA: Polity Press.

Fine, G. A. and Kleinman, S. (1983), "Network and Meaning: An Interactionist Approach to Structure," *Symbolic Interaction*, 6 (1): 97–110.

Fisher, B. M. (2008), "'Freedom for Women': Stories of Baghdad and New York," in C. Mohanty, M. B. Pratt, and R. Riley (Eds.), *Feminism and War: Confronting US Imperialism*, New York: Zed Books, pp. 207–215.

Flynn, V. (2008), *Extreme Measures*, New York: Pocket Books.

Foer, J. S. (2005), *Extremely Loud and Incredibly Close*, New York: Houghton Mifflin Company.

Forest, J. (Ed.) (2007), *Countering Terrorism and Insurgency in the 21st Century: International Perspectives*, Westport, CT: Praeger Security International.

Fosher, K. B. (2009), *Under Construction: Making Homeland Security at the Local Level*, Chicago: University of Chicago Press.

Foucault, M. (1972), *The Archaeology of Knowledge and the Discourse on Language*, New York: Pantheon Books.

——(1980), *Power/Knowledge: Selected Interviews and Other Writings, 1972–1977*, ed. and trans. C. Gordon, New York: Pantheon.

——(1995) *Discipline and Punish*, 2nd edn, New York: Vintage Books.

——(2003), *"Society Must Be Defended': Lectures at the Collège de France, 1975–76*, ed. M. Bertani and A. Fontana, trans. David Macey, New York: Picador.

——(2007), *Security, Territory, Population: Lectures at the Collège de France, 1977–78*, ed. Michel Senellart, trans. G Burchell, Basingstoke: Palgrave Macmillan.

Fowler, J. H., Heaney, M. T., Nickerson, D. W., Padgett, J. F., and Sinclair, B. (2011), "Causality in Political Networks," *American Politics Research*, 39 (2): 437–480.

Frake, C. (1998), "Abu Sayyaf: Displays of Violence and the Proliferation of Contested Identities Among Philippine Muslims," *American Anthropologist*, 100 (1): 41–54.

Freeman, L. C. (2004), *Network Analysis: A Study in the Sociology of Science*, Vancouver: Empirical Press.

Friel, B. (1981), *Translations: A Play*, New York: Samuel French Inc.

Fuhse, J. (2009), "The Meaning Structure of Social Networks," *Sociological Theory*, 27 (1): 51–73.

Fujii, L. A. (2008), "The Power of Local Ties: Popular Participation in the Rwandan Genocide," *Security Studies*, 17 (3): 568–597.

Gage, B. (2011), "Terrorism and the American Experience: A State of the Field," *Journal of American History*, 98 (1): 73–94. Available online at http://www.journalofamericanhistory.org/teaching/2011_06/article.pdf (accessed May 20 2012).

Geertz, C. (1973), *The Interpretation of Cultures*, New York: Basic Books.

George, A. (1991), "The Discipline of Terrorology," in A. George (Ed.), *Western State Terrorism*, Cambridge: Polity Press, pp. 76–101.

Georges, R. A. and Jones, M. O. (1980), *People Studying People: The Human Element in Fieldwork*, Berkeley, CA: University of California Press.

Gilbert, N. and Mulkay, M. (1984), *Opening Pandora's Box: A Sociological Analysis of Scientists" Discourse*, Cambridge: Cambridge University Press.

Glissant, E. (1989), *Le Discourse Antillais (The Caribbean Discourse)*, trans. M. J. Dash, Charlottesville, VA: University of Virginia Press.

Goddard, S. E. (2006), "Uncommon Ground: Indivisible Territory and the Politics of Legitimacy," *International Organization*, 60 (1): 35–68.

Goffman, E. (2001), "On Fieldwork," in Robert M. Emerson (Ed.), *Contemporary Field Research: Perspectives and Formulations*, Long Grove, IL: Waveland.

Gooda, M. (2011), "Strengthening Our Relationships over Lands, Territories and Resources: The United Nations Declaration on the Rights of Indigenous Peoples," Eddie Koiki Mabo Lecture, James Cook University, May 24. Available online at http://www.hreoc.gov.au/about/media/speeches/social_justice/2011/20111024_mabo_lecture.html (accessed May 20, 2012).

Goodin, R. E. (2006), *What's Wrong with Terrorism?* Cambridge: Polity.

Gordon, A. (2007), "Transient and Continuant Authors in a Research Field: The Case of Terrorism," *Scientometrics*, 72 (2): 213–224.

Graham, P., Keenan, T., and Dowd, A. M. (2004), "A Call to Arms at the End of History: A Discourse-Historical Analysis of George W. Bush's Declaration of War on Terror," *Discourse and Society*, 2–3 (May): 199–221.

Gramsci, A. (1971), *Selections from the Prison Notebooks*, London: International Publishers.

Grayson, K. A. (2006), "The persistence of memory: The new surrealism and the 'War on Terror'," in Dauphinée, E. and Masters, C. (eds), *The Logics of Biopower and the War on Terror: Living, Dying, Surviving*. New York: Palgrave Macmillan, pp. 83–108.

Gregory, D. (n.d.), "Research Themes," available online at http://web.mac.com/derekgregory/iweb/site/research%20themes.html (accessed May 20, 2012).

——(2004), *The Colonial Present: Afghanistan, Palestine, Iraq*, New York: Blackwell.

Gruffydd Jones, B. (Ed.) (2006), *Decolonizing International Relations*, Boulder, CO: Rowman & Littlefield.

Guess, R. (1987), *The Idea of a Critical Theory: Habermas and the Frankfurt School*, Cambridge: Cambridge University Press.

Guha, R. (ed.) (1997), *A Subaltern Studies Reader, 1986–1995*, Minneapolis: University of Minnesota Press.

Guilfoil, J. M. (2011), "Van's Fuel Sparks a Terrorism Response," available online at http://articles.boston.com/2011-10-17/news/30290356_1_natural-gas-alternative-fuel-tewksbury (accessed May 20, 2012).

Gunning, J. (2004), "Peace with Hamas? The Transforming Potential of Political Participation," *International Affairs*, 80 (2): 233–255.

——(2007a), "A Case for Critical Terrorism Studies," *Government and Opposition*, 42 (3): 363–393.

——(2007b), "Babies and Bathwaters: Reflecting on the Pitfalls of Critical Terrorism Studies," *European Political Science*, 6: 236–243.

Gupta, M. D. (2006), "Bewildered? Women's Studies and the War on Terror," in R. Riley and N. Inayatullah (Eds.), *Interrogating Imperialism: Conversations on Gender, Race, and War*, Basingtoke: Palgrave Macmillan, pp. 129–155.

Gusterson, H. (1996), *Nuclear Rites: A Weapons Laboratory at the End of the Cold War*, Berkeley, CA: University of California Press.

——(2009), "Ethnographic Research," in Audie Klotz and Deepa Prakash (Eds.), *Qualitative Methods in International Relations: A Pluralist Guide*, New York: Palgrave.

Guzzinni, S. (2011), "Securitization as a Causal Mechanism," *Security Dialogue*, 42 (4–5): 329–341.

Hammond, P. and Barnfield, G. (2011), "Introduction: The War on Terror in News and Popular Culture," *Journal of War and Culture Studies*, 4 (2): 155–161.

Hansen, L. (2006), *Security as Practice: Discourse Analysis and the Bosnian War*, London and New York: Routledge.

——(2010), "Poststructuralism and Security," in R. Denemark (Ed.), *The International Studies Encyclopedia*, Oxford: Blackwell. Available online at http://www.isacompendium.com/subscriber/tocnode?id=g9781444336597_chunk_g978144433659716_ss1-17 (accessed May 20, 2012).

——(2011), "The Politics of Securitization and the Muhammad Cartoon Crisis: A Post-Structuralist Perspective," *Security Dialogue*, 42 (4–5): 357–369.

Harrell, M. (2003), "Gender and Class-Based Role Expectations for Army Spouses," in P. R. Frese and M. C. Harrell (Eds.), *Anthropology and the United States Military: Coming of Age in the Twenty-First Century*, New York: Palgrave.

Haurwitz, R. K. M. (2011), "Business, Academic Leaders Back University Research," *American Statesman*, May 19. Available online at http://www.statesman.com/news/local/business-academic-leaders-back-university-research-1486337.html?printarticle=y (accessed May 20, 2012).

Hawthorne, S. and Winter, B. (Eds.) (2003), *After Shock: September 11, 2001: Global Feminist Perspectives*, Melbourne: Spinifex Press.

Held, D. (1980), *Introduction to Critical Theory: Horkheimer to Habermas*, Berkeley, CA: University of California Press.

Herbst, P. (2003), *Talking Terrorism: A Dictionary of the Loaded Language of Political Violence*, Westport, CT: Greenwood Press.

Herman, E. S. (1982), *The Real Terror Network: Terrorism in Fact and Propaganda*, Boston: MA: South End Press.

Herman, E. and O'Sullivan, G. (1989), *The "Terrorism" Industry: The Experts and Institutions That Shape Our View of Terror*, New York: Pantheon.

Hertz, R. and Imber, J. B. (1993), "Fieldwork in Elite Settings," *Journal of Contemporary Ethnography*, 22 (1): 3–6.

Hesse-Biber, S. N. and Piatelli, D. (2007), "Holistic Reflexivity: The Feminist Practice of Reflexivity," in S. N. Hesse-Biber and D. Piatelli (Eds.), *Handbook of Feminist Research: Theory and Praxis*, Thousand Oaks, CA: Sage Publications, pp. 493–514.

Hindess, B. (2006), "Terrortory," *Alternatives: Global, Local, Political*, 31 (3): 243–257.

Hirsch, P. M. (1986), "From Ambushes to Golden Parachutes: Corporate Takeovers as an Instance of Cultural Framing and Institutional Integration," *American Journal of Sociology*, 91 (4): 800–837.

Hobson, K. "Ethnographic Mapping and the Construction of the British Census in India." Available online at http://www.britishempire.co.uk/article/castesystem.htm (accessed June 10, 2011).

Hodges, A. (2011), *The "War on Terror" Narrative: Discourse and Intertextuality in the Construction and Contestation of Sociopolitical Reality*, New York: Oxford University Press.

Hoffman, B. (2006), *Inside Terrorism, New York: Columbia University Press.*

Hoffman, M. (1987), "Critical Theory and the Inter-Paradigm Debate," *Millennium: Journal of International Studies*, 16 (2): 231–249.

Hollis, M. and Smith, S. (1990), *Explaining and Understanding International Relations*, Oxford: Oxford University Press.

Holstein, J. A. and Gubrium, J. F. (1995), *The Active Interview*, Thousand Oaks, CA: Sage.

Horgan, J. and Boyle, M. (2008), "A Case Against Critical Terrorism Studies," *Critical Studies on Terrorism*, 1 (1): 51–64.

Horkheimer, M. and Adorno, T. (1969), *Dialectic of Enlightenment*, New York: Continuum.

Howard, R. D. and Sawyer, R. L. (2006), *Terrorism and Counterterrorism: Understanding the New Security Environment, Readings and Interpretations*, 2nd edn, Dubuque, IO: McGraw-Hill.

Hughes, G. (2003), "Analyse This," *The Age*, July 20.

Huisman, M. and Van Duijn, M. A. J. (2011), "A Reader's Guide to SNA Software," in J. Scott and P. J. Carrington (Eds.), *The Sage Handbook of Social Network Analysis*, Thousand Oaks, CA: Sage.

Hulsse, R. and Spencer, A. (2008), "The Metaphor of Terror: Terrorism Studies and the Constructivist Turn," *Security Dialogue*, 39 (6): 571–592.

Hunt, K. and Rygiel, K. (Eds.) (2006), *(En)gendering the War on Terror: War Stories and Camouflaged Politics*, Aldershot and Burlington, Vt.: Ashgate.

Huston, J. (2001), *Flash Point*, New York: Avon Books.

——(2002), *The Shadows of Power*, New York: Avon Books.

——(2004), *Secret Justice*, New York: Avon Books.

Hyndman, J. (2003), "Beyond Either/Or: A Feminist Analysis of September 11th," *ACME: an International E-Journal of Critical Geographies*, 2 (1). Online. Available at http://pi.library.yorku.ca/dspace/bitstream/handle/10315/6338/beyond%20either%20or.pdf (accessed June 26, 2011).

——(2008), "Whose Bodies Count? Feminist Geopolitics and Lessons from Iraq," in C. Mohanty, M. B. Pratt, and R. Riley (Eds.), *Feminism and War: Confronting US Imperialism*, New York: Zed Books, pp. 194–206.

Inayatullah, N. and Blaney, D. (2004), *International Relations and the Problem of Difference*, London and New York: Routledge.

Jackson, P. T. (2006a) *Civilizing the Enemy: German Reconstruction and the Invention of the West*, Ann Arbor: University of Michigan Press.

——(2006b), "Hegel's House, or "People Are States Too," *Review of International Studies*, 30 (2): 281–287.

——(2006c), "Making Sense of Making Sense: Configurational Analysis and the Double Hermeneutic," in D. Yanow and P. Schwartz-Shea (Eds.), *Interpretation and Method: Empirical Research Methods and the Interpretive Turn*, New York: M. E. Sharpe.

——(2008), "Can Ethnographic Techniques Tell Us Distinctive Things About World Politics?" *International Political Sociology*, 2 (1): 91–93.

——(2011), *The Conduct of Inquiry in International Relations*, London and New York: Routledge.

Jackson, P. T. and Nexon, D. H. (1999), "Relations Before States: Substance, Process and the Study of World Politics," *European Journal of International Relations*, 5 (3): 291–332.

Jackson, R. (2005), *Writing the War on Terrorism: Language, Politics and Counterterrorism*, Manchester: Manchester University Press.

——(2006), "Genealogy, Ideology, and Counter-Terrorism: Writing Wars on Terrorism from Ronald Reagan to George W. Bush Jr.," *Studies in Language and Capitalism*, 1: 163–193.

——(2007a), "Constructing Enemies: 'Islamic Terrorism' in Political and Academic Discourse," *Government and Opposition*, 42 (3): 394–426.

——(2007b), "Introduction: The Case for Critical Terrorism Studies," *European Political Science*, 6: 225–227.

——(2007c), "Language, Policy, and the Construction of a Torture Culture in the War on Terrorism," *Review of International Studies*, 33 (3): 353–371.

——(2007d), "The Core Commitments of Critical Terrorism Studies," *European Political Science*, 6 (3): 244–251.

——(2008), "The Ghosts of State Terror: Knowledge, Politics and Terrorism Studies," *Critical Studies on Terrorism*, 1 (3): 377–392.

——(2011), "In Defense of "Terrorism": Finding a Way through a Forest of Misconceptions," *Behavioral Science of Terrorism and Political Aggression*, 3 (2): 116–130.

Jackson, R., Jarvis, L., Gunning, J., and Smyth, M. B. (2012), *Terrorism: A Critical Introduction*, New York: Palgrave Macmillan.

Jackson, R., Murphy, E., and Poynting, S. (Eds.) (2009a), *Contemporary State Terrorism: Theory and Practice*, London and New York: Routledge.

Jackson, R., Smyth, M. B., and Gunning, J. (2009b), *Critical Terrorism Studies: A New Research Agenda*, London and New York: Routledge.

Jacobson, S. and Colon, E. (2006), *After 9/11: America's War on Terror*, New York: Hill & Wang.

Jarvis, L. (2009), "The Spaces and Faces of Critical Terrorism Studies," *Security Dialogue*, 40 (1): 5–27.

Jenkins, H. (2006), "Captain America Sheds His Mighty Tears: Comics and September 11," in T. Nardin and D. J. Sherman (Eds.), *Terror, Culture, Politics: Rethinking 9/11*, Bloomington, IN: Indiana University Press, pp. 69–102.

Johnson, A. and Sackett, R. (2000), "Direct Systematic Observation of Behavior," in H. Russell Bernard (Ed.), *Handbook of Methods in Cultural Anthropology*, Boulder, CO: Alta Mira.

Jones, D. M. and Smith, M. L. R. (2006), "The Commentariat and Discourse Failure: Language and Atrocity in Cool Britannia," *International Affairs*, 82 (6): 1117–1124.

——(2009), "We're All Terrorists Now: Critical – or Hypocritical – Studies 'on' Terrorism?" *Studies in Conflict and Terrorism*, 32 (4): 292–302.

Jones, D. M., Smith, M. L. R., and Weeding, M. (2003), "Looking for the Pattern: Al Qaeda in Southeast Asia – the Genealogy of a Terror Network," *Studies in Conflict and Terrorism*, 26 (6): 443–457.

Joseph, J. (2009), "Critical of What? Terrorism and Its Study," *International Relations*, 23 (1): 93–98.

——(2011), "Terrorism as a Social Relation Within Capitalism: Theoretical and Emancipatory Implications," *Critical Studies on Terrorism*, 4 (1): 23–37.

Kahler, M. (2009), "Collective Action and Clandestine Networks: The Case of Al Qaeda," in Miles Kahler (Ed.), *Networked Politics*, Ithaca, NY: Cornell University Press.

Katz, C. (2007), "Banal Terrorism: Spatial Fetishism and Everyday Insecurity," in Derek Gregory and Allan Pred (Eds.), *Violent Geographies: Fear, Terror, and Political Violence*, London and New York: Routledge.

Kellner, D. (1990), "Critical Theory and the Crisis of Social Theory," *Sociological Perspectives*, 33 (1): 11–33.

Kenney, M. (2009), "Turning to the 'Dark Side': Coordination, Exchange, and Learning in Criminal Networks," in Miles Kahler (Ed.), *Networked Politics*, Ithaca, NY: Cornell University Press, pp. 79–102.

Keohane, R. (1989), "International Relations Theory: Contributions of a Feminist Standpoint," *Millennium: Journal of International Studies*, 18 (2): 245–254.

Khan, S. (2008), "Afghan Women: The Limits of Colonial Rescue," in C Mohanty, M. B. Pratt, and R. Riley (Eds.), *Feminism and War: Confronting US Imperialism*, New York: Zed Books, pp. 161–178.

Kick, E. L., McKinney, L. A., McDonald, S. and Jorgenson, A. (2011), "A Multiple-Network Analysis of the World System of Nations, 1995–1999," in J. Scott and P. J. Carrington (Eds.), *The Sage Handbook of Social Network Analysis*, Thousand Oaks, CA: Sage.

King, G., Keohane, R., and Verba, S. (1994), *Designing Social Inquiry: Scientific Inference in Qualitative Research*, Princeton, NJ: Princeton University Press.

Kinsella, D. (2006), "The Black Market in Small Arms: Examining a Social Network," *Contemporary Security Policy*, 27 (1): 100–117.

Klovdahl, A. S., Potterat, J. J., Woodhouse, D. E., Muth, J. B., Muth, S. Q., and Darrow, W. W. (1994), "Social Networks and Infectious Disease: The Colorado Springs Study," *Social Science Medicine*, 38 (1): 79–88.

Knoke, D. (2011), 'Policy Networks', in J. Scott and P. J. Carrington (eds.), *The Sage Handbook of Social Network Analysis*, Thousand Oaks, CA: Sage.

Knoke, D. and Kuklinski, J. H. (1982), *Network Analysis*, Thousand Oaks, CA: Sage.

Knox, H., Savage, M., and Harvey, P. (2006), "Social Networks and the Study of Relations: Networks as Method, Metaphor, and Form," *Economy and Society*, 35 (1): 113–140.

Knudsen, O. (2001), "Post-Copenhagen Security Studies: Desecuritizing Securitization," *Security Dialogue*, 32 (3): 355–368.

Koschade, S. (2006), "A Social Network Analysis of Jemaah Islamiyah: The Applications to Counterterrorism and Intelligence," *Studies in Conflict and Terrorism*, 29 (6): 559–575.

Krause, K. and Williams, M. (1997), *Critical Security Studies: Concepts and Cases*, Minneapolis, MN: University of Minnesota Press.

Krebs, V. E. (2002), "Mapping Networks of Terrorist Cells," *Connections*, 24 (3): 43–52.

Krishna, S. (2001), "Race, Amnesia, and the Education of International Relations," *Alternatives: Global, Local, Political*, 26 (4): 401–424.

Kumar, A. (2012), *A Foreigner Carrying in the Crook of His Arm a Tiny Bomb*, Durham, NC: Duke University Press.

Laclau, E. and Mouffe, C. (2001), *Hegemony and Socialist Strategy: Towards a Radical Democratic Politics*, 2nd edn, London and New York: Verso.

Lafree, G. and Bersani, B. (2012), *Hot Spots of Terrorism and Other Crimes in the United States, 1970 to 2008*, Final Report to Human Factors/Behavioral Sciences Division, Science and Technology Directorate, Washington, DC: US Department of Homeland Security.

Laqueur, W. (1977), *A History of Terrorism*, New York: Little, Brown & Co.

——(2000), *The New Terrorism: Fanaticism and the Arms of Mass Destruction*, New York: Oxford University Press.

Lauderdale, P. and Oliverio, A. (eds) (2005), *Terrorism: A New Testament*, de Sitter publications.

Li, J. (2009), "Intertextuality and National Identity: Discourse of National Conflicts in Daily Newspapers in the United States and China," *Discourse and Society*, 20 (1): 85–121.

Liebow, E. (1967), *Tally's Corner: A Study of Negro Streetcorner Men*, Boston: Little, Brown & Co.

Liljeros, F., Edling, C. R., Amaral, L. A. N., Stanley, H. E., and Aberg, Y. (2001), "The Web of Human Sexual Contact," *Nature*, 411: 907–908.

Lincoln, B. (2006) "An Early Moment in the Discourse of 'Terrorism': Reflections on a Tale from Marco Polo," *Comparative Studies in Society and History*, 48 (2): 242–259.

Ling, L. H. M. (2002), *Postcolonial International Relations: Conquest and Desire Between Asia and the West*, New York: Palgrave.

Linklater, A. (1990), *Beyond Realism and Marxism: Critical Theory and International Relations*, Houndmills: Macmillan.

Linstead, S. (1993), "From Postmodern Anthropology to Deconstructive Ethnography," *Human Relations*, 46 (1): 97–120.

Lord Widgery (1972), *Report of the Tribunal Appointed to Inquire into the Events on Sunday, 30th January 1972, Which Led to Loss of Life in Connection with the Procession in Londonderry on That Day*, London: Her Majesty's Stationery Office, April, available at http://cain.ulst.ac.uk/hmso/widgery.htm (accessed May 20, 2012).

Low, S. M. (2008), "Fortification of Residential Neighbourhoods and the New Emotions of Home," *Housing, Theory and Society*, 25 (1): 47–65.

Lunstrum, E. (2009), "Terror, Territory, and Deterritorialization: Landscapes of Terror and the Unmaking of State Power in the Mozambican 'Civil' War," *Annals of the Association of American Geographers*, 99 (5): 884–892.

Macek, I. (2011), *Sarajevo Under Siege: Anthropology in Wartime*, Philadelphia, PA: University of Pennsylvania Press.

Magee, P. (2001), *Gangsters or Guerrillas: Representations of Irish Republicans in 'Troubles Fiction'*, Belfast: Beyond the Pale Publications.

Magouirk, J., Atran, S., and Sageman, M. (2008), "Connecting Terrorist Networks," *Studies in Conflict and Terrorism*, 31 (1): 1–16.

Mahmood, C. K. (1996), *Fighting for Faith and Nation: Dialogues with Sikh Militants*, Philadelphia, PA: University of Pennsylvania Press.

——(2001), "Terrorism, Myth, and the Power of Ethnographic Praxis," *Journal of Contemporary Ethnography*, 30 (5): 520–545.

Malmvig, H. (2006), *State Sovereignty and Intervention: A Discourse Analysis of Interventionary and Non-Interventionary Practices in Kosovo and Algeria*, London and New York: Routledge.

Marin, A. and Wellman, B. (2011), "Social Network Analysis: An Introduction," in J. Scott and P. J. Carrington (Eds.), *The Sage Handbook of Social Network Analysis*, Thousand Oaks, CA: Sage, pp. 11–25.

Martin, G. and Steuter, E. (2010), *Pop Culture Goes to War: Enlisting and Resisting Militarism in the War on Terror*, Lanham, MD: Lexington Books.

Masters, C. (2009), "Femina Sacra: The 'War on/of Terror,' Women and the Feminine," *Security Dialogue*, 40 (1): 29–49.

Mayhew, D. R. (1974), *Congress: The Electoral Connection*, New Haven, CT: Yale University Press.

McAdam, D., Tarrow, S., and Tilly, C. (2001), *Dynamics of Contention*, Cambridge: Cambridge University Press.

McClintock, A. (1995), *Imperial Leather: Race, Gender and Sexuality in the Colonial Context*, Routledge, London and New York.

McDonald, M. (2007), "Emancipation and Critical Terrorism Studies," *European Political Science*, 6: 252–259.

——(2009), "Emancipation and Critical Terrorism Studies," in R. Jackson, M. Breen Smyth and J. Gunning (Eds.) *Critical Terrorism Studies: A New Research Agenda*, London and New York: Routledge, pp. 109–123.

McEvoy, S. (2008), "Telling Untold Stories: Women in Loyalist Paramilitary Organizations in Northern Ireland 1968–2006," Ph.D. Dissertation, Clark University, Massachusetts.

McLeod, J. (2010), *Beginning Postcolonialism*, Manchester: Manchester University Press.

McSherry, J. P. (2002), "Tracking the Origins of a State Terror Network," *Latin American Perspectives*, 29 (1): 38–60.

Michel, T. and Richards, A. (2009), "False Dawns or New Horizons? Further Issues and Challenges for Critical Terrorism Studies," *Critical Terrorism Studies*, 2 (3): 399–412.

Milliken, J. (1999), "The Study of Discourse in International Relations: A Critique of Research and Methods," *European Journal of International Relations*, 5 (2): 225–254.

Mills, C. W. (1956), *The Power Elite*, New York: Oxford University Press.

Mische, A. (2008), *Partisan Publics: Communication and Contention Across Brazilian Youth Activist Networks*, Princeton, NJ: Princeton University Press.

——(2011), "Relational Sociology, Culture, and Agency," in J. Scott and P. J. Carrington (Eds.), *The Sage Handbook of Social Network Analysis*, Thousand Oaks, CA: Sage.

Mitchell, T. (1991), *Colonising Egypt*, Berkeley, CA: University of California Press.

Mohanty, M. (1988), "Under Western Eyes: Feminist Scholarship and Colonial Discourses," *Feminist Review*, 30 (autumn): 65–88. Available online at http://www.soc.duke.edu/courses/soc197/articles/mohanty.pdf (accessed June 20, 2011).

Molloy, P. (2009), "Terror Time in Toronto: A Response to the Response to the Arrests of the Toronto 17," in A. Closs Stephens and N. Vaughn-Williams (Eds.), *Terrorism and the Politics of Response*, London and New York: Routledge, pp. 112–129.

Montoye, H. J., Kemper, H. C. G., Saris, W. H. M., and Washiburn, R. A. (1996), *Measuring Physical Activity and Energy Expenditure*, Champaign, IL: Human Kinetics.

Moreno, J. (1934), *Who Shall Survive?* Beacon, NY: Beacon House.

Mueller, J. (2005), "Simplicity and Spook: Terrorism and the Dynamics of Threat Exaggeration," *International Studies Perspectives*, 6 (2): 208–234.

Murphy, O. (2003), "'Our Mission and Our Moment': George W. Bush and September 11th," *Speech Communication*, 6 (4): 607–632.

Mutimer, D. (2010), "Critical Security Studies: A Schismatic History," in Alan Collins (Ed.), *Contemporary Security Studies*, Oxford: Oxford University Press, pp. 84–105.

Mutzel, S. (2009), "Networks as Culturally Constituted Processes: A Comparison of Relational Sociology and Actor-Network Theory," *Current Sociology*, 57 (6): 871–887.

Nandy, A. (n.d.), "Narcissism and Despair," *The Little Magazine*, 7 (3 & 4). Available online at http://www.littlemag.com/security/ashisnandy.html (accessed January 24, 2012).

——(1983) *The Intimate Enemy: Loss and Recovery of Self under Colonialism*, Oxford: Oxford University Press.

Nayak, M. and Selbin, E. (2010), *Decentering International Relations*, London: Zed Books.

Neal, A. (2006), "Foucault in Guantanamo: Towards an Archaeology of the Exception," *Security Dialogue*, 37 (1): 31–46.

Neufeld, M. (1995), *The Restructuring of International Relations Theory*, Cambridge: Cambridge University Press.

Neumann, I. (1998), *Uses of the Other: The "East" in European Identity Formation*, Minneapolis, MN: University of Minnesota Press.

——(2007), "'A Speech That the Entire Ministry May Stand For,' or: Why Diplomats Never Produce Anything New," *International Political Sociology*, 1 (2): 183–200.

Newman, M. E. J. (2010), *Networks: An Introduction*, Oxford: Oxford University Press.

Nordstrom, C. (1997), *A Different Kind of War Story*, Philadelphia, PA: University of Pennsylvania.

Nusair, I. (2008), "Gendered, Racialized, and Sexualized Torture at Abu Ghraib," in C. Mohanty, M. B. Pratt, and R. Riley (Eds.), *Feminism and War: Confronting US Imperialism*, New York: Zed Books, pp. 179–193.

Ochs, J. (2011), *Security and Suspicion: An Ethnography of Everyday Life in Israel*, Philadelphia, PA: University of Pennsylvania Press.

Oliverio, A. (1997) "The State of Injustice: The Politics of Terrorism and the Production of Order," *International Journal of Comparative Sociology*, 38 (1/2): 48–63.

——(1998), *The State of Terror*, Albany, NY: State University of New York.

Oliverio, A. and Lauderdale, P. (Eds.) (2005), *Terrorism: A New Testament*, Whitby, ON: De Sitter Publications.

Patomaki, H. and Wight, C. (2000), " After Postpositivism? The Promises of Critical Realism," *International Studies Quarterly*, 44 (2): 213–237.

Peabody, R. L., Hammond, S. W., Torcom, J., Brown, L. P., Thompson, C., and Kolodny, R. (1990), "Interviewing Political Elites," *PS: Political Science and Politics*, 23 (3): 451–455.

Pedahzur, A. (2006), *Root Causes of Suicide Terrorism: The Globalization of Martyrdom*, London and New York: Routledge.

Peterson, V. S. (2004), "Feminist Theories Within, Invisible to, and Beyond IR," *Brown Journal of World Affairs*, 10 (2): 1–11. Available online at http://www.u.arizona.edu/~spikep/publications/vsp%20fem%20inandbey%20ir%20brownj%20pandp2004.pdf (accessed May 20, 2012).

Petras, J. (1987), "The Anatomy of State Terror: Chile, El Salvador and Brazil," *Science and Society*, 51 (3): 314–338.

Pettman, J. (1996), *Worlding Women: A Feminist International Politics*, St Leonards: Allen & Unwin.

——(2004), "Feminist International Relations After 9/11," *Brown Journal of World Affairs*, 10 (2): 85–96.

Pew Research Center (2011), *Public Remains Divided over the Patriot Act*, Pew Research Center for the People and the Press, available online at http://www.people-press.org/2011/02/15/public-remains-divided-over-the-patriot-act (accessed May 20, 2012).

Piazza, J. (2010), "Terrorism and Party Systems in the States of India," *Security Studies*, 19 (1): 99–123.

Plate, T. and Darvi, A. (1981), *Secret Police: The Inside Story of a Network of Terror*, Garden City, NY: Doubleday.

Potter, J. (1996), *Representing Reality: Discourse, Rhetoric and Social Construction*, London and Thousand Oaks, CA: Sage Publications.

Potter, J. and Wetherell, M. (1987), *Discourse and Social Psychology: Beyond Attitudes and Behaviour*, London: Sage.

Pram Gad, U. and Lund Petersen, K. (Eds.) (2011a), "Concepts of Politics in Securitization Studies," *Security Dialogue*, 42 (4–5): 315–328.

——(2011b), "Special Issue on the Politics of Securitization," *Security Dialogue*, 42 (4–5): 315–480.

Puar, J. (2008), "Feminists and Queers in the Service of Empire," in C. Mohanty, M. B. Pratt, and R. Riley (Eds.), *Feminism and War: Confronting US Imperialism*, New York: Zed Books, pp. 47–55.

Qian, Y. (2010), *Discursive Constructions Around Terrorism in the People's Daily (China) and the Sun (UK) Before and After 9.11: A Corpus-Based Contrastive Critical Discourse Analysis*, Oxford: Peter Lang Publishers.

Qin, J., Xu, J. J., Hu, D., Sageman, M., and Chen, H. (2005), "Analyzing Terrorist Networks: A Case Study of the Global Salafi Jihad Network," *Intelligence and Security Informatics*, 3495: 287–304.

Radcliffe-Brown, A. R. (1940), "On Social Structure," *Journal of the Royal Anthropological Institute*, 70 (1): 1–12.

Rai, A. (with Puar, J.) (2002), "Terrorist, Monster, Fag: The War on Terrorism and the Production of Docile Patriots," *Social Text*, 22 (3): 117–148.

Rai, A. (2004), "Of Monsters: Biopower, Terrorism and Excess in Genealogies of Monstrosity," *Cultural Studies*, 18 (4): 538–570.

——(2005), "The Promise of Monsters: Terrorism, Monstrosity, and Biopolitics," *International Studies in Philosophy*, 37 (2): 81–92.

Ranstorp, M. (2009), "Mapping Terrorism Studies After 9/11: An Academic Field of Old Problems and New Prospects," in R. Jackson, M. Breen Smyth and J. Gunning (Eds.), *Critical Terrorism Studies: A New Research Agenda*, London and New York: Routledge, pp. 13–34.

Rapoport, A. and Horvath, W. J. (1961), "A Study of a Large Sociogram," *Behavioral Sciences*, 6 (4): 279–291.

Rapoport, D. C. (1984), "Fear and Trembling: Terrorism in Three Religious Traditions," *The American Political Science Review*, 78 (3): 658–677.

Reid, E. and Chen, H. (2007), "Mapping the Contemporary Terrorism Research Domain," *International Journal of Human-Computer Studies*, 65: 42–56. Available online at http://ai.arizona.edu/intranet/papers/paper-reid-terrorism-researcher.pdf (accessed May 20, 2012).

Reid, J. (2006), *The Biopolitics of the War on Terror: Life Struggles, Liberal Modernity and the Defence of Logistical Societies*, Manchester: Manchester University Press.

Riley, R. and Inayatullah, N. (Eds.) (2006), *Interrogating Imperialism: Conversations on Gender, Race, and War*, Basingstoke: Palgrave Macmillan.

Riley, R., Mohanty, C., and Pratt, M. B. (2008), *Feminism and War: Confronting US Imperialism*, London and New York: Zed Books.

Robben, A. (2010), *Iraq at a Distance: What Anthropologists Can Teach Us About War*, Philadelphia, PA: University of Pennsylvania Press.

Rockwell, D. (2012), *The Little Book of Terror*, Foxhead Books.

Rowley, C. and Weldes, J. (2008), "Identities and US Foreign Policy," in M. Cox and D. Stokes (Eds.), *US Foreign Policy*, Oxford: Oxford University Press.

Rubin, H. J. and Rubin, I. S. (2004), *Qualitative Interviewing: The Art of Hearing Data*, Thousand Oaks, CA: Sage.

Sady, R. (1990), *District Leaders: A Political Ethnography*, Boulder, CO: Westview Press.

Sageman, M. (2004), *Understanding Terror Networks*, Philadelphia, PA: University of Pennsylvania Press.

——(2008), *Leaderless Jihad*, Philadelphia, PA: University of Pennsylvania Press.

Said, E. (1988), "The Essential Terrorist," in E. Said and C. Hitchens (Eds.), *Blaming the Victims: Spurious Scholarship and the Palestinian Question*, London: Verso, pp. 149–158.

——(1995), *Orientalism*, London: Penguin.

Salazar, E. M. (2008), "State Terror and Violence as a Process of Lifelong Teaching-Learning: The Case of Guatemala," *International Journal of Lifelong Education*, 27 (2): 201–216.

Sangarasivam, Y. (2001), "Researcher, Informant, 'Assassin,' Me," *The Geographical Review*, 91 (1–2): 95–104.

Santino, J. (2004), *Signs of War and Peace: Social Conflict and the Uses of Symbols in Public in Northern Ireland*, New York: Palgrave Macmillan.

Schaberg, C. and Thompson, K. (2011), "Special Issue on 'Cultural Productions of 9/11'," *Reconstruction*, 11 (2). Available online at http://reconstruction.eserver.org/112/contents112.shtml (accessed May 20, 2012).

Schatz, E. (2009), "Ethnographic Immersion and the Study of Politics," in E. Schatz (Ed.), *Political Ethnography: What Immersion Contributes to the Study of Power*, Chicago: University of Chicago Press, pp. 1–22.

Schmid, A. and Jongman, A. (2006), *Political Terrorism: A New Guide to Actors, Authors, Concepts, Databases, Theories and Literature*, London: Transaction.

Schwartz-Shea, P. (2006), "Judging Quality: Evaluative Criteria and Epistemic Communities," in D. Yanow and P. Schwartz-Shea (Eds.), *Interpretation and Method: Empirical Research Methods and the Interpretive Turn*, Armonk, NY: M. E. Sharpe, pp. 89–114.

Scott, J. (2000), *Social Network Analysis*, Thousand Oaks, CA: Sage.

Sewert, John J. (1978), "Critical Theory and the Critique of Conservative Mind," *The American Sociologist*, 13 (1): 15–22.

Shapiro, M. J. (1988), *The Politics of Representation: Writing Practices in Biography, Photography, and Political Analysis*, Madison, WI: University of Wisconsin Press.

Sharpe, J. (1994), "The Unspeakable Limits of Rape: Colonial Violence and Counter-Insurgency," in P. Williams and L. Chrisman (Eds.), *Colonial Discourse and Post-Colonial Theory: A Reader*, New York: Columbia University Press, pp. 196–221.

Sheehan, I. S. (2008), *When Terrorism and Counterterrorism Clash: The War on Terror and the Transformation of Terrorist Activity*, Youngstown, NY: Cambria Press.

Shepherd, L. J. (2006), "Veiled References: Constructions of Gender in the Bush Administration Discourse on the Attacks on Afghanistan Post-9/11," *International Feminist Journal of Politics*, 8 (1): 19–41.

——(2008), *Gender, Violence and Security: Discourse as Practice*, London: Zed Books.

——(2010), "Feminist Security Studies," in Robert A. Denemark (Ed.), *The International Studies Compendium Project: International Security Studies*, Blackwell Reference, Online.

Sherman, D. and Nardin, T. (eds.) (2006), *Terror, Culture, Politics: Rethinking 9/11*, Bloomington, Ind.: Indiana University Press.

Shigematsu, S. (2008), "Women-of-Color Veterans on War, Militarism, and Feminism," in C. Mohanty, M. B. Pratt, and R. Riley (eds.), *Feminism and War: Confronting US Imperialism*, New York: Zed Books, pp. 93–102.

Shilliam, R. (2008), "What the Haitian Revolution Might Tell Us About Development, Security and the Politics of Race," *Comparative Studies in Society and History*, 50 (3): 778–808.

——(ed.) (2010), *Non-Western Thought and International Relations*, London and New York: Routledge.

Silke, A. (2008), "Research on Terrorism: A Review of the Impact of 9/11 and the Global War on Terrorism," *Terrorism Informatics*, 18 (1): 27–50.

Silva, N. (2010), "'Gendering' Terror: Representations of the Female 'Freedom Fighter' in Contemporary Sri Lankan Literature and Cultural Production," in E. Boehmer and S. Morton (Eds.), *Terror and the Postcolonial*, London: Blackwell-Wiley, pp. 329–345.

Sjoberg, L. (2011), "Feminist IR 101 Post 5: War and Security," available online at http://duck ofminerva.blogspot.com/2011/01/feminist-ir-101-post-5-war-and-security.html (accessed July 15, 2012).

Sjoberg, L. and Gentry, C. (2007), *Mothers, Monsters, Whores: Women's Violence in Global Politics*, London and New York: Zed Books.

Sjoberg, L. and Gentry, C. (eds) (2011), *Women, Gender, and Terrorsim*, Athens, GA: University of Georgia Press.

Skidmore, M. (2004), *Karaoke Fascism: Burma and the Politics of Fear*, Philadelphia, PA: University of Pennsylvania Press.

Sluka, J. A. (1989), *Hearts and Minds, Water and Fish: Popular Support for the IRA and INLA in a Northern Irish Ghetto*, Greenwich: JAI Press.

——(1990), "Participant Observation in Violent Social Contexts," *Human Organization*, 49 (2): 114–126.

——(2000), *Death Squad: The Anthropology of State Terror*, Philadelphia, PA: University of Pennsylvania Press.

Smyth, M. B. (2007), "A Critical Research Agenda for the Study of Political Terror," *European Political Science*, 6: 260–267.

——(2009), "Subjectivities, Suspect Communities, Governments, and the Ethics of Research on Terrorism," in Richard Jackson, Marie Breen Smyth, and Jeroen Gunning (Eds.), *Critical Terrorism Studies: A New Research Agenda*, London and New York: Routledge, pp. 194–215.

Smyth, M. B., Gunning, J., Jackson, R., Kassimeris, G., and Robinson, P. (2008), "Symposium: Critical Terrorism Studies – an Introduction," *Critical Terrorism Studies*, 1 (1): 1–4.

Soss, J. (2006), "Talking Our Way to Meaningful Explanations: A Practice Centered View of Interviewing for Interpretive Research," in D. Yanow and P. Schwartz-Shea (Eds.), *Interpretation and Method: Empirical Research Methods and the Interpretive Turn*, New York: M. E. Sharpe.

Sparrow, M. K. (1991), "The Application of Network Analysis to Criminal Intelligence: An Assessment of the Prospects," *Social Networks*, 13: 251–274.

Speckhard, A. (2009), "Research Challenges Involved in Field Research and Interviews Regarding the Militant Jihad, Extremism, and Suicide Terrorism," *Democracy and Security*, 5: 199–222.

Spivak, G. C. (1994), "Can the Subaltern Speak?" in P. Williams and L. Chrisman (Eds.), *Colonial Discourse and Post-Colonial Theory*, New York: Columbia University Press.

——(2004), "Terror: A Speech After 9–11," *Boundary*, 2 (2): 81–111.

Staff Reporters (1984), "Inquiry on Security Blunder Starts," *The Times*, October 13, pp. 1–2.

Stampnitzky, L. (2011), "Disciplining an Unruly Field: Terrorism Experts and Theories of Scientific/Intellectual Production," *Qualitative Sociology*, 34 (1): 1–19. Available online at http://iis-db.stanford.edu/pubs/23109/stampnitzky.pdf (accessed February 10, 2012).

Stavrianakis, A. (2011), "Small Arms Control and the Reproduction of Imperial Relations," *Contemporary Security Policy*, 32 (1): 193–214.

Steans, J. (2006), *Gender and International Relations: Issues, Debates and Future Directions*, Cambridge: Polity Press.

——(2008) "Telling Stories About Women and Gender in the War on Terror," *Global Society*, 21 (1): 159–176.

Stephens, A. C. and Vaughan-Williams (eds.) (2009), *Terrorism and the Politics of Response*, London: Routledge.

Sterling, C. (1981), *The Terror Network: The Secret War of International Terrorism*, New York: Holt, Rinehart & Winston.

Stern, J. (2003), *Terror in the Name of God: Why Religious Militants Kill*, New York: HarperCollins.

Stohl, M. (1988), *The Politics of Terrorism*, Basel and New York: Marcel Dekker, Inc.

Streets, H. (2004), *Martial Races: The Military, Race and Masculinity in British Imperial Culture, 1857–1914*, Manchester: Manchester University Press.

Stump, J. L. (2009), "The Risk of 'Terrorism' and the Washington Metro," in M. A. Viteri and A. Tobler (Eds.), *Shifting Positionalities: The Geopolitics of Surveillance and Policing*, Newcastle: Cambridge Scholars Publishing.

——(2010), "Ordinary Terrorism: Interpersonal Security Conduct and the Politics of Danger in the United States," Ph.D. Dissertation, American University, Washington, D.C., United States of America.

——(2011), "On the Future of Critical Terrorism Studies: A Response to Richard Jackson's Minimalist Redefinition of Terrorism," *Behavioral Science of Terrorism and Political Aggression*. Available online at http://www.tandfonline.com/doi/abs/10.1080/19434472.2011.629579#preview (accessed August 16, 2012).

Stump, J. L. and Dixit, P. (2012), "Toward a Completely Constructivist Critical Terrorism Studies," *International Relations*, 25 (2): 199–217.

Sylvester, C. (2010a), *Experiencing War*, London and New York: Routledge.

——(2010b), "Tensions in Feminist Security Studies," *Security Dialogue*, 41 (6): 607–614.

Sylvester, C. and Parashar, S. (2009), "The Contemporary 'Mahabharata' and the Many Draupadis: Bringing Gender to Critical Terrorism Studies," in R. Jackson, J. Gunning, and M. B. Smyth (Eds.), *Critical Terrorism Studies: A New Research Agenda*, London and New York: Routledge, pp. 178–193.

Taylor, D. (2011), *Michel Foucault: Key Concepts*, Durham: Acumen.

Taylor, J. R. and Van Every, E. J. (2000), *The Emergent Organization: Communication as Its Site and Surface*, Mahwah, NJ: Erlbaum.

Temple-Raston, D. (2007), *The Jihad Next Door: The Lackawanna Six and Rough Justice in an Age of Terror*, New York: Publicaffairs.

Tétreault, M. A. (2006), "The Sexual Politics of Abu Ghraib: Hegemony, Spectacle, and the Global War on Terror," *NWSA Journal*, 18 (3): 33–50.

Thomas, R. J. (1993), "Interviewing Important People in Big Companies," *Journal of Contemporary Ethnography*, 22 (1): 80–96.

Tickell, A. (2010), "Excavating Histories of Terror: Thugs, Sovereignty, and the Colonial Sublime," in E. Boehmer and S. Morton (Eds.), *Terror and the Postcolonial*, London: Blackwell-Wiley, pp. 177–202.

Tickner, A. (1997), "You Just Don't Understand: Troubled Engagements Between Feminists and IR Theorists," *International Studies Quarterly*, 41 (4): 611–632.

Tickner, J. A. (1992), *Gender in International Relations: Feminist Perspectives on Achieving Global Security*, New York: Columbia University Press.

——(2002), "Feminist Perspectives on 9/11," *International Studies Perspectives*, 3 (4): 333–350.

Tilly, C. (1995), 'To Explain Political Processes', *American Journal of Sociology*, 100 (6): 1594–1610.

——(1999), *Durable Inequality*, Berkeley, University of California Press.

——(2001), "Mechanisms in Political Processes," *Annual Review of Political Science*, 4 (June): 21–41. Available online at http://arjournals.annualreviews.org/doi/pdf/10.1146/annurev.polisci.4.1.21 (accessed May 20, 2012).

——(2003), *Stories, Identities, and Political Change*, Boulder, CO: Rowman & Littlefield.

——(2004), "Terror, Terrorism, Terrorists," *Sociological Theory*, 22 (1): 5–13.

——(2005a), *Identities, Boundaries, and Social Ties*, Boulder, CO: Paradigm.

——(2005b), "Terror as Strategy and Relational Process," *International Journal of Comparative Sociology*, 46 (1–2): 11–32.

——(2006), "Afterword: Political Ethnography as Art and Science," *Qualitative Sociology*, 29 (3): 409–412.

——(2008), *Explaining Social Processes*, Boulder, CO: Paradigm.

Toolis, K. (2004), "Rise of the Terrorist Professors," *The New Statesman*, June 14.

Toros, H. (2008), "Terrorists, Scholars and Ordinary People: Confronting Terrorism Studies with Field Experiences," *Critical Studies on Terrorism*, 1 (2): 279–292.

Toros, H. and Gunning, J. (2009), "Exploring a Critical Theory Approach to Terrorism Studies," in R. Jackson, M. B. Smyth, and J. Gunning (Eds.), *Critical Terrorism Studies: A New Research Agenda*, London and New York: Routledge, pp. 87–108.

Trinh, T. M. (1989), *Woman, Native, Other: Writing Postcolonality and Feminism*, Bloomington, IN: Indiana University Press.

True, J. (2010), *Doing Feminist Research in Political and Social Sciences*, New York: Palgrave.

Useem, M. (1979), "The Social Organization of the American Business Elite and Participation of Corporation Directors in the Governance of American Institutions," *American Sociological Review*, 44 (4): 553–572.

Vallis, R., Yang, Y. and Abbas, H. A. (2006), "Disciplinary Approaches to Terrorism: A Survey," *Defense and Security Applications Research Centre*, Viewed April 7, 2010.

Van Dijk, T. (2008), *Discourse and Power*, Houndsmills: Palgrave.

Vaughan-Williams, N. (2009), "The Shooting of Jean Charles De Menezes: New Border Politics," in A. Closs Stephens and N. Vaughan-Williams (Eds.), *Terrorism and the Politics of Response*, London and New York: Routledge, pp. 96–111.

Vuori, J. A. (2008), "Illocutionary Logic and Strands of Securitization: Applying the Theory of Securitization to the Study of Non-Democratic Political Orders," *European Journal of International Relations*, 14 (1): 65–99.

Waever, O. (1995), "Securitization and Desecuritization," in Ronnie D. Lipschutz (Ed.), *On Security*, New York: Columbia University Press, pp. 46–86.

Wagner-Pacifici, R. E. (1986), *The Moro Morality Play: Terrorism as Social Drama*, Chicago: University of Chicago Press.

Warren, K. (1993), *The Violence Within: Cultural and Political Opposition in Divided Nations*, Boulder, CO: Westview Press.

Wasserman, S. and Faust, K. (1994), *Social Network Analysis: Methods and Applications*, Cambridge: Cambridge University Press.

Weatherford, M. J. (1985), *Tribes on the Hill*, New York: Greenwood.

Weber, C. (1994), "Good Girls, Little Girls, and Bad Girls: Male Paranoia in Robert Keohane's Critique of Feminist International Relations," *Millennium: Journal of International Studies*, 23 (2): 337–349.

——(2006), *Imagining America at War: Morality, Politics, and Film*, London and New York: Routledge.

——(2011), *'I am an American': Filming the Fear of Difference*, Chicago: University of Chicago Press.

Weick, K. E., Sutcliffe, K. M., and Obstfeld, D. (2005), "Organizing and the Process of Sensemaking," *Organization Science*, 16 (4): 409–421.

Weinberg, L. and Eubank, W. (2008), "Problems with the Critical Studies Approach to the Study of Terrorism," *Critical Studies on Terrorism*, 1 (2): 185–195.

Weldes, J. (1999), *Constructing National Interests: The United States and the Cuban Missile Crisis*, Minneapolis, MN: University of Minnesota Press.

——(2003), Discussion Paper on "Discourse and Identity," Ohio State University Conference, April, available online at https://kb.osu.edu/dspace/bitstream/handle/1811/31957/weldes%20comments.pdf?sequence=30 (accessed May 20, 2012).

——(2006), "High Politics and Low Data: Globalization Discourses and Popular Culture," in D. Yanow and P. Schwartz-Shea (Eds.), *Interpretation and Method: Empirical Research Methods and the Interpretive Turn*, Armonk, NY: M. E. Sharpe, pp. 176–186.

Weldes, J., Laffey, M., Gusterson, H., and Duvall, R. (Eds.) (1999), *Cultures of Insecurity: States, Communities and the Production of Danger*, Minneapolis, MN: University of Minnesota Press.

Wellman, B. and Berkowitz, S. D. (1988), *Social Structures: A Network Approach*, Cambridge: Cambridge University Press.

Wendt, A. (1998), "On Constitution and Causation in International Relations," *Review of International Studies*, 24 (5): 101–118.

Wetherell, M., Potter, J., and Stringer, P. (1984), *Social Texts and Context: Literature and Social Psychology*, London and New York: Routledge.

Wetherell, M., Taylor, S., and Yates, S. (Eds.) (2001), *Discourse as Data: A Guide for Analysis*, Thousand Oaks, CA: Sage.

White, H. C. (2008), *Identity and Control: How Social Formations Emerge*, Princeton, NJ: Princeton University Press.

Whitehead, J. W. and Aden, S. H. (2002), "Forfeiting 'Enduring Freedom' for 'Homeland Security': A Constitutional Analysis of the USA Patriot Act and the Justice Department's Anti-Terrorism Initiatives," *American University Law Review*, 51 (6): 1081–1133.

Whitelaw, V. (1984), "Speech to the House of Lords, October 16, 1984," Parliamentary Debates, Lords, 5th Ser., 455, Col. 885., Viewed January 21, 2011, available online at http://hansard.millbanksystems.com/lords/1984/oct/16/grand-hotel-brighton-bomb-explosion#s5lv0455p0_1984 1016_hol_86 (accessed May 20, 2012).

Whitten, N. E. (1970), "Network Analysis and Processes of Adaptation Among Ecuadorian and Nova Scotian Negroes," in M. Freilich (Ed.), *Marginal Natives*, New York: Harper & Row.

Wibben, A. (2011), *Feminist Security Studies: A Narrative Approach*, London and New York: Routledge.

Wilkinson, C. (2007), "The Copenhagen School on Tour in Kyrgyzstan: Is Securitization Theory Useable Outside Europe?" *Security Dialogue*, 38 (1): 5–25.

Williams, T., Dunlap, E., Johnson, B. D., and Hamid, A. (1992), "Personal Safety in Dangerous Places," *Journal of Contemporary Ethnography*, 21 (3): 343–374.

Winichakul, S. (1994), *Siam Mapped: A History of the Geo-Body of a Nation*, Honolulu, HI: University of Hawaii Press.

Wodak, R. (2007), "What Is Critical Discourse Analysis?" *Forum: Qualitative Social Research*, 8 (2), available online at http://www.ling.lancs.ac.uk/staff/wodak/interview.pdf (accessed May 20, 2012).

Wodak, R. and Meyer, M. (Eds.) (2009), *Methods of Critical Discourse Analysis*, Thousand Oaks, CA: Sage.

Wolfe, A. W. (1978), "The Rise of Network Thinking in Anthropology," *Social Networks*, 1 (1): 53–64.

Wyn Jones, R. (2005), "On Emancipation: Necessity, Capacity and Concrete Utopias," in Ken Booth (Ed.), *Critical Security Studies and World Politics*, Boulder CO: Lynne Rienner, pp. 215–235.

Yanow, D. (2000), *Interpretive Policy Analysis*, Thousand Oaks, CA: Sage.

Yanow, D. and Schwartz-Shea, P. (Eds.) (2006), *Interpretation and Method: Empirical Research Methods and the Interpretive Turn*, New York: M. E. Sharpe.

Young, A. (1975), "Magic as a 'Quasi-Profession': The Organization of Magic and Magical Healing Among Amhara," *Ethnology*, 14 (3): 245–265.

Yuval-Davis, N. (1997), *Gender and Nation*, Thousand Oaks, CA: Sage.

——(1999) "What Is 'Transversal Politics'?", *Soundings*, 12 (summer): 94–98.

——(2010), "What Is Transversal Politics?" Available online at http://geopoliticaleveryday.wordpress.com/2010/03/14/what-is-transversal-politics-nira-yuval-davis (accessed June 10, 2011).

Zulaika, J. (1988), *Basque Violence: Metaphor and Sacrament*, Reno, NE: University of Nevada Press.

——(1995), "The Anthropologist as Terrorist," in C. Nordstrom and A. C. G. M. Robben (Eds.), *Fieldwork under Fire: Contemporary Studies of Violence and Survival*, Berkeley, CA: University of California Press, pp. 206–223.

——(2005), *Terrorism: A Self-Fulfilling Prophecy*, London and New York: Routledge.

Zulaika, J. and Douglass, W. A. (1996), *Terror and Taboo: The Follies, Fables, and Faces of Terrorism*, London and New York: Routledge.

——(2008), "The Terrorist Subject: Terrorism Studies and the Absent Subjectivity," *Critical Studies on Terrorism*, 1 (1): 27–36.

Index